MW00477672

"This book captures the real personalities of the Bushes and reveals some untold vignettes, which makes this book a must read."

—The Honorable Dan Quayle

"Russ Levenson has eloquently captured the essence and dignity of these two beautiful human beings who remain role models of character, decency, and integrity."　　　—The Honorable James A. Baker III

"Russ Levenson's *Witness to Dignity* is a beautiful tribute to God and the faith of George H. W. and Barbara Bush that sustained them during their lives."　　　　　　　　　　　　　　　　—Dana Perino

"What makes this book unique and profoundly moving is Levenson's unapologetically personal account, as if we have been invited to sit at the family table and catch a glimpse of their deep love and abiding faith."

—The Most Right Reverend Michael Curry

"They were not perfect, but as Russell Levenson's personal and pastoral memoir tells us, they strove to be faithful people of God."

—Jon Meacham

"This impressive book by his longtime pastor and friend Russ Levenson is the story of President Bush as a Christian. It is a fascinating read and an important contribution to the literature of our forty-first president."

—Brit Hume, senior political analyst, Fox News

"Russ Levenson's moving memoir of George and Barbara Bush vividly recounts how blessed we were to have people of faith in the White House who worked for the greater good of their country, their community, and their church."　　　—Joe Scarborough, host of MSNBC's *Morning Joe*

"Congratulations to my friend Russ Levenson. He has captured a compelling story of faith, family, love, and leadership."

—Max Lucado, minister, Oak Hills Church, San Antonio, Texas

"Russ Levenson's elegant narrative voice in *Witness to Dignity* is a perfect reflection of the Bush family. I am so grateful for his efforts in capturing these timely stories of this amazing couple."

—Amy Grant, award-winning recording artist

"A remarkable addition to the legacy of our forty-first president."

—Admiral William H. McRaven, US Navy (Retired)

"British admirers of George H. W. and Barbara Bush will be thrilled with Russ Levenson's tribute."

—The Most Right Honourable Dr. George L. Carey,
103rd archbishop of Canterbury

"Russ has written this account in such a way that readers can and should put aside their political or faith affiliation and can appreciate the deep Christian faith embraced and exhibited by these two people who loved all sorts and conditions of humans."

—The Reverend Dr. Robert Certain, former pastor to
President and Mrs. Gerald R. Ford

"Through the lens of a lasting and intimate friendship with President George and First Lady Barbara Bush, Russ Levenson's enjoyable, funny, and insightful book *Witness to Dignity* reveals to us the beauty and the importance of faith and the value of friendships."

—Tom Bradbury, Kennebunkport Conservation Trust

"Russ's book truly reveals the inside story of this remarkable couple and the extent to which their lives were informed by their faith."

—Jean-Pierre Isbouts, historian and *National Geographic* author

WITNESS TO DIGNITY

The Life and Faith of George H. W. and Barbara Bush

THE REVEREND
RUSSELL J. LEVENSON JR.

CENTER STREET

NASHVILLE   NEW YORK

With admiration and gratitude,
this is dedicated to 41 and Bar
and all who seek to live and serve with dignity

And to the precious circle who have lovingly joined me in the journey:
Evelyn, Jones, Luke,
and my beloved,
Laura

———————

Center Street
Hachette Book Group
1290 Avenue of the Americas, New York, NY 10104
centerstreet.com
twitter.com/centerstreet

Originally published in hardcover and ebook in November 2022
First trade paperback edition: November 2023

Center Street is a division of Hachette Book Group, Inc. The Center Street name and logo are trademarks of Hachette Book Group, Inc.

The publisher is not responsible for websites (or their content) that are not owned by the publisher.

The Hachette Speakers Bureau provides a wide range of authors for speaking events. To find out more, go to hachettespeakersbureau.com or email HachetteSpeakers@hbgusa.com.

Center Street books may be purchased in bulk for business, educational, or promotional use. For information, please contact your local bookseller or the Hachette Book Group Special Markets Department at special.markets@hbgusa.com.

All Scripture quotations, unless otherwise indicated, are taken from the Holy Bible, New International Version®, NIV®. Copyright © 1973, 1978, 1984, 2011 by Biblica, Inc.™ Used by permission of Zondervan. All rights reserved worldwide. www.zondervan.com The "NIV" and "New International Version" are trademarks registered in the United States Patent and Trademark Office by Biblica, Inc.™

[NRSV] New Revised Standard Version Bible, copyright © 1989 National Council of the Churches of Christ in the United States of America. Used by permission. All rights reserved worldwide.

The author is represented by Tom Dean, literary agent with A Drop of Ink LLC, www.adropofink.pub

Library of Congress Control Number: 2022010897

ISBNs: 9781546003304 (trade paperback), 9781546003311 (ebook)

Printed in the United States of America

LSC-C

Printing 1, 2023

Contents

Foreword

by Jeb Bush

One of my father's favorite quotes, which some through the years have ascribed to Saint Francis, was "Preach Christ at all times; if necessary, use words." In fact, Dad liked this quote and the sentiment behind it so much that, later in his life, he asked our family friend Dan Gilchrist to etch the phrase onto a wooden plaque that he kept in his desk.

Knowing my father, he kept that plaque handy as a private reminder that one's actions almost always speak louder than one's words, and that the power of a good example far outweighs the impact of most Sunday sermons, parental lectures, and political speeches. Without question, and without fail, George Herbert Walker Bush was a "lead by example" kind of person—a way of living that was inculcated into him by his father, my grandfather.

The truth is, neither of my parents were known to wear their faith on their sleeves. A big part of that, I am sure, was generational. Just as the World War II generation never talked about their war experiences, the prevailing social mores also dictated that there were other things my parents never talked about, especially in polite company—such as the biggest taboo, money.

Nevertheless, when you look at their long and consequential lives, faith was clearly important to them both. It sustained them through times of personal tragedy—such as losing a daughter to leukemia—while also keeping them grounded during periods of heady success.

During his presidency, I particularly recall how my father invited the Reverend Billy Graham to pray with him the night the air war started in Operation Desert Storm. Afterward, he admitted to sharing the experience of President Lincoln, who said that as commander in chief, "I have been driven many times upon my knees by the overwhelming conviction that I had nowhere else to go."

If my parents' faith was a constant in their public and private lives, it was not in any ritualistic sense. They were never simply going through the motions. When they prayed, it was with true intention—not by rote. We went to church every Sunday, of course, but while we were living in Midland, Texas, Dad also taught Sunday school (though not to me, thankfully!). Later, after our family moved to Houston, Dad served as a vestryman at St. Martin's Church.

Mom and Dad also cherished the traditions of their Episcopalian faith, such as marrying within the church. These ceremonies became important family milestones and touchstones, and a source of enormous comfort.

At all times, certainly in my observation, my parents tried to conduct themselves in a Christlike fashion. Indeed, long before my father first uttered the phrase "points of light," both he and Mom were active in their communities, supporting a broad range of causes and groups that lifted the lives of countless others. I am biased, of course, but when it came to serving others, they "walked the walk" like few couples before or since.

A final observation for now: George and Barbara Bush never instructed me or any of my siblings as to what type of Christian we should be, or even that we be Christians at all. Later, when I decided to become a Catholic, my parents supported this personal decision with their take-it-to-the-bank, unconditional love as always. The freedom they gave me and my siblings to chart our own paths in life was truly one of the greatest gifts they could bestow on us.

To be clear, we received the same life lessons so common in so many families—sit up and look people in the eye, say "please" and "thank you"—and to those they added tell the truth, serve others, treat everyone as you would want to be treated, and love your God with your heart and soul.

No doubt, one of the greatest blessings of their long lives was the many opportunities they had to extend those same lessons to their grandchildren.

As we age, it seems our values and priorities shift to an even greater degree to the more purposeful and meaningful aspects of our lives. My parents were certainly not unique in that, as they got older, their faith became even more important to them. Their relationship with God was always important, but never more so than as they neared the end of their journey with us here on Earth.

Which brings me to Russ Levenson and this wonderful book. We can never adequately thank Russ for his tireless efforts to minister to our parents when they needed it—and him—most. He was so incredibly generous with his time and compassion, and as you will discover in the pages that follow, he and his wife, Laura, came to have a very close and special relationship with my parents.

The last time I was with Mom, I asked her about dying. Was she ready to go? Was she sad? Without missing a beat, she said, "I believe in Jesus and he is my savior. I don't want to leave your dad, but I know I will be in a beautiful place."

Our world is not the same without George and Barbara Bush, but their example remains ever before us. This book, then, is a celebration of those two remarkable people who showed us how to live a life of high purpose, with decency, integrity, kindness, and charity for all. In a word, they showed us dignity.

Preface

To be a witness does not consist in engaging in propaganda, nor even in stirring people up, but in being a living mystery. It means to live in such a way that one's life would not make sense if God did not exist.

Madeleine L'Engle

In my vocation as a priest, we often talk about a "calling." There are all kinds of callings. Being a priest is one of them, but so is being a mother, a spouse, a physician, an attorney, a writer, a salesclerk, a cook, a bottle washer. A calling tugs at you and will not let you go until you do something about it—ignore it, dismiss it, or respond to it. I feel I have been called to write this book and share it with you.

The title I chose a long time before I began to put words that respond to this call is simple: *Witness to Dignity*. Many will no doubt say we are living in a time when traits like sound character, integrity, and dignity are in decline, if not gone altogether. Journalistic, political, social, and even religious rhetoric seems devoid of compassion, gentility, and mutual respect or understanding. The shrill voices of division that so dominate the times in which we live make us question whether we have gone too far to turn back. And I would suspect—if not hope and pray—that there rises a hunger within more and more people for what President George H. W. Bush called kinder and gentler times.

At present, I serve as the rector of St. Martin's Episcopal Church in Houston, Texas. My duties include a number of things and absolutely require that I serve people from all walks of life. From August 2007 until December 2018—just over eleven years—two of those people I was honored and humbled to serve were George Herbert Walker Bush and his beloved wife, Barbara Pierce Bush.

A witness observes, becomes privy to a particular set of circumstances, experiences, and relationships unique to that observer. I suspect no one has numbered the words and pages that have been written about these two remarkable people, but to my knowledge, no one has written about their lives from the perspective of being their pastor, their priest, and well—yes, something that comes with my vocation—their confidant.

This is not a book about politics. This is a "tell-all" in that I will, in fact, tell you what I know—experiences that I was fortunate to witness. But if what you are seeking is some hidden story, some dark secret, some twist in the stories we have come to know and admire about our forty-first president and his first lady, you will be sorely disappointed. This is not that kind of "tell-all."

Shortly after the president's death, and just prior to his state funeral in Washington, I was being interviewed by a reporter for a British television program. We met in the Bethlehem Chapel in the bowels of the National Cathedral. The interviewer asked several questions but then got around to one that I suppose might have been considered tantalizing: "Can you tell us something that perhaps no one else knows about President Bush . . . something that might surprise us all?" There are matters with which I had spoken with the president over the years in confidence, and I will not share those; but this I can share, and it is what I told that reporter:

I suppose what would surprise people is that there really are no surprises. There are no skeletons lurking in their closets. The public life and the private life were lived in the same way. What you and I were fortunate to see is what you and I got. There was no broken continuum between the person I came to know and the person the world saw.

This is not a book about the Bushes' family history or political journey. There are plenty of those books. And frankly, I am not qualified to offer a reflection on either of those beyond what you likely witnessed in your own encounters, in your watching or reading of the news or one of the many volumes dedicated to those topics.

My intent is to share with you what was slowly revealed to me, my wife, and my children through relationships that began as many do but ended with an intensity and intimacy that few do.

Over the years, when I shared experiences members of my family and I had with President and Mrs. Bush, people have asked me, "Are you writing these down?" At first, frankly, I was not. I did not think, when I was called to St. Martin's, that I would have as much interaction and as many experiences with the Bushes as I ended up having. I confess that I never dreamed that the first meal my wife, Laura, and I shared with them would be the first of too many to count. I did not think after my first visit to see one of them in the hospital, that that same hospital would become a regular chapel of our meeting and praying together. I believed we might get to be with them from time to time, that they might be occasional churchgoers, that if we were fortunate, we might get to spend more than an hour or two at their home. But from those first visits to the last on the days and at the moments of their deaths, we very much, over time, felt we had another home. So frankly, I did not keep a regular diary or record—until now.

While there is a beginning and an ending, this is not a chronological story. What you have here is a set of vignettes that go back and forth to tell a larger story. It's one that I hope will, as it has done for me, allow you to laugh, to cry, to be inspired to live your life in a particular way that honors the gift it is to you.

Now, some will wonder about my motivation for pulling this together. I can only ask that you read it from beginning to end and make that determination on your own. Anyone who knew President Bush and the First Lady also knew they were not enticed by having the spotlight of attention on themselves. The president's mother often told her children, "Let's not talk about the big 'I.'" Doing so brought down a soft but firm gavel that sounded the judgment that drawing attention to oneself was not in sync with the Bush family ways.

I confess I wrestled with moving forward on this project for a long time, which is obvious as you hold now in your hands a volume that has come out years since the deaths of our forty-first president and his lovely first lady.

But the idea continued to nag me, so I finally turned to the Bushes' children, all of whom endorsed the idea, and all of whom in the end gave the green light. I suppose, with gratitude, I was encouraged the most by Governor Jeb Bush, to whom I turned in June 2020 with the following email:

Dear Governor:

…I touched base with you last year, but wanted to circle back. I'll try to be brief (hard for a preacher). I have thought for some time of writing a book on what Laura and I witnessed for just over ten years—I've toyed with the idea of "Witness to Dignity." We, of course, have no firsthand knowledge of the public lives they led (just pretty much what everyone else knows!)…but we have many memories of their humor, their charity, their kindness—in Houston, in Kennebunkport, in the hospital and of course, at the end—and we never witnessed anything but dignity.

I have spoken with some of our mutual friends at length about this, including Jim and Susan Baker—and while all of them have been supportive, many have also asked me, "…what is the purpose?" I think given the current climate of leadership we have now in our nation, the purpose would be to remind folk that having godly, dignified leaders of character is not only possible, but necessary. That what happens in private life matters in public life (and vice versa). There would be no calling out of current leaders—instead, I think the book offers the opportunity to "light a candle," rather than "curse the darkness." But toward that end, it seems timely…

I also think there should be some "record" of how they lived out their faith…not in a showy, on your sleeve kind of way—but, in the words of the plaque your dad gave to me, "Preach Christ at all times; if necessary, use words."

Then, one last thought, and this is what has kept me from taking the steps—I know your parents were great advocates of not talking about the "big me." Every time I have sat down to write something, it is hard to do without using personal pronouns…because, frankly, it is about what I witnessed… I don't want it to come off as "well, this is about a lot of really neat things we got to do because I was the President's pastor"—though I confess, they were pretty neat!

Do you have any thoughts?…

Many thanks…

Russ+

About two hours later, the governor responded:

I like the idea of shining the light rather than cursing the darkness. I think the point about the "big me" is an important one to tell the story and for your own ministry which in and of itself is important.

Jeb

This is one of many reasons why I asked the governor to write the foreword to this book.

So, I apologize to you on the front end that I am going to break the "big I" rule. One cannot be a witness without speaking of what the "big I" experienced, heard, saw. These are stories told through my eyes and the eyes of those who were part of those stories with me (other witnesses who will come forward as we make this journey together). I take delight in sharing them. I do not do so to prove a particular point, to impress, to turn the spotlight in my direction.

A practical point: I am a bit of a traditionalist. In our many years of friendship, with the exception of the times when I prayed for the president, I always referred to him as "Mr. President." He never corrected me, and so I always honored that. In recounting stories that occurred prior to our formal relationship, I will at times refer to him as "George," or "the future president." Once I cross over into the beginning of our relationship, I will at times in these pages refer to him as "41." But for the most part, when I share something about "the president," you can assume I am sharing something about our forty-first president.

This will not be the case with First Lady Barbara Bush. Not too long after I came to Houston, the Bushes were in Kennebunkport at Walker's Point. I had to call them over the phone to discuss a church matter. The president put me on speakerphone and as I began to talk, I said, "Well, Mr. President and Mrs. Bush," at which point she immediately said, "Mrs. Bush would be my mother-in-law... You can call me Barbara or Bar... but please don't call me Mrs. Bush." I learned early on the importance of following her directives! So, from this point forward, you will read "the First Lady," "Barbara," and "Bar" interchangeably.

In the pages that follow, I will share conversations, emails, and letter exchanges—moments, but mostly observations—as a proper witness should. Some are simply descriptive, some are basic correspondence, and some are rather intimate and personal. I began this project by asking the permission of the president and Bar's children—our forty-third president, Governor Bush, Marvin, Neil, and Doro—all of whom have become friends to one degree or another. Anything you read here is offered with their review and blessing.

Then, lastly, and most importantly, while a good part of this story will have connecting points between President Bush and the First Lady and their church and faith, this is not so much a religious book as it is a book about how they lived their faith. I am not offering a long sermon to prove a particular point, but I am unapologetic in that I write as a Christian about two Christians. President and Mrs. Bush had a deep commitment to Jesus Christ as their Lord and Savior, and they were (as you will see) active in their church, but their faith was generous in many ways. You did not have to believe as they did—they had friends from every Christian faith tradition and every major, and many minor, religious traditions. They were religious, yes, but they were believers, and I hope to offer a snapshot of the innumerable ways their belief shaped their lives—and the lives of those around them.

Inscribed on the face of the great sundial designed by Sir Christopher Wren in 1653 at All Souls College in Oxford is the ancient Latin proverb *Pereunt et imputantur.* Ascribed to the first-century Roman poet Martial, the literal translation is "The hours perish and are laid to our charge." For some, that has come to mean to spend wisely the hours one is given. But of course, it also implies that the hours we experience are, in fact, our possession until life's end, perhaps beyond that as well.

We capture perished time through the wonderful gift of memory. In the pages that follow, the stories you will read about the personal experiences my wife, Laura, and I shared with President Bush and Barbara are the fruit of cherished memories.

The opening quote by Madeleine L'Engle reminds us there is more to being a witness than mere observation, in the sense of what I have been describing here. I am that kind of witness. But what I am bearing witness to here is the faith of these two extraordinary people—the inward faith that nourished them, strengthened them, upheld them.

And I will submit that their witness was *to live precisely in an authentic way such that their lives would not make sense if God did not exist.*

Thus, my reader, let's begin. This is what I offer because I deeply love the president and Barbara Bush, and for reasons that I hope will become clear, I want to be a witness for them...and for you.

RJL+

CHAPTER ONE

LIFE LESSONS FROM WALKER'S POINT

Have to touch a rock...
Barbara Bush

S omething was wrong.

It was time for breakfast on July 15, 2015, eight years since I was called to be the rector of St. Martin's Episcopal Church, and with that, the birth of the friendship between my wife, Laura, and I and George and Barbara Bush. This was our sixth trip to Kennebunkport, Maine, where the Bushes' summer home—Walker's Point—has been a respite for members of the Bush family and their legions of guests for decades.

By now, we had worshipped together hundreds of times, shared meals and times of prayer, and worked together on projects at the church and in our community.

The night before, Laura and I were dinner guests of the president and Mrs. Bush's (Bar's) daughter, Doro Koch. The president and Bar needed to attend the intimate family birthday dinner of the president's younger brother, Bucky—an important family get-together, in large part because Bucky's wife, Patricia, had been battling a hard case of cancer for over two years. Bar had apologized no less than three times before our arrival at the Point that the president and she could not be with us since we had only arrived just hours before. "No worries," Laura and I both offered. "We'll have a great time."

Before dinner, Bar, Laura, and I sat on the porch of the "Wave," one of several small cottages on the grounds of Walker's Point—each, to some degree, designated to one of the children. The Wave was typically where Jeb and Columba stayed. We talked for nearly an hour—catching up on things in Houston, on Jeb's presidential run, on our shared concerns about the far extremes of both major political parties and the danger there is in capitulating to that kind of extremism. We talked about plans for the next few days and then Bar left to join the president, and Laura and I cleaned up for dinner.

Doro provided some light snacks and a great meal—salad, corn, "lobster potpie," and some light dessert. Doro's house is the "Bungalow," and we talked about how when we first came to the Point in the summer of 2008, we stayed in her house. We told her how anxious we were in large part because the Bushes had invited all three of our children—who at the time were fourteen, nineteen, and twenty-one. God only knows what children would do in such a setting!

However, within an hour of that visit, the president and Mrs. Bush were treating the kids like their own grandchildren, and the children felt like they were with new grandparents. Late in the afternoon of our first day, I was dressing in the bedroom when I heard in the other room a knock at the front door. I heard Laura say, "Well, hello there!" Then I heard the president's voice. He came over to "check on you, see if there is anything you need." He wanted to make sure the kids knew they had the "run of the place," and he encouraged them to make use of the bikes, tennis racquets, and boats. He was most concerned that they each learn how to ride a Segway, as the Bush family had acquired several and they were much fun.

The real testament to our kids' comfort level with the president, we told Doro, was that in the middle of the president's visit, our youngest, Luke, came walking out of the bathroom, dressed in his boxer shorts and brushing his teeth! The president just smiled, said, "Hello, Luke!" and patted him on the head. There would be many more memories like that at Kennebunkport, but none as memorable as the morning after our dinner with Doro.

The rule for eating at the main house was that all guests were welcome to come get coffee in the morning (without knocking), and if you wanted a hot breakfast, you came at 8:00 a.m.; if you wanted something cold (cereal and milk), you could come later. As I rolled over and picked up my phone, I had a text from Doro: *Mom wanted to make sure you joined us for breakfast at 8!* Since it was 7:45, Laura and I quickly got our act together and got over to the main house.

Bar was still out walking her pups, Bibi and Mini—part of her regular morning ritual was to walk them on a nearby beach. As we had so many times before, we came in a side door that leads into a hall between the kitchen and the Bushes' master bedroom.

But as we entered, it was clear something had happened. Paula, a longtime member of the Bush staff, looked at Laura, who speaks Spanish fluently, and said, "Está enfermo" (Is sick), pointing back to the president's bedroom. We could hear whispers only steps away. "Go...go," Paula said to both of us. The president was being tended to by an aide and his medical aide, Evan Sisley.

I saw him sitting in his recliner, but I came up from behind. We had not seen each other since our arrival at the Point. "Mr. President?"

"Yes? Who is that?"

"Russ Levenson, sir."

Laura added, "Laura too, Mr. President."

"Russ...Laura..."

You could tell he was smiling while he said it. He held out his hand to greet us. As we rounded the chair, we could see he had a large ice pack on his neck.

"What's going on, sir?" I asked.

"My neck. I fell and hit my neck."

"Does it hurt?" I said.

"Yep—hurts bad," the president said.

I had been with him many times over the years before, during, and after medical procedures. I had never heard him complain of pain.

Evan came in and asked the president a few questions. "Do you know when you were born?"

In a clear, strong voice, the president said, "June 12, 1924."

"Do you know what year it is?"

Again, a strong voice: "Twenty fifteen."

"Do you know where you are?"

"Yes…I am sitting in this ugly brown chair in my bedroom!"

"Between zero and ten, with ten being the worst, what is your level of pain?" Evan asked.

"An eight," the president said without hesitating.

"That's good enough for me," Evan said. "We need to get him to the hospital."

Of course, we did not know the extent of the injury at that time. So as Evan went off to call an ambulance, I told the president, before it arrived, that we should pray. He held out both hands and I prayed for God's presence, for healing, for a speedy recovery, and that he would be home before the day's end. The president was often moved to tears in prayer—and this time was no exception. "Thank you, Russ," he said when I had finished. Then Laura and I stepped back.

In the meantime, Bar had arrived, and while not panicked in any way, she was obviously deeply worried. As the ambulance headed our way, one of our concerns were the "Bush-watchers." The Bush-watchers were people who, almost around the clock, arrived by car or on foot and "watched" from the cliffs across the inlet from Walker's Point. They came with cameras and binoculars with the hope of getting a glimpse of a member of the Bush family. Clearly, seeing the president taken out on a stretcher with a brace around his neck would start the rumor mills around the globe.

Fortunately, by the time the ambulance arrived, a thick fog had covered the little hill across the way, and to my eyes, there was only one car. As discreetly as possible, the president was taken to the ambulance. Bar did not want to raise additional alarm bells when he arrived at the hospital, so she decided to see him off, and then we would wait for the initial report from the hospital.

We had a quick breakfast, then Laura and I walked to the rectory of St. Ann's Episcopal Church, the summer worship home for many in the Kennebunkport community, including the Bush family. We had just sat down for a cup of coffee with the summer priest, the Reverend Peter Cheney, and his wife, Kiki, when the phone rang. Peter answered it and then handed the phone to me, saying, "It's for you."

It was Jean Becker, the president's chief of staff, who would become a very close friend in the years to come. "What's going on?" I asked her.

"You and Laura need to get back to the house. He's broken his neck and they are about to call Barbara and tell her. I think you need to be there when she gets that call."

I did not hesitate. "We are on the way." I shared the news with Peter, asked for his confidence, which was rock solid, and asked for his prayers. Laura and I hightailed it back to the Point.

We walked in the front door this time and called out to Barbara just as the phone rang. Barbara, Laura, and I all sat down together in a small sitting room just off the kitchen where the family often gathered for a drink before dinner, or just to talk or watch television.

I sat on the sofa next to Barbara as she said, "So, how's my boy?" She listened carefully and began to wince and grimace. "I understand; we'll be right there." She hung up the phone. I was still in my walking clothes, and she looked at me. "You need to go clean up. We're going to the hospital—he's broken his neck."

I took those orders about as seriously as any I had received. Again, Barbara was concerned that we not cause a spectacle. So without the regular Secret Service entourage, she and Doro would ride with two agents, and I would follow. Laura and Barbara decided it was best for Laura to stay at the Point—we had no idea how big the room was at the hospital. But even in our departure, Barbara was concerned that Laura might feel as though she were being abandoned and invited Laura to use the car at the house to go into town—to make herself at home, a phrase we had heard dozens of times from the hosts of Walker's Point.

We took off. In midjourney, it seemed that we were no longer going to the local hospital, so I called Doro. She said they had made the decision to go ahead and transport the president to the hospital in Portland, Maine. Something had happened—something changed. "Just follow us," Doro said. I hung up and began to pray out loud.

As we pulled up to the emergency room bay, there were Secret Service agents waiting for us. One pointed at me and told me where to park, and he said he would meet me outside the emergency room and show me where to go. I parked, and my phone started ringing—it was Doro. I rounded the corner and she was waving for me to come on. She looked ashen and I was even more worried at that point.

As we walked into the hospital, the staff was careful to "cover" areas where other patients might be as the retired First Lady made her way down the hall with agents and hospital administrators, staff, and security in tow. As we came into the president's room, Bar announced, "We're here…"

"Who's that? Bar?" the president asked.

"It's me—Bar—Doro, and Russ."

Bar kissed the president; Doro and I took his hands and patted him a bit. Bar introduced the ER staff to Doro, and then she introduced me. "This is our priest, Russ Levenson—but he's like family." We all stood back and let the staff begin their extensive evaluations.

It was decided the president needed a CT scan to make sure the break had not impinged on his spinal cord in any way. So he was taken out, and the three of us—Bar, Doro, and me—were left sitting alone for a few moments. The feelings were palpable. We were deeply worried. Bar was a rock. "Well…I hate this for my boy," she said. Doro had held it in since morning and she began to cry. "I hate this for Dad…He already has to deal with so much." And I knew that for the rest of my time with them that day, my primary job was not to try and explain, or to talk much—but to sit, listen, and to offer simply my ministry of presence.

After a bit, the president came back. We took turns standing with him—holding his hands, talking to him. At one point, he looked up at Doro and said, "My wonderful, beautiful daughter." The president loved the warmth of embraces—he liked a good handshake, a gentle handhold; he liked hugs, kisses, and massages. He liked to have his back and head scratched. It comforted him, particularly since his battle with Parkinsonian syndrome had made him less mobile than he was only a few years before. So Bar comforted him in this way: she began to scratch his scalp with her wonderfully manicured fingernails. The president smiled and let out a little hum letting her know her touch was welcomed.

After a few minutes, she said, "What is this?" She ran across a rough patch on his scalp, the result of some oversunning on the water in his boat, *Fidelity*. "It's a scab! And here's another one!" She looked at me. "Feel that!" she said, encouraging me to join her on this little exploration mission. "Yep...I do," I said as now three hands were rubbing the president's scalp.

"Well," the president said, "you can call me Old Scabby-Head, I guess."

"Better Scabby-Head than another kind of head that starts with the letter *s*," she said. The Bush humor was alive and well.

As we waited for the results of the CT scan, things shifted significantly when the heart monitor went off—for several seconds, beeping quickly and loudly. The president showed no signs of distress, but the nurse came over quickly. "Mr. President, are you okay, sir?"

"Yep," he said, and then the beeping stopped.

The staff was clearly concerned. There were whispers in the room and out. Evan was called into the room and asked if this was normal. "Never happened before," Evan said.

A few more whispers, and then the ER doctor came over to talk to us: "Here is what is going on. We know the president has a broken bone in his neck, and we are waiting on the neurosurgeon to take a look at the CT scan before we can determine the best path of treatment [he was in surgery and hoped to be out soon]. But what just happened a few moments ago was the president experiencing some tachycardia—an unusually rapid heartbeat. Sometimes that can come on from coffee—but sometimes there are other reasons. We're going to have to keep an eye on it and, regardless of what happens, probably move him to an ICU room."

Then he continued, a bit more somber. "Have you all discussed the lengths to which the president and family want to go should his heart stop?"

It was as if someone had dropped an anvil into the conversation.

"What?"

Evan was brought back into the room, and the parameters, which had been made clear by the president a long time ago, were reiterated. But for some reason, everything now seemed to go from bad to worse. They took the president off for X-rays.

We waited and waited some more—probably a few hours. During that time, Doro went to the cafeteria and picked up three chicken salad sandwiches. When she returned, Barbara read aloud a new article on Jeb's run for president and the potential role of his wife, Columba, as first lady. Overall, it was very positive, laying out "who" Jeb was—a normal kid who partied in college and was known to be a "toker." Bar paused, looked at Doro and me, and said, "What is that?"

Doro saved me from having to answer. "Someone who smokes pot, Mom . . ."

Bar raised her eyebrows and said, "There you have it—the mother's the last to know!" The article helped pass the time. It was a diversion from what we were really thinking.

The hospital staff could not have been any more professional in any way. About the only laugh Doro and I got was when a nurse came in to ask Mrs. Bush to sign a form acknowledging that she understood the general Medicare policy coverage. I turned to Doro and said, "Well, if the First Lady does not know, we're all sunk!"

After the president was brought back to the room to wait on the results of the X-rays, an administrator came to tell Mrs. Bush that the hospital was often 100 percent full and they were waiting for a room that had another connected to it so Mrs. Bush and the agents would have a place to sit and relax. Mrs. Bush did not pause. "You don't have to do that—if need be, I'll sleep on the floor."

"That would not be good for my image, Mrs. Bush," the administrator said.

Soon, Dr. William D'Angelo, the hospital's neurosurgeon, came in and explained that though the vertebra was broken, it had not impacted the spinal cord or column. He said he believed the president could recover with the strict immobility of a brace and no surgery. The questions began. "Can he resume regular activities? Can he eat? Will he be able to sit up? Ride in a car? Ride in the boat?" The doctor's answer to all of those questions was, "Yes, depending on how long it takes to heal, but probably not the boat, unless it is perfectly calm water." He went on: "He'll have to be in that brace for about three months." He was clear, professional—and as he finished up, the president did not complain or seem overwhelmed by the news. He just held out his hand and said, "Thank you, Doctor."

As the doctor left, Bar said, "Now that we know, we are going to ask Russ to offer a prayer, and then you," she said, pointing at me, "are going to take Doro home." We came over to the bed and circled the president. Bar took his right hand in her left, and Doro took my left hand. As we prepared to pray, the president said, "I'm not completely sure what is going on."

"You have a broken neck, dear, and now we are going to get you better."

His eyes filled a bit with tears. "So I am going to make it?"

"Yes," Bar said on his left.

"Yes, sir, you are going to make it," I said.

He smiled, but Bar quickly reminded him, "It is serious—now, let's pray."

I had brought my oil stock, a small round silver box with holy oil. It was the same oil stock I had used in prayer with the president on dozens of occasions during my regular visits to Houston Methodist Hospital over the course of two months in the winter of 2012–2013, when he was battling a severe case of bronchitis, and on Christmas Day in 2014 in that same hospital when he returned for a few days. We had prayed this way many times over the last years, but this would be one of the most important prayers we had ever shared. I anointed his head with a cross, and the president, Bar, Doro, and I circled up as I prayed for his healing, those tending and caring for him, and for the presence and peace of God. With the amen came some more tears. I gave the president a kiss on the forehead with my farewell: "I love you, Mr. President."

"Love you too, Russ," he said, words that came easy to this former leader of the free world.

Doro and I headed back to Kennebunkport. I was driving, and she called her siblings one by one to give them updates: Marvin; the forty-third president, George; and Jeb, who was on the campaign trail in California. Neil had learned about the accident just before getting on a plane to Singapore but did not know the full extent of the injury. Doro called a few other close friends, and then we spent the rest of the drive talking about her faith—a lively, real, abiding faith.

Doro had been baptized as a teenager in an underground church when her dad was the US ambassador to China. She had no miraculous conversion moment, but the older she got and as life went on, her faith just became more and more meaningful to her—her relationship with our Lord became all the more real.

We returned, and Laura quickly came out to join us. We sat on the porch of the Wave for about an hour. Now 4:00 p.m.—some eight hours after Laura and I first came over for breakfast that morning—I walked her through the events in Portland.

"Is he in pain?" Laura asked.

"He is," I told her and then talked about everything else that had happened.

Her face turned red and her eyes filled with tears. "I hate it for him. I hate to think of him hurting. He is the sweetest man, one of the sweetest men I have ever known—even if he were not the president, I know he would still be as sweet as he is."

Bar had stayed until the president got settled in his room and then decided to come home for dinner. She pulled up shortly after Laura and I finished talking. I came out to the car and she gave me a quick update. "Is Laura okay?" she asked. "I hated to think about her here all day without you."

We talked for a bit and then she asked, "Have you all been to the new house?" She was referring to the latest addition to Walker's Point—a house Jeb and Columba were building on the grounds that was in the final stages of construction.

"No," I said.

"Well, go get Laura. I want to show it to you all."

It was, well, another diversion. Bar, the pups, Laura, and I walked from the main house to Jeb's house. As we did, Bar talked about things other than what we were all thinking. She talked about her relationship with the president's father—Prescott—who, she said, could be a "hard man."

She recalled when she and George were first married that she was a smoker. She came out of the house one day smoking, and her father-in-law said, "Who said you could smoke?" Bar quickly retorted, "When you marry me, I'll tell you." The serious Prescott burst out laughing and they became fast friends.

She also remembered how kind he was to her when their daughter Robin was so ill with leukemia. He was in his own senior years and asked Bar to join him as he "picked out a spot" for his burial. Bar knew he was doing this to help her ease toward the inevitable and to think about Robin's burial. "That was very kind," she said, and then her voice cracked and her eyes filled with tears.

Often people who imagine Walker's Point say how "extravagant" it must be—but nothing could be further from the truth. The houses that have welcomed countless guests over the years are more like homes—they are comfortable, modestly decorated, and simple. There is no question that the view is unmatched—something only God could paint—but as to the homes, they are in no way what some might call "over-the-top," and they are designed as much for family needs as they are for the guests that are ubiquitous in the May-through-October season. The Wave, our temporary home, had no air-conditioning, but frankly, open windows allowed nature's cooling system and sound machine to work just fine.

Jeb's house-to-be was much the same. We toured the downstairs, with Bar's pups, Bibi and Mini, at our heels.[1] Knowing Bar, who by then traveled virtually everywhere with the aid of a walker, would find the stairs hard to manage, Laura and I offered just to take a quick tour of the second level on our own. "No," Bar said. "I want to go with you...Watch this!" And she made her way on hands and feet—like a crab crawling up the stairs—to the top level.

As we finished up and headed back to the house, Laura and I knew Bar must be very tired. We offered to go into town and have dinner on our own. "No," Bar said. "I want you all to have dinner here. Let's go get a drink. I think bourbon and water." And that's what we did.

Laura, Bar, and I all filled our glasses and went into the sitting room before dinner. Just as we turned on the television, Jeb Bush was being interviewed about his presidential campaign platform. Bar did not smile or point or shush her guests. In fact, she was going through her mail—some of the countless letters she receives each day—most of which she tries to respond to personally in the morning before the day begins.

I turned and looked at my Laura, who was looking at Bar—as Jeb was talking about his own hope to be president. It was surreal—no other way to put it.

We hit the dinner table and offered a prayer yet again for the

---

1. More on these ferocious animals later!

president. About the time we dug into a delicious meal of salad and chicken enchiladas, the phone rang. It was the president! He talked to Barbara and Doro, and then Doro handed the phone to me.

"Hello, Mr. President," I said.

"Hey, Russ."

"I hate that you are going through this, but we are all praying for you."

"Thanks, Russ."

"I hope you sleep well, Mr. President... We love you."

As we finished up, Bar told us she would rise early to walk the dogs on the beach. "You want me to come along?" I asked.

"Sure!" she said. "We'll go at six a.m."

Laura and I, exhausted from the day, returned to the Wave, talked for a bit, and went quickly to sleep.

I rose early on July 16—less than twenty-four hours after the beginning of that dreadful day before. But we had a better picture of where things were. I grabbed some coffee and joined Bar. Two female Secret Service agents rode in the car front and Bar and I rode in the back with the pups.

As I noted earlier, on most days, Bar would begin her day with a brisk stroll at a nearby public beach where people were allowed to walk with their dogs until 9 a.m. As Bar pushed her walker in front of her, with her pups circling her feet, we made our way to the water.

By now, of course, the public knew. People were coming up to Bar, expressing their concern and sympathy. Bar never seemed to make anyone feel like they were interrupting or intruding—she often greeted with a hug, a "Good morning," or—frankly—an "apology" for Bibi and Mini, who liked to take on any passing dog, regardless of size.

She was always on the lookout for one of her pups to leave behind a little fertilizer—and she had her own poop-scoop bag. As she always did, she cleaned up after her own pups—no aide or agent was asked to even consider it. And when they tried, as I had on these walks, she always refused the offer and cleaned up "nature's gift" herself.

As we walked, Bar kept saying how beautiful it was. It was chilly, and the wind was whipping us both a bit. She pointed to the intricate designs painted by the waves—traveling snails on the surface and worms beneath, carving subterranean trails that looked like tree branches into the wet sand, only to stay for a few brushes of the waves before changing or washing away altogether.

Bar had a fun habit on this beach. The bookends of the walking area were two boulder-filled jetties jutting out into the rough North Atlantic. Bar liked to make her way to one bookend and when she reached it, she tapped it with her foot. "Have to touch a rock," she said.

After touching one, we turned and made our way toward the other—perhaps half a mile down the beach. As we walked, Doro joined us. A friend came up to speak with Bar, and Doro and I broke away with Doro's large dog, Rocky. We talked for a bit before stating the obvious—we were still worried about the president.

Doro said, "You don't know what life will throw at you until you get old." I told Doro I'd been working through C. S. Lewis's autobiography, *Surprised by Joy*, again, in which he described the childhood years as the "dark ages." But he did not necessarily mean that in a pejorative way. He was simply saying what Doro was—that as children, we still live in the age of fantasy, magic, and wishful thinking. Much of the "hard" of life has not stung us yet—we have yet to be "enlightened" as to what life is all about.

Doro and I agreed that's probably a good thing—it's good we don't know it all from the beginning. Finally, as we reached the other end of the beach, and without looking up or breaking the conversation, I noticed Doro—like her dear mother—tapped a rock with her foot and turned around. We then joined Barbara and made our way off the beach and back to the Point.

Cleanup, another breakfast, circling up for prayers—and off we went. Laura and I returned to Houston as Bar went to the hospital to be with "her boy." As we flew home, I thought about how wonderful this family had been to so many. Some call the family a dynasty (an adjective they modestly decline). But in the years following my call to St. Martin's, Laura and I have come to know them as a family. And if you take the public roles away, they are like most families. They have great and not-so-great days; celebrations and sadness; smiles, laughter, tears, and memories.

But like those great boulders on that beach, they have weathered the storms of life—and seem to incredibly continue to. Their loyalty to one another is unparalleled; the fidelity to one another and to their countless friends is rarely matched in a family that spends so much of its time in the public eye. Their commitment to caring for others is not pretend. It is earnest, real. It's not for show; it is sincere.

And their faith. It's not a wear-it-on-your-sleeve, in-your-face, holier-than-thou kind of faith. But it's one that bespeaks of the need for God when it is time to give thanks—and when sad, or afraid, or uncertain about what the future holds.

It has been a tremendous honor to serve this family alongside my wife—and to be welcomed as part of many public, and many more private, moments. While I hope this friendship will last for many years to come, what happened on July 15, 2015, solidified for me the belief that this family is rock solid. On one side of the shore that is their life, there is the rock Barbara; and at its other end, George. And if you touch the rock once, or a hundred times, or a hundred times more than a hundred, you've been blessed to know that things like character, integrity, honesty, kindness, loyalty, faith—and love—still matter, still have value, still give life its greatest meaning and purpose.

I am so glad to have had the opportunity to touch those rocks—and have them touch my life as well.

What you have just read was written about a week after the president's accident.

What I hope the above story offers is a bird's-eye view of the regular lives of two remarkable people who just happened to be the forty-first president and first lady of our United States. I hope it also unveils a faith that manifests itself as courage, compassion, kindness, tenderness, and an earnest desire to invite God into the room.

There is a wonderful thought-provoking bit of verse by American poet Edgar A. Guest titled "I'd Rather See a Sermon." The opening salvo reads,

> I'd rather see a sermon than hear one any day;
> I'd rather one should walk with me than merely tell the way.
> The eye's a better pupil and more willing than the ear,
> Fine counsel is confusing, but example's always clear;
> And the best of all the preachers are the men who live their
>   creeds,
> For to see good put in action is what everybody needs.

As a pastor and priest, I am certainly in the sermon-giving business, but now I would like to allow George and Barbara Bush to preach for the remainder of these pages. I suspect by the time you finish reading, you will have witnessed, as I have, two people who lived their creeds and spent their lives to the very end putting in action the kind of authentic life of faith, love, and service that everybody needs.

Let the sermon begin.

CHAPTER TWO

OVERTURE

The checks will continue to come in until it is definitely established that I am safely in heaven.

G. H. W. Bush in a letter to his parents[1]

A saint is never consciously a saint; a saint is consciously dependent on God.

Oswald Chambers[2]

One of the things Laura and I learned over the years as our friendship with the president and Bar grew is that they were, personally and as a couple, amazingly adept at recounting stories. Things that are revealed in the various books and their own memories and volumes of correspondence were in many ways living memories that they liked to share again and again in gatherings with friends and family. As with any new relationship, what I would describe as an appropriate veil of discretion was slowly lowered the better we got to know one another. At the

---

1. George H. W. Bush, *All the Best, George Bush: My Life in Letters and Other Writings* (New York: Simon & Schuster, 1999), 39.

2. Marin H. Manser, comp. *The Westminster Collection of Christian Quotations* (London: Westminster John Knox Press, 2001), 331.

same time, what you saw publicly is what I witnessed privately, which, frankly, makes their stories all the more remarkable. Before I begin sharing with you those things I witnessed personally as they relate to their personal faith and lives, it behooves me to provide a bit of history.

Church, Love, Sex, Choices, War, Marriage, and Destiny

The president was reared in the Episcopal Church and faith of his parents. When he was a child, the family attended Christ Church in Greenwich, Connecticut. His mother, Dorothy, with whom the president was very close until the day of her death, was firmly planted in the Episcopal Church and often took the time to read to her family from the Book of Common Prayer. Barbara grew up in the Presbyterian Church. Church attendance from the president's and Barbara's early years to their last ones remained central to their lives.

The Bushes loved—*loved*—to tell the story of their meeting, and I suspect if my own wife, Laura, and I heard the story once, we heard it a dozen times.

During a Christmas break from their respective schools, they met at a vacation dance in Greenwich in 1941 and took to each other immediately. Often when the president told the story, he would make it clear that he remembered her wearing a green-and-red dress. George Bush was seventeen at the time; Bar, only sixteen. She would later write that she went home and told her mom, "On this night...I'd met the nicest, cutest boy, named Poppy Bush."[3]

Fanning the flame of that initial spark was not an easy task. The future president was attending Phillips Academy in Andover, Massachusetts, and Barbara was a student at Ashley Hall, a private school in Charleston, South Carolina. So letter writing was the tether that kept

---

3. Barbara Bush, *Barbara Bush: A Memoir* (New York: Charles Scribner's Sons, 1994), 16.

them bound, but as time went on, they tugged firmly on that binding, growing closer with each visit.

After the attack on Pearl Harbor, George Bush joined the navy in 1942, and the young couple did not kiss until just before he left for basic training. There is something quite poignant in that bit of revelation. From what I have read, and from what I know, George H. W. Bush never felt the compulsion to be a moralist, in that he never necessarily felt it his Christian duty to spend a lot of time evaluating the moral fiber or ethical choices of others. But in his own life, he was personally committed to living his faith, and one area where that proved true was in his own decision to honor chastity outside of marriage.

Evidently at one point, George and his mother had some discussion about just how far young couples should carry their physical desire for one another if the couple was not betrothed, after his mother found his younger sister, Nancy, kissing her beau in the summer of 1942. In reflection, he thought it necessary to fess up to his mother regarding his own personal convictions and wrote her a letter from his training grounds at the naval air station in Minneapolis, Minnesota.

Dearest Mum,

Now about your question, Mum. I do love to kid you and did this summer, but I agree with you in part...Kissing is not an obligation a girl owes a boy regardless of how often he takes her out or how much money he spends...but I don't think that it is entirely wrong for a girl to be kissed by a boy... I kissed Barbara and am glad of it. I don't believe she will ever regret it or resent it, and I certainly am not ashamed of it. I'd tell you, Mrs. Pierce, or anybody at the same time I might as well tell you I have never felt towards another girl as I do towards her. Whether the feeling is mutual I cannot say...if Barbara sort of forgets me, which is not unlikely, as I have no chance to see her at all, I don't believe she will ever dislike me more for having kissed her. She knows how I felt towards her *and she must have shared some of the same feeling or she would not have allowed me to kiss her. I have never kissed another girl...For a girl to be kissed by someone whom she loves (or <u>thinks</u> she love [sic]) and who—she is sure cares for her—O.K. This is a very uncoordinated piece of writing and unorganized but I've said about what I mean.*

...Now for me to continue and tell you the facts of life—of the life I'm living in 1940's—Apparently Mum you seemed so terribly surprised when Pressy[4] and I hinted around about the "things that went on?" Pressy and I share a view which few others, <u>very few</u> others even in Greenwich share. That's regarding intercourse before marriage. I would hate to find that my wife had known some other man, and it seems to me only fair to her that she be able to expect the same standards from me. Pres agrees as I said before, but not many others our age will. Daddy has never discussed such things with us—of this I am very glad. But we have learned as the years went on by his character what is right and what is wrong. Most fellows here—true some are engaged and some believe as I do—but most fellows take sex as much they can get...I would be most facetious were I to deny ever having experienced said feelings. The difference is entirely in what we have been taught; not only in "what" but in "how well" we have been taught it.

This pertains not only to the N.A.S. [Naval Air Station] Minneapolis, Minn., but to every town in the country, to college campuses—yes, even to Yale University. Boys you know—boys I like very much—and even boys I admire have had intercourse with women...

4."Pressy" was Prescott S. Bush Jr., elder brother of George by two years. When they were children, they actually shared a room together, and for that reason and many more, the two were very close siblings.

... To think all this was brought on by your asking me what I thought about kissing.

Much love,

Pop[5]

professor "sexology" Ph.D.[6]

I share this letter from the president's personal collection of letters, *All the Best*, for a number of reasons. First, it shows the strength of the young navy pilot's inner moral compass. He had thought it through and in his own mind had landed squarely with a decision to remain chaste until marriage.

Second, it reveals that while that was his personal choice, he realized it put him in an infinitesimal minority of men, and perhaps even less so of military soldiers who often made decisions based upon the possible last opportunities put before men who might very well die in combat. Personally, he felt it was wrong; but he understood why men and women, given a particular set of circumstances, might make a decision to be sexually active before marriage.

Third, it speaks to "how" the president incorporated many of his own decisions about what is right and what is wrong. He noted that sexual intimacy was not something he discussed with his father but that his own compass was drawn to a moral north not so much by words but by observation. Being a man of moral fiber to the future president would be the effective tutor above and beyond one's words. The Bush methodology toward an ethical and moral life was not just to speak of it. It was to live it, something the future statesman would model himself, a theme I will return to often in the pages that follow.

---

5. The president often signed his letters "Pop" or "Poppy," a nickname given to him by his uncles when he was born. His paternal grandfather, George Herbert Walker, was called Pop, so GHWB became Poppy, or sometimes "Little Pop." When my wife and I were with the president and Bar, she often called him Pop, and his children and grandchildren almost always did as well.

6. G. H. W. Bush, *All the Best*, 30.

Fourth, it also speaks to a remarkable intimacy that existed between George and his mother. Few men have this kind of open relationship with their parents, but George clearly did not draw back from anything other than full engagement with his parents about virtually all matters, even the most personal.

Fifth, we see here the president's humor and the way he employed it to disarm uncomfortable or tense interactions (i.e., "professor 'sexology' Ph.D."). It is fair to say this is a trait that served him well in every station of his life.

But I think the most critical reason I share this note is that it may speak to our own time. Who now in the twenty-first century delves this deeply into a decision-making process about sexual intimacy?

These days, there are few, if any, portrayals in film, television, in music or books that suggest anything other than sexual intimacy is something that happens nearly from the get-go in a romantic relationship—regardless of its depth, length, or orientation. Teens who publicly make promises to abstain from sexual intimacy before marriage are often ridiculed by their peers and the media. It is no longer questioned when film stars, music idols, and sports figures choose to live together with a "partner," have children without the benefit of marriage, or laugh off a leaked sexting exchange or "sex tape." And suffice it to say, our culture, especially in the West, has grown accepting of and comfortable with the sexual antics of our elected leaders—whether they be the local mayor or the president of the United States.

Prior to sharing this letter from his collection, the president wrote, "Please keep in mind as you read this letter that I was a very innocent eighteen-year-old, and it was 1942. Things were very different way back then. Having said that, I do not think it would be a bad thing if more eighteen-year-olds today were just as innocent." That wisdom speaks to our own time and it speaks for itself.

Despite this decision, which was no doubt a struggle for this young pilot, George was deeply and passionately in love with Barbara. The two decided to have what the president would later describe as a "secret engagement." Given his closeness to his parents, it was not a secret long and became public knowledge once it was published in his hometown paper in December 1943.

The distance between them only made their love grow stronger, and this was perhaps nowhere more obvious in the early days of their relationship than in his letters. Sometime after our relationship with the Bushes grew, we learned what was already public knowledge—that during the war, Bar had actually lost all of George's letters to her, with the exception of one. Shortly after news of their engagement hit the papers, he wrote her the only letter she did not lose from those early days, from December 12, 1943.

> My darling Bar,
>
> ...I love you, precious, with all my heart and to know that you love me means my life. How often I have thought about the immeasurable joy that will be ours some day. How lucky our children will be to have a mother like you...
>
> ...Bar, you have made my life full of everything I could ever dream of—my complete happiness should be a token of my love for you...
>
> Goodnite, my beautiful. Everytime I say beautiful you about kill me but you'll have to accept it—
>
> ...All my love darling—
>
> Poppy
> public fiancé as of 12/12/43[7]

"Why Had I Been Spared?"

Less than a year later, the possibility of moving from engagement to marriage was put to its greatest test—one that in the end would set

---

7. G. H. W. Bush, *All the Best*, 38–39.

George Bush on a path of pondering even more deeply the mysteries and ways of God.

After completing his flight training, he served as a photographic officer for a torpedo squadron based on the USS *San Jacinto*. In the spring of 1944, the *San Jacinto* was part of a task force that took part in operations against Marcus and Wake Islands in May, followed by operations in the Marianas in June.

On June 19, the task force won one of the largest air battles of the war, but during the return of his aircraft from the mission, then ensign Bush had to make a forced water landing. The plane was lost, but the crew survived unscathed, being rescued by the destroyer USS *Clarence K. Bronson*. In July, George was one of two pilots who received credit for sinking a small cargo ship.

Beating-the-odds stories are not uncommon in times of war, but when you beat them more than once, you begin to stretch those same odds. That is exactly what happened to George only months after the June 19 water rescue.

In August 1944, George was promoted to lieutenant junior grade, and the *San Jacinto* began operations against the Japanese in the Bonin Islands. On September 2, Lieutenant Bush piloted one of the four TBM Avenger aircraft from Torpedo Squadron VT-51, attacking the Japanese installations on Chichi Jima. For this mission, George's crew included Radioman Second Class John Delaney and Lieutenant Junior Grade William White.

After the attack got underway, all four of the Avengers from the Squadron came under attack, including George's aircraft, which was hit. When he talked about the experience, he would say there was a huge jolt—like a giant fist crunched into the belly of the plane. The cockpit was filled with smoke, and he said he could see fire creeping across the edge of the wing toward the fuel tanks. And yet, he pressed on, completing his part in the raid by releasing four five-hundred-pound bombs on the target. There were already stories aplenty about what happened when pilots survived crashes near enemy islands, only to swim into the hands of their would-be capturers, who would often then torture, execute, and even cannibalize their prisoners.

With his plane still on fire, Bush decided to fly away from the island, where he instructed the crew to bail out. Tragically, of the three, George was the only survivor. One crewman's chute did not open and he fell to his death. It was never clear what happened to the other, nor was it clear which airman jumped with George, who hit his head on the tail of the plane on the way down, tearing a portion of his chute. Delaney and White were both listed as killed in action.

Once George hit the water, he began to get stung by jellyfish, and he swallowed so much water that he began to vomit profusely while floating in his inflated raft. Soon, several flyers circled around him in the air until up popped the submarine USS *Finback*, and its crew pulled him to safety.

This is a harrowing tale for any human being, perhaps even more so for a navy pilot who already brushed up against water peril once. But to survive an air attack, fall from a burning plane with a torn parachute, and suffer a head wound only to land in the added dangers of perilous water near enemy territory—it was, well, extraordinary.

This is a story I had read about a number of times, but the president I came to know would often reluctantly, sometimes in a whisper, retell the story to friends, family, and to his priest. Even to his last days, despite surviving and the passing of decades, he would still wince at the loss of his two comrades.

He could have easily been one of them. About one hundred thousand airmen died in World War II—nearly 25 percent of the total United States fatalities. For all Allied nations in the war, about a quarter of pilots would be killed or seriously injured each month in major combat missions, and in some battles the loss rate reached as high as 40 percent.[8]

---

8. Jesse Greenspan, "George H. W. Bush's Role in WWII Was among the Most Dangerous," History.com, February 13, 2019, https://www.history.com/news/george -hw-bush-wwii-airman.

Given these odds, and the fact that George successfully flew over fifty combat missions in the Pacific, his own survival was nothing short of miraculous.

Though survival was key after the perilous moments that day in September, Bush would become a temporary crewman of the *Finback*. For the next thirty days, he participated in a number of other rescues of downed pilots. But beyond his duties as a navy pilot, he dove deeply into a question he would ask for most of the days of the rest of his life: "Why had I been spared and what did God have in store for me?"

In the years that followed, many would speculate: Was he spared so he could rise to the office of president? Was his survival part of the plan to bring an end to communist dictatorship in Eastern Europe nearly a half century after the twenty-year-old pilot was pulled to safety from the rolling Pacific? Was it to lead a coalition of nearly thirty nations to liberate an invaded people in the Middle East? Was it to be part of the mystery of helping to bring into this world children with particular gifts for particular times, including one who would serve as a governor and another who would serve as a president during the worst attack on United States soil in American history? Or was it, as he sometimes liked to quip especially in his later years, to simply be married to Barbara?

Was it to show the world that it is quite possible, if not preferable, to lead a nation—a world—with character, dignity, honor, and integrity?

I think it is safe to say that perhaps it was all of these things. But this pivotal moment suddenly transformed the life of our forty-first president. He was not just a young man from an established family who was thrust into the role of a surviving hero, but a survivor who began to consider deeply the ways of God.

I was struck in our conversations about moments like these that the president never questioned the existence of God but only—perhaps— God's methodology, God's reasonings. In reflection, he would say that he had a number of spiritual experiences—connecting points—that inspired the growth of his faith. And his rescue from sea was certainly among them, even if it begged the question as to why he had been spared. That would be a question we would return to a number of times once our relationship began.

I have worked with enough people in thirty years of ordained ministry to know that sometimes when someone experiences horrible tragedy, they pitch in the towel on any belief in God or even the enduring and eternal qualities of goodness, holiness, meaning, and purpose. Nihilism is an easy book to pull off the shelf when things in life do not turn out as one had hoped. George H. W. Bush never opened that door and, in fact, crept more and more intentionally beyond the open door of faith—a faith he would need again and again as life began to unfold.

Following his harrowing escape from death, he would waste no time getting onto more important matters. During his next trip home, he and Barbara married on January 6, 1945, at the First Presbyterian Church in Barbara's hometown of Rye, New York.

Their newlywed season was spent in a variety of places as the president continued to serve in a newly formed squadron. Sometimes Barbara joined him, and other times she could not. But in the months leading up to the end of the war, they lived at bases in Maine, Michigan, and Virginia Beach. At the time, of course, no one knew that the end of the war was drawing nigh, so the unspoken reality of George returning to battle was constantly present—until V-J Day, September 2, 1945.

Barbara recalled many times people pouring into the streets in jubilant celebration at the end of the war. But before that day ended, George and Barbara, together, found their way into a small local church where they prayed together—thanking God for the end of the war and praying for those who had lost their lives.[9]

With the end of the war, George was honorably discharged with two air medals and a Distinguished Flying Cross, and the two youngsters who had already experienced more "life" than most twice their age

---

9. B. Bush, *Barbara Bush*, 25. On occasion throughout this book, I will recall memories that the president or Barbara shared with my wife, Laura, and/or me, but when possible, I have tracked down a reference that might expand the story—such is the case here.

headed off to Yale to pursue George's college degree. There, he played baseball, began collecting more friends, and grew more deeply in love with his Bar, as she with him. Barbara often recounted that even in the early days of marriage, she came to experience what her father had told her: "Every day you are married, you grow more deeply in love with your husband or your wife."

After graduation, the Bushes headed to Odessa, Texas, where George began a career in the oil business. In the years that followed, the family began the emotional roller coaster of celebration and grief. George W. was born in 1946. But three years later, in September 1949, Barbara's parents were in a horrible car accident and her mother died. Barbara was pregnant with her second child at the time and could not attend her mother's funeral. But when the baby was born, George and Barbara named her Robin, after Barbara's mother. They moved to California for a brief period before returning to Texas in 1950, a place that would be "home base" for several years, as the family grew with yet another son, Jeb, born in 1953.

Put to the Test . . . Again

By now, George and Barbara had been put to the test by life a number of times, but perhaps no more than in the winter of 1953, just weeks after Jeb's birth. Most people who have read anything about George or Barbara will know that little Robin was diagnosed with leukemia the same year her younger brother was born.

The months that followed were filled with grueling treatments, travel, waiting, and praying. At the time, the Bushes attended First Presbyterian Church in Midland, and it was there that George stopped *every morning at 6:30 a.m.* on his way to work to pray for Robin. A sustaining friendship, and prayer partnership, during that time was with the Reverend Dr. Matthew Lynn. Though Robin had brief periods of remission, her precious days would not continue on this earth into the new year, and she passed peacefully from this life to the next on October 11.

The subject of Robin's death, and life after death, is something that I discussed with the Bushes many times—more with the president than with Barbara. But again, much like the president's query about surviving being shot down in the Pacific, in this moment, neither Barbara nor George abandoned their faith. I think it is fair to say any of us would have had reason to do so, but even at the darkest moment, Barbara would sense the presence of God. In her memoir, she wrote,

> Eventually the medicine that was controlling the leukemia caused other terrible problems. We called George, and by the time he got there [home] our baby was in a coma. Her death was very peaceful. One minute she was there, and the next she was gone. I truly felt her soul go out of that beautiful little body. For one last time I combed her hair, and we held our precious little girl. I never felt the presence of God more strongly than at that moment.[10]

The family had a funeral, though no burial, as they made the decision to donate Robin's body to research. The months that followed were agonizing, but to hear Barbara tell it, they literally survived because of their love for one another, the love and support of their family and friends, and, in Barbara's words, "Not the least, we believed in God. That has made an enormous difference in our lives, then and now."[11]

No parent expects to bury their child, and even after officiating at more funerals for children than I can now count or recall, I still shudder at the anguish that such a death brings.

While we did speak about Robin's death on a number of occasions, the president rarely discussed it publicly. One exception was a poignant exchange he had with a reporter who was trying to portray President Bush as a distanced New England elite who had no real understanding

---

10. B. Bush, *Barbara Bush*, 45.

11. B. Bush, *Barbara Bush*, 41.

of the way people lived in the real world, by asking Bush if he had ever experienced any "personal difficulty." The father spoke through the statesman with heartfelt clarity: "Have you ever sat and watched your child die?"

"No," answered the reporter.

That was a "no" the majority of human beings can, mercifully, answer. It was not an experience that eluded George and Barbara Bush.

Saints Alive

I began this chapter with two quotes. The first was a bit from a letter George wrote to his parents on December 29, 1943. It reveals, yet again, his winsome approach to life, but there is yet another layer pulled back as well...

> *Dear Mum,*
>
> *...I changed my allotment check, so starting either at the end of January or the end of February the check for 143 dollars will come to you every month. The reason for this is because if I left it made out to the bank and I should become lost the payments would immediately be stopped. If it is made out to you and I am lost the checks will continue to come in until it is definitely established that I am safely in heaven*[12]

Here we have the realities of war: the young navy pilot, paid $143 a month, could be lost at sea, shot down, captured, and executed—he was, in fact, at least one of those things. This was reality—this was the way things were, so he was making the point that should his life end, he wanted his survivors to have whatever benefit they could...not until his death, but until he was "safely in heaven."

---

12. G. H. W. Bush, *All the Best*, 39.

This, along with the other observations your witness author has made in this chapter, says much. The possible end of life at the hands of the enemy did not mean the end of life. "Yes, well, we all say things like that," one may be tempted to say. But look before and, more importantly, after the writing of this letter, and you will see it was not an empty hope offered from a young man to his mother—it was actually a statement of fact, a belief, a matter of faith.

The second quote is that of Scottish pastor Oswald Chambers, best known for his book *My Utmost for His Highest*, who wrote, "A saint is never consciously a saint; a saint is consciously dependent on God." I believe if the president were sitting with you or me right now, he would scoff at being called a saint. Unfortunately, those in my vocation have too often taken the word *saint* and transformed it to mean something otherworldly—ethereal, unattainable. Chambers's words reboot that for us: a saint is one who is not so much interested in being a saint as they are mindfully and consistently dependent on God.

George and Barbara Bush learned the need for that dependence early on. And it would be a dependence that would carry them into the remaining six decades of their lives together.

Thank God for saints like these.

CHAPTER THREE

TO HOUSTON AND BEYOND

He cannot have God for father, who refuses to have the Church for mother.

Saint Augustine of Hippo

Worship is basic to my life. Our family has endeavored to uphold our faith by participation in the life of our Church.

George H. W. Bush[1]

St. Martin's has been Church for our family for over fifty years . . . . . . It is a wonderful Church home!

Barbara Bush[2]

Finding St. Martin's

Over the next few years, George and Barbara were blessed with three more children: Neil (b. 1955), Marvin (b. 1956), and Doro, born about the same time they moved from Midland to Houston, in August 1959.[3]

---

1. President George H. W. Bush, in "An Open Letter to the Clergy on the Eve of His Inauguration as President," January 18, 1989.

2. Barbara Bush, September 7, 2009.

3. The Bushes moved twenty-nine times during their marriage, remaining deeply in love the whole way through—that might be counted as a miracle in and of itself!

Only months later, that same year, St. Martin's Episcopal Church would be formally dedicating its first formal worship space. The parish began as a small "neighborhood" church. The third bishop of the Diocese of Texas, the Right Reverend Clinton S. Quinn, had tapped a young but extraordinarily gifted and energetic priest, the Reverend Dr. Tom Bagby, to plant a church in the Tanglewood subdivision of Houston, and Bagby agreed.

The parish began with about 250 members that met first in a large home, not far from where the church is now. Within no time, under Dr. Bagby's dynamic leadership, the parish grew, and by 1959, the parish was home to over 2,000 baptized members.

George and Barbara attended St. Martin's as visitors for a while before joining more formally. Since George was already baptized and confirmed into the Episcopal Church, his membership was merely a matter of paperwork. He transferred his membership to St. Martin's from Christ Church in Greenwich, Connecticut, in December 1964.

However, earlier that year, as a lifelong Presbyterian, in order to be a "confirmed member," Barbara would need to go through adult confirmation classes. One of her "classmates" was James A. Baker III, who had been attending St. Martin's with his first wife, Mary Stuart, who became a member of the parish in 1961. Bar would be confirmed some fifty years later—but that is a story for later in the book. Nevertheless, the Bushes (and Bakers) found their church home, and they never questioned whether or not this was the place to be. The parish became the beating heart for the Bush family.

Though George and Barbara's lives began to take a significant shift from oil to politics, this did not keep them from their participation in the life of the parish—a participation that mirrored that of any other active members. They were regulars in church, with Barbara teaching Sunday school and George serving in leadership (and he had no resistance to serving as an usher or working the coffee and breakfast line on Sunday mornings).

A New Mission and a Moral Choice

As time wore on, Houston would be home—but a new life's mission was about to launch. In 1966, George Bush was elected to the House of Representatives for Texas's Seventh Congressional District. It would be the first of many posts that took the Bush family to the nation's capital. In 1970, Congressman Bush ran for the United States Senate. Though he suffered a bruising defeat by Lloyd Bentsen, the disappointment was short-lived. He accepted President Richard Nixon's appointment to be the tenth US ambassador to the United Nations in March 1971. He left the post in January 1973 after being tapped to serve as the new chairman of the GOP.

Chairman Bush had great admiration for President Nixon, having key roles in his election campaigns and supporting many of the president's policies. But as the shadow of the Watergate scandal grew long, George Bush's strong moral compass would drive him to make a clear choice.

When the now infamous Nixon recordings about the Watergate break-ins were made public, George realized President Nixon, who had been instructing his staff to block the FBI's investigation of the Watergate break-ins, had lied. George Bush was crushed. He lost all faith in this man whom he had admired, endorsed, and served. On August 6, 1974, the future president would write in his journal,

> *It is so hard to know what is fair and right. It is so easy to get a headline. It is so difficult to assess how the sublimation of one's views in a position of leadership might be detected as softness. All of this is quite clear to those on the outside but it is never clear to those on the inside. I don't want to pile on. I don't want to add to the woes of the President, I don't want to increase the agony of his family. And yet, I want to make damn clear the lie is something we can't support. But this era of tawdry, shabby lack of morality has got to end... I will take Ford's decency over Nixon's toughness because*

what we need at this juncture in our history is a certain sense of decency.[4]

George Bush's burning internal certainty about right and wrong, about decency and propriety up and against decadence and immorality was not the fruit of a desire for political gain or historical notoriety but a natural outgrowth of his innate goodness and faith.

On August 7, George Bush would write a private letter in which he made his position clear: *It is my considered judgement that you should now resign . . . Until this moment resignation has been no answer at all, but given the impact of the latest development, and it will be a lasting one, I now firmly feel resignation is best for this country, best for this President.*[5] The next day, Nixon announced he would resign as president of the United States.

This was no easy task for George Bush, but he felt he had no choice but to be honest, and clearly his honesty, borne of a desire to restore dignity in the office of the president, may very well have been the final straw that ended the Nixon era.

Unlike many politicians, however, George Bush did not cut and run from his former mentor. The two kept in close touch over the years, and President Nixon and George Bush would exchange letters and, when the occasion provided, would visit with one another until Nixon's death in 1994.

But with Nixon and his vice president, Spiro Agnew, gone, House Minority Leader Gerald R. Ford stepped into place. Among many, George Bush was considered for the role of vice president, but Ford eventually settled on Nelson Rockefeller. But then Ford tapped George Bush to be the chief of the US liaison office in the People's Republic of China, essentially making him ambassador to China. After that, George returned to Washington and accepted the president's appointment to head up the Central Intelligence Agency.

When President Ford lost to the governor of Georgia, Jimmy Carter,

---

4. G. H. W. Bush, *All the Best*, 191.

5. G. H. W. Bush, *All the Best*, 193.

George and Barbara decided it was time to head back to Houston, but it would be a short season back in his beloved Texas. Within four years, Ambassador Bush would be returning to Washington DC as Vice President Bush for the genesis of twelve remarkable years of leadership.

As I noted at the beginning, this is not a book about a political career but about the faith of a husband and wife who lived in a number of spheres—but those public lives were informed by their private faith and strengthened by their consistent commitment to their church family. Though the vice president and second lady were settled into their new home in Washington, they kept a tight spiritual umbilical cord that bound them to their church in Houston. While in Washington, the vice president and Barbara would frequent several Episcopal churches, including the National Cathedral and St. John's on Lafayette Square.

Often, when someone moves from one city to another, that person becomes a member of a church closer to their new home. Not so with the Bushes. Despite their years away, they never abandoned their St. Martin's loyalty, and they remained closely tied to the clergy and members of the parish.

I stay in touch with Tom Jr., son of the now late Dr. Tom Bagby. He has told me that on a number of occasions—in fact, almost every Sunday evening like clockwork—close to the dinner hour, their home phone would ring and it would be Vice President Bush. He would ask his priest and pastor, "How did church go today? Who was there?" and then go on to ask about various members of the church by name. Though it was 1,500 miles from the vice president's office, St. Martin's remained a lifeline throughout his eight years in that office, and perhaps no time was that made clearer than in a speech the vice president gave at the invitation of Dr. Bagby, just months before Dr. Bagby's retirement.

A Special Trip Home

Sometime in the fall of 1982 and knowing his retirement would take place in the new year, Dr. Bagby reached out to the vice president and asked if he would be willing to address his home church near Christmas of that year.

The vice president agreed, and on Sunday morning, the day after Christmas, 1982, he spoke with heartfelt devotion but also intimate transparency about the depth of the love he and Barbara had for his church and for the faith that sustained them.

At one point, according to the text of that speech held in our archives at St. Martin's, the then vice president told a story about his recent trip with Barbara to Red Square in Moscow to represent the United States for the funeral of Soviet Union leader Leonid Brezhnev.

But…there was no mention of God. There was no hope, no joy, no life ever after, no mention of Christ and what His death meant to so many. It was very different. So discouraging in a sense, so hopeless, so lonely in a way.

I thought of St. Martin's Church, of our joy all year long, but especially at Christmas. If only their country was one nation under God, if only the kids there had grown up with a Christmas angel and maybe a shepherd in the family, if only, if only they had Tom Bagbys and others taking the hopeful, joyous message of Jesus into their lives…peace would be so much easier to achieve.

We shall continue to pursue peace. We must succeed in achieving it. After all, St. Martin's has given us a clear shot; in so many subtle ways we have been strengthened here.

Blessed are the peacemakers for they shall inherit the earth!

The vice president would have his chance to forge that plea for peace six short years later. He and Barbara would return to St. Martin's many more times in the years that followed, but his return to the nave of St. Martin's in November 1987 would not be to offer remarks but to pray for a new beginning.

CHAPTER FOUR

THE NEW CHALLENGE

George wanted to begin his first day as President-elect by going to church.

Barbara Bush

Please guide us and guard us on our journeys—particularly watch over Dad and Mother. We pray that our lives be beacons to you by remembering the words of David: "May that which I speak and that which I have in my heart be acceptable to thee, oh Lord."

George W. Bush

D r. Tom Bagby retired as the first rector of St. Martin's in 1983, and the parish called Claude Payne as his successor. Payne had been serving as rector of St. Mark's Episcopal Church in Beaumont, Texas, for the previous fifteen years, and the newly elected president called upon his new rector a few days prior to the election, asking if he and the family could gather for a worship service the day after the election.

"George wanted to begin his first day as President-elect by going to church," Bar would later write, adding, "It seemed the natural thing to do since we both were fortunate enough to grow up in families where God played an integral part."[1]

The president-elect and Barbara and their children, along with former pastor Tom Bagby and new priest Claude Payne, gathered in the nave of St. Martin's for prayers. But no prayers meant as much to Barbara and the president-elect as those offered by the future forty-third president, George W., who was forty-five at the time:[2]

> Our Heavenly Father, we thank you for your many blessings: We thank you for our health and safe passage during the past months. We thank you for our country and the freedom to exercise our free will. And we thank you for our greatest gift of all—your Son...Please give us strength to endure and the knowledge necessary to place our fellow man over self... We ask that you open our hearts and minds to prayers so we can feel the solace of your gentle love. Please guide us and guard us on our journeys—particularly watch over Dad and Mother. We pray that our lives be beacons to you by remembering the words of David: "May that which I speak and that which I have in my heart be acceptable to thee, oh Lord."

Beginnings are, of course, important. How one begins a new job, a new relationship, a new venture often sets the course for how that same person will manage what is to come.

In the mid-1970s, the Moral Majority movement was launched with a series of "I Love America" rallies across the United States. The movement jumped into the American culture where division was growing on a wide range of moral hotspots. It was not long before conservative leaders had to court the Moral Majority crowd for support, and

1. B. Bush, *Barbara Bush*, 248.

2. B. Bush, *Barbara Bush*, 248–49.

this was certainly the case in the Reagan and Bush years. But clearly Bush believed the old adage that religion and politics make strange bedfellows.

Yes, Christianity and Christ were his way, but as he would say in his inauguration speech, "A President is neither prince nor pope, and I don't seek 'a window on men's souls.' In fact, I yearn for a greater tolerance, an easy-goingness about each other's attitudes and way of life."[3]

This was, in fact, a subtle message that he believed firmly in the separation of church and state. His own commitment was to preserve the principles of the First Amendment primarily as a guardian of religion from the government. But he would not be coaxed into believing the government's task was to evangelize the world.

But that separation in no way meant that George H. W. Bush would hold back from either exercising or speaking of his faith. For the forty-first president, that dividing line was put in place by our Constitutional framers to protect one's personal faith from being controlled or squelched by elected leaders; but it did not imply those leaders could not draw upon their faith to inform or guide their own decisions.

However, like most Episcopalians, Bush would make no "show" of his faith. As I would preach many years later at his state funeral, he did not wear his faith on his sleeve. But he did depend on his faith each and every day of his life—whether in or out of an appointed or elected office. His faith was inclusive, not exclusive. During his run for president, he would be pushed by more fundamentalist elements to take a firm stand on how he came to faith—in short, whether or not he had a conversion, or a new birth experience. He would push back by saying there was not one moment but many—a gradual though nonrelenting deepening into a personal relationship with Jesus Christ as both his Lord and his Savior.

The campaigning vice president was not averse to welcoming the support from religious conservatives, and I think it is fair to say that he felt himself a religious conservative. But this was a man who, with

---

3. George H. W. Bush, "Inaugural Address," January 20, 1989.

his wife, had traveled the world, had lived abroad, and had made close friends from every language, race, and nation. Theirs was a serious faith that took even more seriously the chief Christian ethic to love. Among the closing words of his inaugural speech were, "If our flaws are endless, God's love is truly boundless."[4] George and Barbara Bush lived that truth and shared God's love with others as a reflection of their experience of the abundant love they had received from God.

And so . . .

The stage was set. Buoyed by his decisive win, President-elect Bush would make plans for his inauguration.[5] His speech was marked by a fresh and buoying optimism, setting that stage for putting into practice two phrases he embedded in the lexicon of American history: "a kinder and gentler nation" and "a thousand points of light."[6]

Those phrases could very well have been mirror images of the Episcopal liturgies the newly elected president had heard his life through. But he clearly felt that the gift of his election, which now purposed his life for the highest office in the land, could only begin in one way—with an oath and a prayer.

From what I know, President Bush was not superstitious, but he did place tremendous value in history and tradition. So he chose to take the oath of office not on one Bible, but two—the Bush family Bible and the Bible upon which George Washington began his presidency.

Then, having been sworn in by the chief justice of the Supreme Court, William Rehnquist, after a few words of recognition, the newly

---

4. G. H. W. Bush, "Inaugural Address."

5. In the 1988 election, George H. W. Bush took all but ten states and the District of Columbia. Since that election, to date, no winning candidate has exceeded the number of states won, the percentage of popular votes (53.4 percent), or the number of electoral votes (426).

6. Upon his nomination to run for the GOP ticket, Vice President Bush employed "kinder and gentler nation" as part of his hope in his acceptance speech. His "thousand points of light" was birthed on the campaign trail, but he would use it again in his inaugural address and State of the Union speech.

inaugurated president would bow his head before the Authority of the whole human family and invite the citizens he was called to serve to join him:

> And my first act as President is a prayer. I ask you to bow your heads:
>
> Heavenly Father, we bow our heads and thank You for Your love. Accept our thanks for the peace that yields this day and the shared faith that makes its continuance likely. Make us strong to do Your work, willing to heed and hear Your will, and write on our hearts these words: "Use power to help people." For we are given power not to advance our own purposes, nor to make a great show in the world, nor a name. There is but one just use of power, and it is to serve people. Help us to remember it, Lord. Amen.[7]

And for the next four years, President George H. W. Bush did just that.

---

7. G. H. W. Bush, "Inaugural Address."

CHAPTER FIVE

THE "ST. MARTIN'S WAY"

Lord, if your people need me, I will not refuse the work. Your will be done.

Martin of Tours, d. AD 397

You are welcome to come and worship with us.

Charles Kraft, parish leader of St. Martin's

To this day, when you speak with one of the clergy or the lay ministry team at St. Martin's of Houston or with the lay leaders and membership, you will likely hear something about the "St. Martin's Way."

As the fourth rector of this large parish, I have often been asked what the "secret sauce" is that fosters such organic growth and ministry. My answer would be to say something about this "way," which is really quite simple: to faithfully proclaim the Gospel of Jesus Christ and to live into the two great laws of our Judeo-Christian history—to love God and to love our neighbor. In other words, the St. Martin's Way takes seriously the Christian faith, but it is a faith lived out not only with one's lips, but in one's life.

The parish has worked hard not to be pulled left or right into church or societal controversies and planted itself deeply in this crucial work of the church and its members. Allow me to share a few notable moments in which the contagious nature of St. Martin's played itself out. I will do this by backing up a bit to describe when and how things changed when our two parishioners, George and Barbara, became vice president and second lady.

When Claude Payne took the reins from Tom Bagby as the second rector of St. Martin's, he knew, as did his two successors, that if the Bushes were in town, they would be in church. And if they were coming to church, that usually began with a routine telephone call from the Secret Service, or a member of Vice President Bush's staff.

In those days, they usually attended the early service at 8:00 a.m. Father Payne never "announced" that the vice president and Mrs. Bush might be attending, and yet no one expected it to be a secret.

One exception to the practice of subtle security occurred when Father Payne invited the vice president to speak at the 11:00 a.m. service in recognition of Veterans Day, which quickly made the local press. The Secret Service made an advance visit, and on the day of the vice president's address, a bulletproof plexiglass shield covered the pulpit.

All of this generated some attention beyond the Houston area, and not one to miss an opportunity to jump in the spotlight, Madalyn Murray O'Hair, a well-known atheist and public critic of all things religion, showed up with a group of protestors holding highly visible placards.

The church rests at the corner of Sage Road and Woodway Drive in the Tanglewood subdivision of Houston, and that is where the atheist brigade set up shop. A commotion began to break out a bit with the chants and jeers from O'Hair and her noisemakers. Father Payne appointed Charles Kraft, a lay leader who happened to be on usher duty that morning, to go out and see what he could do to cool things down a bit.

Charles had no problem presenting himself verbally, and nonverbally, as someone who was in charge of the presenting opportunity. He approached Ms. O'Hair and politely said, "Ms. O'Hair, you do believe in the separation of church and state, don't you?"

Predictably, her reply was "Of course."

Then Charles continued: "Well, Ms. O'Hair, you see the curb right there? Up here on the sidewalk is the church. Down there in the street is the state. Separate. Now, if you would like to come in and worship with us, you and your folk will be most welcome."

She pressed the point by waving an envelope in the air and saying bellicosely, "I have a letter for the vice president!"

In response, Charles said, "Well, Ms. O'Hair, this is not a post office . . . That is right down the street. This is a church, and you are welcome to come and worship with us." At this point, there was little the group could do but retreat.

This little exchange reveals a bit about the character of St. Martin's: clear about identity, gentle and loving in living it out. St. Martin's would be neither afraid nor dissuaded from being the church it was called to be—rooted in solid biblical principles lived out in a kind of gracious, gentle, and consistent hospitality. It was a day that President Bush and Barbara would recall as being "well-handled" by Claude Payne and the leadership. And I do not know, but I suspect the Secret Service could not have done a better job of busting up the little crowd of disrupters. They were armed—so too was Charles Kraft; he just happened to be armed with his faith. Indeed, a "soft answer turns away wrath" (NRSV).[1]

Another historic moment for the city of Houston and St. Martin's that reveals a bit more about the nature of the church and its intersection with the Bush presidency came in the summer of 1990 on the parish's annual "Bring a Friend to Church Day."

Claude Payne had encouraged the members of St. Martin's to put the Great Commission into practice by going out into the community and inviting friends and strangers to St. Martin's. It just so happened that this particular Sunday was the day before the launch of the sixteenth G7 summit, when the heads of the world's largest industrial nations would gather on the campus of Rice University in Houston on July 9–11, 1990.

---

1. Proverbs 15:1.

Well, what did St. Martin's most well-known member do? He invited his visiting friends to church! Members still recall the day when Prime Minister Margaret Thatcher and her husband, Denis, as well as Prime Minister Brian Mulroney and his wife, Mila, joined the Bushes for worship.

As he began his presidency and carried out the policies and work of his administration, President Bush's heart was never far from his faith or his church. This was perhaps most crucially revealed in yet another "invitation."

When Iraq invaded Kuwait on August 2, 1990, the president and his team, including Secretary of State and St. Martin's member James A. Baker III, began to build a worldwide coalition of response. Kuwait was an ally; Kuwait was a friend; and the growing abuses of Saddam Hussein's advancing Republican Guard pushed the allied coalition first to attempt a pullout, and when refused, plans for an all-out war began.

The president not only prayed fervently about what would be required to get Iraq out of Kuwait, but he sought spiritual counsel of several, including then presiding bishop of the Episcopal Church, Edmund Browning. Bishop Browning was a strident pacifist, but the president felt compelled to bring the spiritual leader of his own denomination into his circle of discernment. For the president, it was not all about developing a strategy for victory; it was about a thoughtful ethical and moral foundation for moving forward. Toward that end, the president and his team actually spent time studying the just war theory, developed by the ancient church father, bishop, and theologian, Augustine.[2] Essentially, the theory proposed the coming together of several factors that, in some cases, proved that war, though horrible in nature, was just in order to deter, prevent, and/or defeat evil.[3]

---

2. D. AD 430.

3. Augustus developed seven necessary elements in his just war theory: (1) war must be the last resort; (2) war must be carried out by a legitimate authority; (3) war must be in response to a wrong that has been suffered; (4) the war must have some probability of success; (5) there must be a right intention in moving forward with the

With this in hand, along with atrocities cataloged by Amnesty International, the Red Cross, and other watch groups, the president and Secretary Baker met with the presiding bishop seeking his support, or at the very least his silence on the matter. Despite the evidence, the presiding bishop refused to support the war to come and he made it clear that he felt more at home with the protestors that were growing in number outside the White House gates than he did with a member of his church who sought his counsel and spiritual comfort and support.

That said, from what I know, there was no major religious leader in the world that did not understand that President George H. W. Bush was not just making a strategic decision but a moral one.

As the deadline for Hussein to pull out loomed, on the night of January 15, 1991, the president was in and out of prayer. He received a supportive cable from the pope—a cable he would describe as "beautiful." He heard from his longtime friend and spiritual counselor, Billy Graham. And, when all was said and done, he did hear from Bishop Browning, who called with a word not of support, but as a bishop to a member of his flock carrying, literally, the weight of the world.

We know what happened once the war began—it was one of the shortest, and most successful, military accomplishments in world history. Operation Desert Storm was launched on January 16, 1991, and it was over six weeks later, on February 28, 1991.

However, what we witness here is a common thread—the faith of George and Barbara Bush. Again and again, they turned to their faith, and their church, as the foundation for the enduring stories they built with every aspect of their service.

I happened to be attending Virginia Theological Seminary (VTS) in Alexandria during most of President Bush's presidency. I entered VTS in the fall of 1989 and graduated in the late spring of 1992. Though I never met the president during those years, many spouses of seminarians

---

war—specifically that the peace sought must exceed the peace that occurred without use of force; (6) proportionality; and (7) civilian casualties must be taken into account.

served in various positions on his staff, many of whom were very good friends of Laura's and mine.

They would often report that the president, before major decisions around any matter, would invite members of the staff who would like to join him and Barbara for prayer or for worship. This often occurred at St. John's Episcopal Church in Lafayette Square, only steps from the White House and the de facto church "home away from home" during the president's years in the Oval Office.

But these invitations were not out of character or inconsistent with the practiced theology of the Bushes that, in many ways, played itself out in generous invitations—an invitation to worship offered to a protesting atheist; an invitation to world leaders to worship in the pews on a Sunday morning in the Bushes' small neighborhood church in Houston; an invitation to the president's church leader to offer counsel—even if it was counsel that was a voice of opposition. This was, and remains to this day, a fruit of the St. Martin's Way.

I am confident there are many more such examples that could fill many more pages, but these three speak a great deal to the unbroken continuity in the lives of George and Barbara Bush in those years in the White House—their faith, their church, their Lord.

To St. Martin's second rector, Claude Payne, this would be no surprise. Shortly before the November 1988 elections, Father Payne was sitting at a Women of St. Martin's meeting when a member of the staff slipped in to say the vice president had called, was holding, and wanted to speak to him.

Father Payne made his way to the phone: "Hello, Mr. Vice President." Then the vice president said,

Claude...I have a favor to ask. We feel very good about our election prospects next Tuesday. My favor is that you plan a special service early on Wednesday morning for our family and friends at St. Martin's. This would be a Prayer Service in thanksgiving for our nation. Though we are optimistic,

> we want to have the service regardless of the outcome. We
> don't want to publicize this and don't want the press. Yet we
> do want you to spread the word among friends of ours that
> they are encouraged to join us, as well as all the clergy.[4]

As you read that, may I ask you just to sit with that for a moment?

You know from the last chapter that this service happened, that it was a moment of wonderful celebration and expectant hope. But before all the other invitations—before asking the nation to pray together at his inauguration, before gathering with world leaders who would together forge a new world by presiding over the dissolution of the Soviet Union and the collapse of the Berlin Wall, before waging one of the most pivotal wars in the Middle East—George and Barbara called their pastor and invited him to gather friends and family to pray, regardless of win or loss, and to give thanks. No cameras. No press. No fanfare. Just prayer.

Again, may I ask you just to sit with that for a moment?

Before we turn the page from the St. Martin's Way, what follows is just a bit more on how that is lived out among and through the parish members. The patron saint of the parish is Martin of Tours. He grew up in Pannonia, became a Christian at an early age, and went on to join the Roman cavalry in Gaul.

Perhaps the most well-known story from Martin's life emerges not from his days in service to the church, but from when he was a soldier. He was stationed in Gaul, modern-day France, when one day he was approaching the city of Amiens on horseback. As he reached the city's gates, he was met by a half-naked beggar. Almost without thinking— impulsively, some have written—Martin immediately cut his cloak in half and covered the man.

That evening, Martin had a dream of Jesus robed in that same half cloak, and then he heard Jesus say to the angels, Martin... clothed me in

---

4. From notes given to me by the Right Reverend Claude Payne on September 7, 2021.

this robe. This was, without a doubt, a practiced faith, for Jesus taught his disciples: "I needed clothes and you clothed me...Truly I tell you, whatever you did for one of the least of these brothers and sisters of mine, you did for me."[5]

Martin would go on to become a priest, a monk, and finally the third bishop of Tours before his death in AD 397. He is one of the most revered of Christ's followers in the Christian faith, and one can find tributes to his ministry in churches and shrines all over the world—including Houston, Texas.

As we will continue to read the sermon that was George and Barbara Bush's lives, we will see time and time again how they lived into the legacy of Martin of Tours. They, like Martin, believed if the people of God needed their service, they were ready to render it.

Claude Payne was still the rector of St. Martin's when the Bushes moved back to Houston after the president's loss to Bill Clinton in 1992. It is no secret that the loss was crushing and disappointing. Historically, if Texas billionaire and independent candidate Ross Perot, who had no reasonable chance of winning the election, had not entered the race, President Bush would have won a second term.

Governor Clinton garnered 43 percent of the popular vote, while Perot took roughly 19 percent. President Bush had 37 percent, and virtually every study of the 1992 election suggests that Perot drew on dissatisfied members of the president's base. Had Perot stuck to the oil business, the president would have likely easily captured the election and begun another successful term. Alas, it was not to be. So he returned to the Lone Star State and sought solace and strength from his family, his friends, and his faith.

Of high priority when they settled back into Houston was plugging back into church. Within days, they would take their place and renew their friendship with Father Claude Payne and his wife, Barbara. But it

5. Matthew 25:36, 40.

was a short reunion, as Payne was elected the seventh bishop of the Episcopal Diocese of Texas in 1993.

By this time, the small neighborhood church that began in 1952 had grown to nearly five thousand baptized members, and a nationwide search began to find a skilled preacher and pastor to take the helm of St. Martin's. The search committee and vestry landed on the dean of the Cathedral Church of the Advent in Birmingham, Alabama, the late Reverend Dr. Larry Gipson.

Larry's widow, Mary Frances, has remained a good friend and she still loves to tell the story of the day President Bush called their home after Larry accepted the post. Larry was already running up against the clock as he dressed to officiate at a baptism.

The phone rang, Mary Frances picked up, and the president said, "Hello, Mary Frances, this is George Bush." Mary Frances, thinking it was one of their friends pulling a prank on the Gipsons as Larry prepared to move to Houston to take on this new and massive mission, rolled her eyes and sarcastically said, "Right! Sure! Of course it is!"

"Mary Frances," the president said, "This IS George Bush." Mary Frances was horrified, but her initial disbelief was no surprise to the president. Almost everyone who ever got a call from him once he stepped into public office could not believe that the former congressman, CIA director, vice president, and now president would take the time to pick up the phone and call you himself.

The president and Barbara took the Gipsons under their wings and welcomed the friendship of their new priest and his wife. They ate together, worshipped together, and learned from Larry's outstanding preaching and teaching as he continued to extol the St. Martin's Way.

The "retired" president and first lady began to jump back in with both feet. When Larry Gipson and the vestry decided to launch a multi-million-dollar campaign to replace the old fifties-era church with a new neo-Gothic church well suited to hold a congregation that continued to flourish and grow, the president and Bar offered to publicly endorse the campaign, bringing it to a successful conclusion and completing one of the most massive building projects in the history of any mainline denomination.

In 2000, when it became clear that Houston would be home for good, the president and Barbara made the decision to have Robin's remains shipped from Putnam Cemetery in Greenwich, Connecticut, to Houston. They wanted Robin to be buried on the campus of Texas A&M in College Station, Texas.

When the time came, the Bushes wanted no attention or press brought to the moment. They only wanted their priest and his wife. Together, the four of them circled up, prayed together, and buried the remains of George and Barbara's precious child in a small patch of land—where, many years later, they, too, would be buried by their fourth rector.

They would return to their church family week after week, always accompanied by Secret Service but never with the kind of falderal that could so easily surround such public figures.

One of the favorite stories often told among the usher crew at St. Martin's comes from one such Sunday morning. It seems it was a very cold morning, quite atypical for the Bayou City. Secret Service had arrived before the president and Bar to go through the regular safety protocols.

Moments before the service, the Bushes' small motorcade pulled up. The president helped Bar out of the car and as he approached the church doors, he noticed one of the ushers had on a blazer, but no coat or jacket.

"Aren't you cold?" the president asked.

"No, sir; I'll be fine," the usher replied.

With one hand the president received the worship bulletin from the young usher, but with the other, he whipped off his coat, wrapped it around the usher, and walked away to find a place in the pews and begin his morning prayers.

There you have it: the St. Martin's Way. A faith not only of lip service, but life service.

CHAPTER SIX

"LET'S SHARE"

A cheerful giver does not count the cost of what he gives. His heart is set on pleasing and cheering him to whom the gift is given.

Julian of Norwich

Let's share . . .

Barbara Bush to Laura Levenson

My mentor, Episcopal priest, and preacher extraordinaire, the late John Claypool, used to say to me, "History turns on slim hinges." What he meant was that sometimes when we look back at our life's timeline, we see intersections that might foretell more. And certainly, there were more—many more—than I could ever imagine.

During the run-up to the '84 election, I had a chance encounter with then vice president Bush when he made a campaign stop not too far from Birmingham-Southern College, where I was a rising senior.

A long period of bipartisan political leadership was firmly established in the Reagan/Bush years, ushering in a long season of economic prosperity and diplomatic policies that were literally bringing an end to oppression around the world and thawing the long, dark season of the Cold War. The stage was set for what would be a second historic landslide.

The feeling in the auditorium where we were gathered to await the vice president is, even now, hard to describe. The Reagan/Bush accomplishments were palpable, and it was hard, even for their critics and opponents, to argue with their successes—something that became evident in the election results: Reagan and Bush would take forty-nine states, while Vice President Mondale would take only one and the District of Columbia.

Though I am now more independent than fully invested in one political party or another, at the time, I was a fully engaged member of the College Republicans. On the day of the vice president's rally, my roommate at the time and I were part of a small circle of young supporters, perhaps no more than a dozen of us, who were ushered into a room to be met by Vice President Bush. We stood nervously for a few moments before the tall, stately, exuberant Bush entered the room and began to make his way around, taking time to speak with each student and asking a question or two. I confess I was a bit starstruck.

Weeks later, I received a large manila envelope and opened it to find a photo that was snapped of the two of us in that moment that I thought would never be again. It came with a kind note and a signature that decades later would become more familiar to me than I could have ever imagined.

I share that little story with you because it shows a consistency of character and generosity that George H. W. Bush showed through his entire life. Yes, he was campaigning, but the election was all but secured. He did not *have* to take the time to visit an admiring crowd in Birmingham, Alabama. He did not *have* to step aside and visit with a small group that had little, if any, influence on what the future held, and he certainly did not *have* to go to the trouble to have his staff take a photo, track down a nameless undergraduate, and send off a piece of memorabilia that I actually have to this day. He did not have to do any of these things—but it was in the then vice president's DNA to give of himself.

Would You Hold, Please, for President Bush?

In 2007, I was in my fifth year as rector of Christ Church in Pensacola, Florida. The previous few years were tough. In 2004, the city was slammed by one of the largest hurricanes in American history, Ivan. Lives were lost, tens of thousands of homes and businesses were destroyed, and Christ Church sustained substantial damage to its worship space that had been built at the turn of the twentieth century.

But within three years, the city had recovered, the economy was growing, the parish had been rebuilt. Laura and I were looking forward to a long, fruitful season of ministry along the Gulf Coast with our three children—Evie, Jones, and Luke.

But then came the call to consider entering the search process for St. Martin's fourth rector. I confess it was a very difficult decision. Our family loved living near the beach, hurricanes and all. Most of our lifelong friends and family lived east of the Mississippi. My predecessor at Christ Church had served as its rector for over thirty years, and I had planned to do the same, if not more.

But the process moved along, and after months of discussions, interviews, and prayer, as a family we agreed this was a vocational call from our Lord to start a new season of ministry.

I was intent on working every day until my last day. One morning, I was preparing to leave my home for a pastoral visit, when the phone rang. I picked it up and saw the name on the display screen: OFFICE OF GEORGE H. W. BUSH. Here I was presented with a small vocational dilemma—do I rush off for my pastoral visit? Or do I answer this call from what appears to be the forty-first president of the United States and a parishioner at the church where I would soon begin a new season of ministry?

I took a deep breath and picked up the phone.

"Is this Father Levenson?" came the voice of Linda Casey Poepsel, the president's executive assistant and longtime aide.

"Yes, ma'am, it is."

"Would you hold, please, for President Bush?"

I do not remember his exact words, but I remember they were warm and familiar. He welcomed me to the new role and said that he and Barbara looked forward to meeting Laura and our children. He said we would be cared for and supported. It was not rushed—it was, frankly, generous.

Unfortunately, Laura was not at home at the time. She worked at a locally owned jewelry store and I tracked her down to say we had just been welcomed by the president. She was thrilled, as was I. And as the day unfolded, we called family and friends.

But more poignant than this call was something the president chose to do. The chair of the St. Martin's search committee, Scott McLean, knew this move would be hard for us, so he put in a call to the president's office sometime after our initial phone conversation. Scott said the president called him back within fifteen minutes. They talked a bit about their new rector, and Scott passed on what he knew about our particular family situation: that we had four aging parents, all within a few hours' drive of our home in Pensacola—that this move meant some heartache and tears for us.

About two weeks after the president and I had talked by phone, a hand-addressed envelope arrived at my parents' home in Birmingham and Laura's parents' home in Roanoke, Alabama. Enclosed in each was a handwritten two-page personal letter from the president. In it, he told them how happy the Bushes were that the Levensons would be coming to Houston. How he knew this must be hard for them, but he wanted them to know St. Martin's was a great church, that he and Barbara looked forward to meeting all four of our parents, and that they had no reason to worry, for he would be "taking care" of us.

That proved to be truer than we could have ever hoped.

There are lots of adjectives I could use to describe the way the president and Barbara lived their lives, but toward the top of the list is clearly *generous.* When one thinks of generosity, it is often linked to wealth and the giving away of that wealth. The Bushes were generous in that way for sure, but generosity has to do with so much more.

George and Barbara Bush knew from whence they came, and they no doubt had ingrained within them the biblical principles about giving as an expression of gratitude for what had been given. "Freely you have received; freely give" was the counsel of Jesus.[1] The apostle Paul wrote that generosity is both a gift and a fruit of the Holy Spirit—evidence, if you will, that the Spirit of God dwells within the giver.[2]

People can be generous in all kinds of ways—sharing their wealth, yes, but their time, their wisdom, their knowledge, their energy, their gifts. In these, and in so many other ways, George and Barbara gave away what they had, who they were. But also like most things, their generosity came as easy as breathing—something I witnessed from our first meeting.

"Let's Share..."

The move to Houston was a bit grueling. We packed up all of our belongings, pets, and children into cars and U-Hauls and drove up onto I-10 West. On the way, one of our three cars had a blowout on the bridge crossing Atchafalaya Basin. We could not get AAA to rescue us, so I had to squeeze up against the guardrail, jack the car up, and replace the tire myself, while Laura and the kids drove on ahead. Once I put on the spare, our caravan reconnected in Lafayette, Louisiana. By late that hot and humid August night, after some wrong turns and twists, we arrived in Houston at a rental house we had captured in the tight housing market that would be our first home in H-town.

The first weeks were a bit overwhelming. I was leaving a church of

---

1. Matthew 10:8.

2. Romans 12:8; Galatians 5:22—the "goodness" in this verse is often interpreted as "generosity."

about twenty-five hundred with a staff of about a dozen for a church of nearly eight thousand with a staff of nearly two hundred. The Bushes were still in Kennebunkport, and just to be honest, at that time, I had no idea if, when they did come to Houston, they were regular worshippers or what we clergy sometimes call "C&E" (Christmas and Easter) Christians.

So time marched on, August gave way to September, and then one morning as we were preparing to go into the 8:00 a.m. service, one of my associate clergy, John Bentley, came back and said, "They are here. The Secret Service is here, so they will be here shortly."

The guidance I received from my predecessor, Dr. Gipson, was that they wanted no special attention, no recognition. They typically sat about two-thirds back on the west side of the nave, under the "Saint George and the Dragon" window, a beautiful stained glass window made possible by a gift from the five Bush children in honor of their parents and installed in 2004 at the time of the completion of the large worship space. George is shown in shining armor, with his foot pressing down on the neck of the great dragon. But once the window was installed, the family and church members would, with tongue pressed firmly into cheek, say of the images, "That's a good representation of George, I wonder who the dragon might represent?"

And true to form, that first Sunday when we were all together in church, we just worshipped together. When church was over, the president and Barbara greeted Laura and me at the door.

That is probably the way this will go, I thought. *We will see them in church from time to time...* Their motorcade drove away and I prepared for the 9:00 a.m. service.

It was late September when I had my first real "day off." I had been at the job about six weeks, but there had yet to be a break as we tried to set up house, get our youngest, Luke, settled in his school, and do the same for our eldest, Evie, who was enrolling in nearby Houston Baptist University. And I would be less than honest if I did not say we were suffering some heartache as our middle child, Jones, was beginning his freshman year at Florida State University, hundreds of miles from Houston in what used to be our home state. Couple all of this with duties surrounding a job that, at the beginning at least, was just a bit overwhelming. So I was looking forward to a day off... when the phone rang.

It was my executive assistant, Carol Gallion. She said the president's office called and wanted to know if Laura and I wanted to go out to dinner. After catching my breath, I said, "Um, well, I think that's a yes, don't you?" I asked Carol to get the details, and I called Laura in from the other room: "Our plans this evening are canceled. We are going to dinner with the president!"

We were nervous the rest of the day. Carol called back and said we were to drive over to the president's home, then we would all leave together for dinner out. Laura picked out a pretty sundress, and I made the decision not to wear my clerical collar. It would be a button-down with a tie.

As it got closer to dinnertime, I think my mind was swimming a bit. I came out of the bedroom and Laura burst out laughing. I was so nervous my "tied" tie was tucked neatly under one side of my collar but was on top of the other, now buttoned-up side. We corrected my wardrobe malfunction and made our way to the president and Bar's home.

When the Bushes moved back to Houston in 1992, they first took up residence in the Houstonian, a large hotel very near their former neighborhood and not too far from St. Martin's. The president had purchased a lot in the late 1980s, and eventually he and Barbara designed and built a house at 9 West Oak Lane South. This, too, was only minutes from his office and his church.

Laura and I later became keenly aware through our many shared moments with the Bushes that what we were experiencing was a tremendous honor and opportunity. But it would prompt within me something I would think and say out loud many times: *Why am I here?*

This is truly a question Laura and I would ask again and again as our years increased. *Why am I here? What do I have to offer? What can I possibly contribute to this conversation?* In time, the answer to these questions would become crystal clear—something that I will return to at the conclusion of this book. But at this point, at this moment, in September 2007, I had no idea what this Alabama-raised boy and his lovely Alabama-raised gal would have to discuss with a former leader of the free world and his first lady.

We arrived at the gate of the subdivision and punched in the code we had been given earlier in the day by a member of the president's staff. The Secret Service answered and buzzed us through. We pulled up in front of the house. At that point, all we could see was a modest two-story redbrick home behind a large stone wall and a steel door, with cameras aplenty posted about the property.

We hit the button on another box—and the large metal door slid open. To this day, I think Laura and I will always remember that moment.

The president was in excellent health at the time. He was barely eighty-three but looked every bit a man of the age of seventy. He was dressed in casual slacks and a black long-sleeved turtleneck. When we came through the gate, he was stretching up as if to reach the top of the porch right outside of the home. A big smile came across his face. "Russ...Laura...welcome!"

"Mr. President, it's great to see you!" (Honestly, what else does one say at a moment like this?)

"Come in...come in."

Here is the thing about the president's home in the West Oaks subdivision—it was, by all accounts, modest for a former president and first lady. Yes, it was outfitted with Secret Service quarters over the two-car garage area, and there were extra security walls around, but it was much smaller than many homes of many other well-known Houstonians and much smaller than many of the homes in their same neighborhood.

We came in the foyer, and Barbara rounded the corner. She took us on a "mini tour" of the downstairs: A living room covered with a large hooked rug that Barbara completed by hand while the president was still in office. Nearby, a small dining room. A small, modest yard with a few water features. A sitting room—which, over the next few years, would become a functioning chapel in many ways.

We ended in the kitchen where the president offered us drinks. "What would you like?" he asked.

"What are you having?" I said.

It was then that we learned the president's favorite drink was a Grey Goose vodka martini, with a little tonic. Barbara preferred a manhattan with a capful of sweet vermouth, a cherry, and cheap bourbon (she said no one knows the difference). But when there was a time squeeze or when she didn't have all of the ingredients, Bar would just go for bourbon, which is what she chose for our first drink together. We chose to follow the president's lead, and he said, "Good. We just got this gift of vodka today. Let's try it out!"

Honestly, it was funny watching him wrestle this wood-encased vodka to the floor. He finally had to get out a knife, then a screwdriver to pop the cover of the box open. In time, drinks all around and things began to loosen up a bit.

Barbara was full of questions—about our children, about what we liked to do in our spare time. The president wanted to know about the church. At the time, with about eight thousand baptized members, St. Martin's was the largest Episcopal church in the US. On a fairly regular basis over the following years, he would ask, "Are we still the largest Episcopal church?"

Barbara wanted to know what we were doing in the way of mission, outreach, and service to the community and beyond. She wanted her church engaged in service to the community—something we would discuss many times, and with her prompting, year after year, our commitment grew and grew.[3]

---

3. St. Martin's has grown about 20 percent since 2007, with nearly ten thousand baptized members. Inspired in large part by Barbara Bush, the parish has now consistently given roughly 25 percent of its annual budget outside of its doors to serve mission and

"Where would you all like to eat?" was the next question.

"We're the newbies in town" came our answer.

"Do you like Chinese food?"

Honesty required us to say, almost in tandem, "We like all foods."

"Chinese it is!"

The president got on the phone, called the Secret Service, and set up dinner for the four of us at YAO Restaurant & Bar, a wonderful spot on the west end of one of Houston's main drags—Westheimer Road—named after the famed Houston basketball star Yao Ming, who was still, at that time, wowing as the Rockets' seven-foot-six-inch center. He would occasionally visit the restaurant, which was run by members of his family.

Needless to say, we had never before been in a motorcade. We loaded up in a large, long, tan Suburban. The Secret Service up front, the president and Mrs. Bush behind them, and Laura and I in the rear seats. There was a Secret Service car ahead of us and behind us.

But Barbara kept the conversation going. She wanted to know about our hometowns and more about our children. There was not a moment of awkward silence, something I had internally predicted the entire day through.

When we arrived, security was already at the door, but the next few moments struck me with a measure of surprise that I had not anticipated. The president and Bar were, of course, immediately recognized. All the way through the restaurant they greeted patrons. They did not choose a private table, nor did they choose one in the center of the room. The president pulled us aside to show us Ming's family table with tall barstool chairs that would have made a man of my frame look like a toddler.

This was, mercifully, I suppose, the season before anyone and everyone felt comfortable asking anyone and everyone for a "selfie." But

---

ministry in Houston, Texas, and beyond. Between 2007 and 2022, over $40 million has been given by St. Martin's members to support its outreach initiatives.

several people did come by the table to greet the Bushes—and they smiled at, greeted, and chatted with everyone. I could only imagine most of them were thinking, *And who are those peons with them?*

Dinner started. The president ordered appetizers, then his favorite dish at the restaurant—Peking duck. It should not have come as a surprise, but it did when the food arrived and Barbara looked at me and said, "I think you should say a blessing." I was put on the spot just a bit, but it was perhaps the first time we would pray together, just the four of us. We took hands, bowed our heads, and prayed.

We talked all the way through dinner. Laura and Bar got closer and closer, to the point of whispering. The president and I kept it pretty much on the surface. Secret Service filled a table away—and were at the door and outside of it.

When the waiter cleared the table, he asked if we wanted dessert. At first, demurely, we declined. The president loved dessert—especially ice cream. "Oh, come on... We have to have dessert," he said. Barbara and Laura were both looking over the menu. The president and I picked out our own; Bar closed the menu and said to Laura, "Let's share." She looked at the waiter and said, "Bring us an ice cream and two spoons."

A few minutes later, I looked across the table at my beautiful wife sitting with the First Lady, and they were both smiling, laughing, talking, and spooning vanilla ice cream out of the same bowl. For the second time that night, I am confident I thought to myself, *And what are we doing here?*

But soon, what seemed very unnatural began feeling natural. What seemed like an acquaintance (of note, no doubt, but acquaintance nonetheless) was possibly becoming a friendship.

It was an evening of generosity that clearly broke the proverbial ice and would be the beginning of untold numbers of outings in the years to come.

An Ongoing Observation

This is something I will return to a number of times as we walk through this relational observatory together: the president and Bar really, earnestly, loved being with other people. Obviously, not every person has the same disposition—but not once in over a decade of observation did I witness anything other than an ongoing generosity of engaged interactions.

And beyond their propensity to strike up conversations with everyone they met, they seemed to have an endless supply of energy to bless the lives of others in small ways and large.

Toward that end, let me share a few stories.

While Laura, the children, and I moved to Houston in August 2007 and I began working virtually the day after we moved, my formal "institution" would have to wait. Over the years, Laura and I had been fortunate to become close friends with the 103rd archbishop of Canterbury, Lord George Carey, and his wife, Lady Eileen Carey. I had asked ++George if he would be present and preach at my institution.[4] As the former archbishop, he still had a very busy schedule, and it took a bit of wrangling to land on the right date and put all the pieces in place. In addition, they lived in Newbury, England—so international travel was also a factor in timing. But we finally agreed that the sixth day of January 2008 would work—the feast day of the Epiphany, the twelfth day of Christmas.

Epiphany had special meaning to me, as I was ordained a priest on January 6, 1993. So, once we nailed down the archbishop's availability, I turned to four of St. Martin's most important and well-known members: the president and Bar, as well as the Honorable James A. Baker III and his wife, Susan. It is no surprise that their calendars were full as well, but fortunately, they made it clear that they wanted to be there to be supportive of their new fourth rector. Laura and I were thrilled, and

---

4. The designation "++" before the name of the archbishop denotes his office as the Primate of the entire Anglican Communion, whether retired or not.

the church began to put into place plans for a wonderful celebratory service.

Once ++George and Eileen were headed stateside from their home in the UK, we got word that the president and Bar wanted to take the four of us out to dinner the Saturday evening before Sunday's events. We were to bring the Careys, and the Bushes would meet us at the Houston Country Club.

We arrived early and were greeted by a few of the folk in the dining area. Soon, Secret Service arrived, and the buzz (as we would normally experience it) began. And the buzz was well-founded, for soon the president and Bar arrived, and they stopped at virtually every table, greeting and talking with almost everyone in the room on the way to our little circle.

The president's staff had arranged for us to have the room to ourselves. All well and good, it seemed. Then—another one of those moments. The president and Bar immediately—and I mean *immediately*—hit it off with ++George and Eileen. They also quickly figured out they had previously all been together at some point. But where? When? The back-and-forth went on for a bit until ++George recalled, "Oh yes— I remember where it was! It was the G7 summit." He was referring to the seventeenth gathering of the prestigious leaders of the industrialized nations of the world in July 1991. The president and Bar were in the last year of his term in office and ++George had just begun as archbishop in March of that same year.

"It was at Buckingham Palace," ++George said, and then the four of them quickly recalled the gathering, noting the celebratory fireworks they all watched with the queen and other members of the royal family.

I looked at Laura, square in the eyes, and whispered, "Really, what are we doing here?" She smiled. "What can we possibly add to this conversation?" I said. Laura smiled again, and together we let out a little sigh and shrugged our shoulders.

Dinner began, and much like that first outing at YAO, it was no time at all before we actually *did* find a lot of things about which to talk.

We all ordered drinks before dinner. Barbara ordered a manhattan, and I followed suit.

Somewhere in the midst of dinner, Laura mentioned that she had given me airline tickets to Las Vegas for my forty-fifth birthday, which fell on January 2, but then said, "But I am letting Russ choose where we will stay."

One heartbeat later, Bar said, "George, Laura has given Russ tickets to Vegas for his birthday—but they don't know where they want to stay...Why don't you contact Sig and see if he can help them out?"

I had no idea who Sig was, and while I appreciated the offer, I tried to decline.

"No...no, we can help take care of that." I will circle back to that in a moment.

The dinner was great, not rushed, and conversation was lively without, much to my surprise, any awkward silences. So here, again, was the president and first lady, the archbishop of Canterbury and his bride, and two new Texans without an ounce of pedigree to our names or our bloodline, and yet we were made to feel as though we had been friends for years. When we parted and dropped off the Careys, Laura and I began to laugh out loud in the car...noting again, "What on earth did we have to offer those four?"

The next day was full of celebration, and then somewhere in the mix, I was doing some reading as preparation of offering my gratitude to the Bushes and Bakers for making time in their busy schedules to attend the service. An institution of a rector is no short event. It easily lasts two hours, and we had scheduled photos before and celebratory fireworks outside the church on the grounds of St. Martin's after the service. Then I came across the importance of January 6 in the Bushes' story. They married on the feast of the Epiphany, 1945, and this was to be their sixty-third wedding anniversary! I was horrified! I could not believe how selfish and self-centered I had been. It never occurred to me that this date could actually be important to someone else beyond my own preference!

When we began to gather for photos an hour or so before the service, I apologized. "Don't you worry about it," Bar said. "We want to be here."

And so, we circled up—the president and Bar, the Careys, the Bakers, my parents, Laura's mother, and our three children. Sadly, Laura's father had died shortly after I had accepted the post, but he lived long enough to get that letter from the president, and he took great delight in sharing the news with anyone who would listen in the small rural town of Roanoke in eastern Alabama.

I made some comment that if the president and Bar had to leave for any anniversary celebration, they should obviously feel free to do so. I think Bar jokingly rolled her eyes and said, "It is sixty-three! We have had a few!" but they both said this was how they were celebrating and they stayed until the last firework popped.

Back to Sig and that trip to Vegas. I had a call from Jean Becker, whom you will recall from the first chapter was the president's chief of staff, telling me that the president had asked her to help us out with that trip to Vegas. A few weeks later came an email to "Sig" and me.

February 7, 2008

By way of this email, I am introducing two of my favorite people.

Sig, as you and I discussed yesterday, Dr. Russ Levenson is the new pastor of St. Martin's Church...so therefore has the salvation of our favorite former president and first lady in his hands. He and his lovely wife Laura hope to escape to Las Vegas for a few days of R & R post Easter, after which he hopefully has saved a few souls. President Bush would love for you to make some recommendations to his pastor about where they should stay, what they should do, etc.

Russ: Sig Rogich is one of 41's oldest and dearest friends and was at his side at the White House until 41 appointed him Ambassador to Iceland. President Bush now calls him "Mr.

Las Vegas" as he knows all, sees all, but tells nothing. He has some advice for you on where to stay, etc.

I will get out of the middle unless you two feel you need my sage counsel on anything.

Jean

That next day, I got a call from Mr. Rogich. He said we would be staying at the Venetian and we should let his staff know what shows we might want to see. I suspected the Venetian might be a bit out of our budget, and I brought that up, at which point he said, "There won't be any costs; this is a gift. I am happy to do anything I can to help my friend, the president."

When we arrived, we realized the "gifted room" would have surely been out of my budgetary reach. Moments after we settled in, Mr. Rogich called to make sure we were happy and told us to contact his staff if we needed anything or had any questions. We had a ball.

I suspect, my reader, that you may run down a rabbit trail here: *Well, of course the president would do something like that for his new priest . . .* My answer would be *Well, yes and no. Yes,* because from time to time, parishioners do treat their clergy to special gifts and opportunities that they might not otherwise be able to enjoy or experience. But *no,* in that they certainly did not *have* to do this. At the time, they were in their eighties. Time and energy are precious commodities at any age, but certainly more to octogenarians.

But here is the important point I want to impress upon you. They did this for anyone and everyone they could. The president was no longer running for office, and history continues to show that he was the most accomplished one-term president in our nation's history. He and Bar had friends aplenty. They had nothing to gain from continuing to pour out their lives in little ways and big. What it reveals is the kind of people they were.

For instance, in February 2009, I got a personal letter from the president:

Dear Russ,

I hate to bother you with this matter, but I am writing on behalf of Braden...a young "toddler."[5] His mother, Danielle is our friend and massage therapist...

Braden has applied for the St. Martin's Toddler Group this summer. Because of our respect for Danielle, I strongly urge that her son be placed in the Group.

Sincerely,
George Bush

St. Martin's Episcopal Preschool began in 1986 as an outreach ministry to the local community. Little Braden had no need to be concerned about being admitted to the summer program, not because the president made the request, but because the preschool is open to anyone who applies, meets the criteria for admission, and can pay the tuition. If there is a financial need, assistance is available.

The point is, once again, the president went out of his way to make a "pitch" for a toddler. Little Braden was admitted, and a few days later, I got an email from the president:

Dear Russ, Jean told me that you arranged for little Braden... to get into the Toddler Group. His mother will be very happy; and if she's happy, she will not hurt me when she's working me over as a trainer.

Many thanks. George Bush.

I am aware these are small stories—little things—but I think because of who the Bushes were, they were big things. Forgive the metaphor that may make more sense to Texans than most people, but George and Barbara Bush could have chosen to metaphorically dismount from

---

5. I have refrained from sharing this toddler's last name.

public life, hang up their spurs, and move quietly out to pastures that offered nothing but applause and emulation for jobs well done.

Now, many years later, and perhaps thousands of conversations later, we would learn that George and Barbara were not just this way with "some" people—they were, frankly, this way with everyone.

If they could improve someone's life, they would. If they had the chance to model compassion, empathy, or self-sacrifice, it seemed to come as easy to them as breathing.

This is the ongoing observation that Laura and I had. Beyond that first dinner in September 2007 came more invitations than we can now number. Sometimes it would be with other friends or family. If my children were in town, they were always included.

Restaurants, plays, movies, and musicals became opportunities to not only deepen our friendship but observe that innate generosity. The president and Barbara were huge fans of Texas A&M's Aggies and Houston's Texans and Astros. When pulling for their favorite baseball team, they usually sat behind home base, and they took us along for the ride from time to time.

Once, we were seated way up in the stands at Minute Maid Park rooting for the Astros. Bar happened to turn around and spot us. Moments later, an aide came and tapped me on the shoulder and asked if we would please come sit with the president and Bar. What does one say to that but "Of course!"? We settled in, but one learned quickly not to interrupt Barbara—she was keeping careful score of all hits, runs, and errors.

But in and out of the stadium, up and down the stairs—everyone was treated with an equal respect. The Bushes were not operating with any agenda other than what came naturally to them—generosity, pouring their lives out for the sake of others. Often—not always, but often—when they entered the room, the theater, the stadium, the ballpark—crowds would instinctively stand and applaud.

As their years increased, these outings did also. There were far more conversations and visits in their home, and in the hospital, than in these arranged social outings.

A Last Night Out

As the years went by, the page had long turned on aides calling for any outing or visit at the house. Bar would call Laura or me when they wanted to get together.

Not knowing it would be the last time we would go out, we got a call one evening from Barbara. She wanted to know if we could go out before they headed back to Kennebunkport for the summer. We all agreed it was time to return to YAO.

Though we tried from time to time, the president *always* paid for meals out, and he *always* covered the cost of whatever Secret Service agents were on duty. This night, Laura and I were bound and determined to pick up the check. So we arrived early and gave the manager our credit card and told him to ring up our meals and those of the agents who would arrive shortly.

They all pulled up, greetings all around. Great conversation, laughter as always, and food aplenty. Lots of conversation about plans for the summer, children, and so on.

As we were finishing up, the president waved for the check.

"No, sir—tonight, I've got it," I said.

In all of our years, in any and every circumstance one can imagine, I never saw the president (or Bar, for that matter) get mad or be upset— with this exception. "No...no! You can't do that!" He waved at the waiter and told him to tear up the check. When I persisted, he resisted! I turned to look at Barbara, thinking she would side with me, and she just smiled and shook her head.

The president seemed a bit unnerved by it all and took my card from the waiter and handed it back to me. One more attempt on my part and Laura added her voice, and then we were told in no uncertain terms to forget it. *Forcefully* is a word I might use here. He waved me completely off, pulled out his card. It was the only presidential veto I had received in my life, and it was made clear it should not happen again!

Generous to the Core

Indeed, what I was fortunate to witness in an infinite number of settings and in immeasurable ways were two people who embraced and welcomed Jesus's invitation: "From everyone to whom much has been given, much will be required; and from the one to whom much has been entrusted, even more will be demanded" (NRSV).[6]

The Bushes knew and lived what Jesus taught. They had been given much and they freely gave, blessing the lives of all God, providence, and happenstance sent their way—all of whom are the better for it. They were, without question, generous to the core.

---

6. Luke 12:48.

CHAPTER SEVEN

SPECIAL MOMENTS

Is prayer your steering wheel or your spare tire?

Corrie Ten Boom

Russ, please pray hard for him. He's gone insane. He wants to parachute on his 90th birthday!

Chief of Staff Jean Becker

The president and Bar were people of prayer. They believed in, practiced, and asked for prayer. One of the ways this began to unfold as our friendship grew was when they would ask Laura and me to attend special events and to offer prayers at those moments.

If one ever attended any event associated with the president and Barbara, there was never a frown in the crowd. There was a kind of contagious optimism that preceded them and followed them—there was usually a measure of humor, sometimes a surprise, and almost always moments of inspiration. Such was the case when, much to my surprise, quite early in my tenure, Laura and I received a request to attend the tenth anniversary of the dedication of the George H. W. Bush Presidential Library in College Station, Texas, on November 10, 2007.

Jean Becker reached out with an invitation to offer an invocation at this gathering. Over the years, I have "invocated" at more events than I can recall, but this, for me and for Laura, was important. It was a kind of debut moment for the president's new priest, and I did not want to flub it up. I worked on it for days and ran it by Jean and the president (most likely in that order) to get the okay.

Later that day, Nancy Lisenby from the president's office sent an email, inviting Laura and me to a "small open house" in their apartment at the library, and Nancy said we could take a quick early bird tour.

Honestly, we were thrilled. When we arrived, the president apologized that we had to stay in a local hotel and said he had hoped to have us stay at the apartment, but all the guest suites were full! Frankly, it was another "What are we doing here?" moment, but we were slowly getting used to those.

It was a full evening of celebration and we were, frankly, astounded at the energy the president and Bar exuded. But we had no idea what was in store for the next day.

We were asked to arrive early. Laura would be seated with Bush family members on the front row in front of a podium, and I was ushered back to be with the master of ceremonies and close friend of the Bushes', sports broadcaster Jim Nantz; the director of the Bush library, Warren Finch; and others.

But then Bar came out and pulled us aside—"Well, he's decided he's going to parachute in!" Unbeknownst to the waiting crowd, the president had decided days before to make one of his then increasingly famous parachute drops onto a patch of ground only yards away from the presentation platform. The jump could not be confirmed until the morning of the tenth, because of weather conditions.

It was a cool, crisp Texas fall morning without a cloud in the sky. Barbara knew. President George W. Bush, who could not attend the event, knew, and Doro knew, but the other children of the president and close family members did not know! I can still see the look on the faces of the front-row club when Jim Nantz announced that the president would be parachuting into the event—tethered to a member of the US Army Golden Knights Parachute Team, but an octogenarian parachute jump nonetheless.

It went off without a hitch, and when he landed, he unzipped his jumpsuit and stepped out in a sharp coat and tie. It was like watching Superman in reverse. He greeted as many people as he could, climbed up the steps to uproarious applause, and then I was invited to pray:

A PRAYER FOR THE REDEDICATION OF THE GEORGE H. W. BUSH PRESIDENTIAL LIBRARY

Almighty God, Whose love and grace and mercy surround us on every side. Today, as we gather in this precious circle of family and friends, we offer our heartfelt thanks for the sacrifice and service, the witness and the sacrifice of President George H.W. Bush and First Lady Barbara Bush.

The witness of their lives reminds us all that You often call on us with tasks that demand our best efforts and offer us the opportunity to boldly serve the human family.

Now we ask this day for Your blessing on this Presidential Library. Send Your Spirit into our midst and fill these halls and spaces with Your Presence, that all who visit or serve this place may be reminded of the freedoms we share in these United States.

…As these doors open again today, and all the days yet to come, may this place call on us to sustain all the leaders of our nation with our prayers and support.

Amen.

It was one of many moments that I still consider to be one of the greatest honors in my life. And then, well, the party began—well, the first party.

Immediately after, a huge barbeque with the 750 close friends and family members got underway—lasting for hours. When it wound down, a late-afternoon party began, and we stayed as long as we could, when we learned there was to be yet another meal and party to follow. Keep in mind this was a Saturday, and Sunday is game day for a pastor. Once the sun was well set, Laura and I drove back to Houston to prepare for Sunday services.

It had been the custom of the president and Bar to attend our earliest service, an 8:00 a.m. Eucharistic service without music. As we drove home, I said to Laura, "There is no way they will be at church tomorrow! They have got to be exhausted." We were, and their priest was ready, willing, and able to give them a "bye" the next morning.

Sunday rolled around faster than I would have liked—we were up early and off to church. We got beyond the 8:00 a.m. service, and then, moments before the 9:00 a.m. service, the Secret Service arrived. *No way*, I thought. In the Bushes came, just before the service began, with as much energy as two teenagers.

"I cannot believe you made it today, Mr. President, Bar." They smiled and made their way to their pew. The 9:00 a.m. service does have music and a full choir. The Bushes had not attended that service in years, and when it was over, as they came out, Bar said, "I *loved* the music! Do we have that every week?"

"Yes, ma'am," I said. "At the nine a.m., eleven fifteen a.m., and six p.m."

I do not think I ever saw them at an 8:00 a.m. service again, as they settled into services where they could listen to the music, the anthems, and raise their voices in songs of praise and prayer with their other church members.

About a week later, another one of President Bush's "packages" arrived at my office. But this was the largest one ever—a full-size poster of the president and those on the grandstand moments after the celebration began. The president had written on it, *Russ—Thanks so much for being with me on a special day . . . George Bush.*

This wasn't the last big occasion the president alarmed those close to him by expressing a desire to parachute yet again. A few years later, ahead of his ninetieth birthday, I got a message from Jean Becker. *Russ, please pray hard for him. He's gone insane. He wants to parachute on his 90th birthday!*

I informed Jean of my upcoming travels to Israel, Turkey, and Italy on the date of his birthday. *I will be in Israel... prayer there is a local call... but are you serious?*

Jean wrote back: *Yes. I am in denial. He's just thinking out loud now. Pray for wisdom. And don't tell a soul!*

I'm a locked vault; but will pray for sure... I guess if I make it to 90... I might do the same thing! I wrote back.

He is determined, Jean said.

On June 12, 2014, the president made the jump on his ninetieth birthday into Kennebunkport. Laura and I watched on the international news from our hotel room in Jerusalem.

A Lesson about Prayers for the President

It was our practice at St. Martin's, as it is at virtually every Episcopal church in the country, to pray for the president at each public service. It is up to the parish rector whether or not the actual name of the president is prayed or not. Needless to say, this took on a completely different feel at St. Martin's during 41's years. When the parish prayed for "George, our president," there was a heartfelt feeling behind the word *our!*

There was one exception, however. The Reverend John Bentley has served at St. Martin's a number of times, and as a young man, he was actually ordained there. Though he retired, I was very fortunate to "inherit" John as a part-time priest when I began my tenure at the parish, and he remains a gifted and loyal member of my staff today.

However, after service as rector of a smaller church, John was called back to St. Martin's to serve as an associate priest under my predecessor. On his first Sunday, John happened to be assigned to say the prayers at the 8:00 a.m. service, but President George H. W. Bush was no longer in office. It was 2004, and Bush's son, the forty-third president, was just ending his first term and revving up for a reelection campaign. It was John's first time back in public worship at St. Martin's and his first time to wear a microphone, and he prayed for the president, but not by name!

When the service was over, Barbara sought John out in the narthex and said, "Please be sure to pray for the president by name. He needs all the help he can get."

John offered a quick "Yes, ma'am."

However, John would later tell me he fretted all week about how to make it right with Bar, and just when he thought he was going to be given the chance, she came up to him in the narthex and said, "I have been worrying all week about apologizing to you. That was a terrible way to welcome you back to St. Martin's." John and Bar had a great relationship after that, and in fact, John's wife, Pam, became one of Barbara's closest friends at St. Martin's. That said, that error never happened again—regardless of who was in the White House!

But the president and Bar did want prayers for their son, his wife, and their children. No one can know the full burden of the office of president and role of first lady, except those who have lived it. Forty-One knew the weight his son carried, and Bar knew the weight her daughter-in-law carried.

Forty-Three had courageously led the US through the aftermath of the ruthless terrorist attacks of September 11, 2001. Who can forget the photo of the president father reaching over to hold the hand of the president son at a prayer service held at our nation's National Cathedral?

His effective leadership during that dark season in our nation's history would give him an edge over his opponent, Senator John Kerry. In November, President George W. Bush won his second term. While the electoral vote margin was slim—thirty-five votes—President Bush did win with the most popular votes in the history of the nation.

Though, like any president, 41's son had his critics, some harsh and severe. I am not going to run down that rabbit trail with you; I can only say I know from numerous discussions with 41 and Bar that when their son took a hit, they felt it. They did want those prayers for their son, and they knew he needed them.

We had received our first invitation to Kennebunkport in the spring of 2008, to join the president and Bar in September. The timing meant, obviously, that we would arrive as their son's second term came to a close and the race for his successor was well underway. Laura and I watched closely the polls, the primaries, and the debates, knowing it would be much fodder for our mealtime conversations.

Knowing the president and Bar would be at the GOP convention, Laura and I tuned in for most of the speeches and were particularly touched by the "gathering of Bushes" and the warm welcome and well-deserved recognition the presidents and first ladies received.

After watching the last night of the convention, I shot an email off to the president:

September 3, 2008
Dear President and Mrs. Bush,

Tonight, as we gathered as a family...so very proud of our members of St. Martin's—the 41st President and his first Lady. You both look absolutely fantastic...and I know your presence meant so much to John and Cindy McCain... Despite the hurricane diversion, we are confident that this week's boost will make a lasting impression. Keeping you all in our prayers.

Laura, the kids and I look forward to seeing you next week.

Faithfully,

Russell+

The next morning, the president replied,

Thanks Russ. Can't wait to see you both hastily from Minn. Gb

Later that day, I replied,

> Looking forward to it sir... Talked with your good friend, and our wonderful member, Jim Baker last night and he said, "We're in the race now!"
>
> Hopefully, if we can skirt the hurricane, we'll see you next Thursday.

We did skirt the hurricane on the way up to Maine, but our prayers took leave from presidents and politics once we arrived safely in Kennebunkport.

And Then There Was Ike

In August 2008, a tropical wave developed off the western coast of Africa and began to move west. By the first week of September, it had strengthened to a Category 4 hurricane and began to make its way toward the Texas coast following much the same track as the infamous 1900 hurricane that decimated Galveston.

By now, we had arrived in Kennebunkport for our first-ever visit to Walker's Point. A few days in, fresh off the heels of the convention, First Lady Laura Bush joined us, as did Margaret Bush, Marvin's wife.

We all watched the slow creeping of what was now Hurricane Ike as it continued on that historic track. And on September 13, the comparison became more than that, as the storm slammed into the shore, with water surging over a seventeen-foot seawall to flood the streets of Galveston. Winds blew out windows some forty miles away in downtown Houston, homes and businesses were flooded, damaged, and destroyed. Over thirty lives were lost. When it was all over, it had wreaked havoc from the Louisiana coast to Corpus Christi, causing over $35 billion in damages. The search-and-rescue operation became the largest in Texas history.

To say Ike was adding insult to injury would be an understatement, for only weeks before Ike's landfall in Texas, Hurricane Gustav had whacked the Gulf Coast regions of Alabama, Mississippi, and Louisiana, killing over fifty US citizens and causing upwards of $6 billion in damage.

The double blow to the Gulf Coast was more than the president could take, and so he rebooted an unlikely partnership with his former presidential rival, Bill Clinton.

You will no doubt recall that despite President Bush's disheartening defeat to the former governor of Arkansas, he left a letter waiting for his successor in the Oval Office, revealing the depth of his own love for his nation and respect for the office of president: *Your success is now our country's success . . . I am rooting hard for you.*

Needless to say, President Clinton did go on to have his own successes, and an all-too-public collection of failures, but President Bush did not let political rivalry or one's personal demons get in the way of a relationship no one could have ever predicted.

It was actually spawned by President Bush's son, our forty-third president. In the winter of 2004, when a tsunami washed over the coasts of Indonesia, Sri Lanka, and Thailand, President George W. Bush was looking for ways to bring America's helping hand to the people and lands of Southeast Asia, and he turned to his predecessors.

In no time, Presidents Bush (41) and Clinton were touring that part of the world together, bringing hope and aid to a gaping hole of need. This would not be the first effort of the presidential duo to reach out— they did it again after Hurricane Katrina in 2005. With their method tested and approved, they set out to do it yet again with the Bush-Clinton Coastal Recovery Fund in 2008.

Before September was out, Secretary James A. Baker had put together a group of forty business and civic leaders, and invited a few religionists along, including the president's rector. The goal was to create and establish a fund that would serve as a resource for long-term recovery from the destruction wrought by both Gustav and Ike.

We were all invited to a small conference room just off an airstrip at Ellington Airport for a simple box lunch and an open discussion on how best to raise awareness and funds. Secretary Baker would chair the meeting, but Presidents Bush and Clinton would be there as well.

This would be the first time I met President Clinton, and I was struck by the different styles of the two men. Everyone arrived on time, except President Clinton, who was late. There was some general conversation until he got there. I had heard of his charisma and natural gift he had to connect, or try to connect, with everyone he met. When President Bush came in, he smiled, sat down in a simple folding chair, greeted attendees. He opened his box lunch and I saw him fiddling with the mustard pack to try to open it. He then put it up to his teeth to bite it open, and he caught me eyeballing him. He smiled and waved but kept at it until it cracked open and he could doctor his sandwich.

While he was putting his light lunch together, President Clinton was making his way around the room. I noticed how he took each person by the hand, looked them in the eye, and talked until he felt the connection was "made" before moving on to the next person.

I am not making any kind of editorial comment here, just noticing a difference in styles, perhaps personalities. President Bush was more than comfortable in his skin—sitting in a circle of friends and snacking away like it was recess at grade school. President Clinton, well, seemed "on." In any case, both made an impression. We talked for an hour or so, and President Clinton left before the meeting was over.

I was vexed about what the president's church could do. Around the table had been extraordinary leaders in the business community, many of them millionaires and at least one, Tilman Fertitta, a well-known Houston billionaire. What could St. Martin's do?

Pray, of course, and prayers for recovery became a regular part of the worship services of St. Martin's. But then it occurred to me that we had a unique chance to bring together not just the members of St. Martin's but differing faith traditions. I got on the phone and began reaching out to a diverse coalition of religious leaders from the greater Houston area. We crafted a lean service of prayer and music with the added gift of both President Bush and Secretary Baker speaking and calling on attendees to join others around the nation in supporting the Coastal Recovery Fund. Coincidentally, one of Houston's most well-known television personalities, KPRC weatherman Frank Billingsley, and I not only attended high school together, but Bible study, some thirty years prior when we were both growing up in Birmingham, Alabama, and I asked Frank to emcee.

In the end, over sixty thousand people had donated over $165 million to the fund. St. Martin's and its religious partners made only a slim contribution to that gargantuan amount, but for the first time in decades, faith communities from different backgrounds and traditions intentionally erased any doctrinal differences and prayed and worshipped together.

A few weeks after the service, I got a letter from the president and Secretary Baker that said it well:

May 12, 2009

Dear Russ,

We want to offer our sincerest thanks and warmest appreciation for the effective work that you have done for the Bush-Clinton Coastal Recovery Fund, and especially for the donations at St. Martin's...as you know, more than $50,000 was contributed—an impressive sum!

The generosity of our St. Martin's family, led by...those who attended that unique prayer service, is truly inspirational. Their response to the needs of the victims of hurricanes Ike and Gustav provides a wonderful reminder of the good things that can happen when people of different faiths join hands in order to confront a common social calamity...

George H.W. Bush, James A. Baker, III

I think what I was beginning to understand more fully is that for George and Barbara Bush—and I should add here Jim and Susan Baker—folding their church and faith into their lives was not just important; it was essential. It was not seen as an add-on, but foundational. There was no resistance to their allegiance in their faith, and in fact, it became increasingly clear that it was a matter of the first priority.

An Enduring Lesson, an Oval Office Visit, and a Fuzzy Hat

After we crept out of a myriad of post-hurricane challenges, it was clear that the majority of Americans had a very different feeling than Laura and I did about who should be the next president. Illinois senator Barack Obama soundly defeated Senator John McCain, winning roughly 53 percent of the popular vote to McCain's 46 percent. President-elect Obama's decisive capture of 365 electoral votes to Senator McCain's 173 sent a clear message—the nation was ready to hand the wheel to the Democrats. Laura and I were disappointed and naturally assumed the president and Bar felt as we did. But I was about to be schooled in the Bush approach to those who find comfort in hunkering down with one's own party.

On November 5, the day after the election, my political—and frankly, moral—compass was about to be recalibrated. I watched President Bush 43 offer his own remarks about the defeat of his party and the election of America's first African American president—and it was a bit of a gut check.

I, of course, knew well President Bush 41's record of working across party lines, and I knew he really did mean what he said when he wanted that "kinder and gentler" nation. But he evidently passed that lesson on, as President Bush 43 offered an inspiring bipartisan and hopeful look to the future.

I felt compelled to email the president and Barbara.

November 5, 2008

Just a note to let you know I am thinking very much about you today. I watched your son, and our President, deliver a moving, heartfelt speech this morning in the typical "Bush" way—with integrity, compassion and the positive spirit that so dominates the ethos of the Bush family. We will continue to pray for you, and for he and Laura as this period of transition begins...

With affection and admiration,
Russ and Laura

He emailed me later that afternoon:

Dear Russ,

You are one thoughtful man. Thanks for these good words. Our country will do just fine, though I wish our man had won. Barack is our President and we will of course support him... All best, gb

We all have moments in our lives when the tectonic plates of our being shift and we are standing on new ground. This was such a moment for me. Watching how President Bush 43, and 41, expressed not just their support for the electoral process but their buoyant and effervescent confidence in the leader of the opposing party spoke volumes. I should mention, per previous lessons from the Bushes, that the following Sunday, we continued praying for President Bush but added President-elect Obama—ergo, the lesson that helped turn my head and my heart in the direction they belonged.

A few months after that, President Bush 41 was kind enough to invite Laura and me, along with fifteen thousand other guests, to Norfolk, Virginia, for the commissioning of the USS *George H. W. Bush* to be held on January 10, 2009. It was a great event—with loads of his Houston friends and St. Martin's members in the crowd.

But knowing we were going to be very close to Washington, I reached out to Jean Becker to see if there was any chance Laura and I might have an opportunity to visit the White House. After some back-and-forth, the answer was a resounding "yes." Though our two eldest were ensconced in their respective college courses, our youngest, Luke, was available to join us for the trip.

We got word that the president would be at the White House that day, that he would arrange a private tour for us, and that we would then finish up with a visit with him in the Oval Office. Needless to say, we were thrilled—as was our thirteen-year-old son, Luke.

As we were on our way by car down to Pennsylvania Avenue, I suggested to Luke that if he had any questions he wanted to ask about anything...this would probably be the time to do it, because there won't come a chance like this again. Luke smiled and said, "Then I'd like to ask him about Area 51!"

It was a great tour but a bit dreamlike—not as in dreamy, but as in strange. We were roughly ten days away from a change in administrations, and it could be felt—carpets were being rolled up, there was not a lot of activity, and as we moved from room to room (most public, a few private), we saw a few staff here and there, and no other visitors.

As we finished up, someone from the president's staff caught up with us and said, "The president is ready to see you now."

I suspect some of you reading this book have walked through those doors. We had not—and it was a take-your-breath-away kind of moment for us. I have come to learn that many public events for politicians are held providing a "grip and grin" moment—a hello, a photo, and a farewell. I thought that is what we were in for, and that would have been plenty. My presumption could not have been further from the truth.

As the door opened, the president greeted us with a boisterous "Laura...Russ...welcome. And this must be Luke."

Standing with us was the White House photographer, who snapped virtually every moment. What followed was a good twenty- to thirty-minute visit. The president showed us around the office and told us about the art in the room and why he chose the paintings he did.

He laughingly remarked that he was "fired" as an acolyte by St. Martin's first rector, Dr. Bagby, for acting up. He asked Luke about what he liked at school and then said, "Do you like baseball?"

I was thinking to myself, *Say yes, Luke...say yes. He owned the Rangers!* Luke said yes and that he had played for a number of years but that football was his game now.

The president made his way over to a bureau and opened it up and pulled out a baseball. As he was signing it for Luke, he said, "You have any brothers or sisters?"

"Yes, sir. One of each," Luke said.

The president reached in and pulled out two more.

Then he called out for a staff member to bring a bag into the office. He began pulling out pens, golf balls, notepads, presidential M&M's, and dumping them all in the bag. "Here—take some of this also..."

Laura started laughing and said, "I guess you are trying to get rid of all of this before next week."

"Dang right!" the president said.

We talked for a moment or two about his parents and he said, "I appreciate you taking care of Mom and Dad." Of course, they had had a few health challenges by then, and so I felt compelled to say I was glad they were doing so well and hoped they would live a long, long time.

Then the president said, somewhat prophetically as we would see a few years later, "Well, we better pray that he goes before she does; because if she goes first, he is going to be a mess. Mom and Dad are strong, but he's going to want to have her around to the end."

I had no idea, of course, at the time that Laura and I would be part of both of those moments, and at the time, I did not even want to think about it.

A few weeks later, we were back in Houston, but Presidents 41 and 43 were in Washington for the inauguration.

I happened to be at work as the news of the forty-fourth president's swearing in began when my middle son, Jones, started texting me.

> Dad...what's with the hat...?
> (Me) What hat?
> Bush senior! Ru watching...!?
> (Me) No...I am at work...what's he wearing?
> Some sort of Eskimo thing...very fuzzy.

That was the last time I heard from Jones on Inauguration Day, but I thought it pertinent to send the exchange to Jean Becker, who emailed me late that day:

> I HATE THAT HAT AND HE KNOWS IT.
> But your son made me laugh...

My relationship with the Bushes opened up doors to interact with other Republicans running for president. In 2010, I got a call from Jean Becker. She said possible presidential candidate Mitt Romney would be coming to Houston with one of his campaign advisors, longtime Republican strategist Ron Kaufman. The president wanted to know if I could come and meet with Governor Romney to discuss any concerns that mainline Christians might have with a Mormon running for office.

I went out on a limb and asked if my son could come along, and the president welcomed us. It was another "What am I doing here?" moment. But we did discuss Romney's potential run, and I certainly encouraged him to do so. I reminded him that we were not looking for a "theologian in chief" but a "commander in chief," and he certainly had all the right qualifications for the job. Luke was, as he always is in such settings, polite, and I remember thinking, *I hope he realizes what he is witnessing here...sitting with a president and a potential presidential candidate!* We took photos, shook hands, and parted ways. Ron and I committed to staying in touch, which we did.

In an email to Barbara on March 17, 2010, I wrote,

The President was so very generous to include Luke and me in a wonderful meeting with Mitt Romney today…it is my deep hope he will run (and win!) in 2012—Lord we need him! Please tell the President how much that meant to Luke and me. Thank you so much for your friendship and support…it means more than you know.

I received this message from her later that night:

Mitt is my choice and we hope he will loosen up a bit, but not in blue jeans, but in showing the American public that he is decent, honest, a successful businessman who has a great family. Mormons are perhaps as great public servants as you and I will ever meet…I don't need to tell you this, but Iowa needs to know that!

I also wrote Governor Romney a short note thanking him for meeting and including Luke. A few days later, I received a handwritten letter from Governor Romney on April 8, 2010. He was certainly taking his cue from President Bush, the master of communicating!

Reverend,

  It was an honor to meet in the President's office. And it was particularly generous of you to send such a gracious and complimentary letter. I too hope we will meet this summer again. I look forward to a time when we can take more time to discuss the path ahead for America.

All The Best,
Mitt

I stayed in touch with the campaign staff for Governor Mitt Romney, who went on to win the Republican nomination in 2012. His team invited me to give the opening invocation at the GOP convention in Tampa, Florida, on August 27, 2012. It was my first experience with the "national press." When I stepped to the podium, it was the only time in my entire ministry before or after that my legs began shaking as I heard the cameras clicking.

It was about as nonpartisan a prayer as one could imagine, but as soon as I stepped off the stage and down onto the campaign floor, I was swamped with reporters asking me, "What did you mean by that?" and if I was trying to subtly take a swat at President Obama. My response was "No. If you listened, that prayer could also have been given at the Democratic convention." So, well, it was then I learned the value of just following the advice of my wife, who had told me, "Just say, 'No comment!'"

Romney would, of course, lose that election in November.

A few years later, during the 2016 campaign, I would join Jeb Bush's Religious Liberty Advisory Committee and meet regularly by phone to discuss issues related to faith, service, and religion until he dropped out of the race.

If you are keeping count, that is 0 for 2 for those who sought my spiritual counsel before running for president. So if you are contemplating a run, my suggestion would be you look for another chaplain!

Two Shining Stars

The back-and-forth over the president's hat was not the only email exchange I had with Jean Becker on Inauguration Day. In the midst of witnessing the president's extraordinary leadership in the wake of the coastal calamities we had endured, and watching how he and Barbara had witnessed to the nation that there was, in fact, such a thing as political civility, even when your party takes a licking, I felt there had to be some way the parish could recognize the president and Bar for these kinds of acts, and so many more. Annually, St. Martin's holds a parish meeting to conduct business, approve a vestry, report on the year gone by, and to recognize those who, for lack of a better phrase, have been models of the St. Martin's Way—by being faithful in worship, service, and touching the lives of others beyond our doors with the good news of God's love.

I confess, knowing all I already knew about the many contributions made by the Bushes, I was surprised they had never received such recognition. So, after some prayer and reflection, I thought I would make that move on the Sunday of my first parish meeting in January 2008.

Having learned that it was best to run any such idea through Jean Becker, I reached out and asked her to see if the president and Bar would be willing to receive the Star Award.

A few weeks out from the meeting, Jean emailed me, saying the president was happy to accept the Star Award, as well as on behalf of Bar.

> What cinched it was that you would do this during the church service, instead of a separate event. He appreciates that very much. So you have the green light.

As we gathered on Sunday, January 27, I asked the president if he would not mind if they sat up front, rather than in their typical place under the St. George's window. During the announcements, I acknowledged that it should be a surprise to no one that we were giving the well-deserved Star Award to two of St. Martin's "shining stars." "President George Bush and First Lady Barbara Bush have made no secret of their personal faith, nor have they worn it on their sleeves; they have openly witnessed to it but also lived it in thought and word and deed," I said in my remarks that morning.

At the conclusion, those packing the pews that Sunday instinctively stood and broke out in long, thunderous applause. The president motioned for me to bring the handheld microphone over to him, as he wanted to say something (which was not in our script).

Bar was standing behind the president as he smiled, took the microphone, and started to speak, but then, his voice broke. Bar dropped her head and put her hand on his back. He collected himself, teared up again, and then just said, "This church just means so much to us... Thank you."

If there was a dry eye in the church at that moment, it must have belonged to a cold heart or stoic. We were all deeply touched.

The next morning, the president wrote me a note and dropped it in the mail:

> *Dear Russ,*
>
> *Thanks so much for presenting Barbara and me with the Star Award. We both view it as a real honor.*
>
> *I am sorry I choked up. I find I cry more at 84 than I did before and I feel badly.*
>
> *Life is so good and I am grateful to you and to our Church.*
>
> *George Bush*

In... All the Way

As the months and years began to pass, it became increasingly evident how very much the president and Bar did love their church. They made every effort to stand behind the leadership of their rector and the initiatives of the parish. I cannot think of a time when they said no to anything I asked of them. Though there was a moment when I wondered!

I had only been at St. Martin's for a year and change when we decided, in the midst of the financial crisis of 2008, to launch the Building for the Ages campaign to raise $25 million. The goal was set to help pay for three acres we recently acquired and to construct several new buildings to expand our youth ministries and a new Hope and Healing Center to provide behavioral, emotional, and mental health care services to the community.

I knew if the campaign was to be any success whatsoever, it would have to have the backing of the president and Bar. I called the office to set up an appointment and they called back and said they would rather have me come to the house (gulp).

When I got there and checked in with the Secret Service, I was told to ring the doorbell. The president opened the door and welcomed me into the sitting room. He asked me if I wanted anything to drink (at the moment, a glass of water and a Valium might have helped). I had never made a "pitch" to a president (they do not teach you that kind of thing in seminary). In addition, I had decided to ask them if they would be honorary co-chairs of the campaign (pass that Valium).

As we sat down, he said, "Bar's upstairs; she'll be down later. She hates to talk about money stuff." At that point, I assumed he knew why I had come, so we settled in and I went through the entire project, the finances, the time frame.

He said it looked good, and then I asked him, "Sir, it would really help us if you and Barbara would be honorary co-chairs of the campaign."

He smiled and said, "Well, who is going to ask me for the money?"

(Did I mention they do not teach you this kind of thing in seminary?) I said, "Well, I guess that would be me, Mr. President."

He smiled a big smile and said, "We are all in."

A few minutes later Barbara came down the stairs. "Are you all through talking about money?"

"Yes... He says you all are 'all in.'"

"He did, did he?" I could "hear" the smile in her voice.

I confess I am not sure who said it, but one of them asked, "How about a drink?"

Um, I did not decline.

That kind of support unfolded in more ways than I could imagine. We raised the funds, built the buildings, and George and Barbara Bush—along with James and Susan Baker, I should add—were there all along the way.

It was not only bricks-and-mortar projects where 41 and Bar helped garner support. In my first full year of service at St. Martin's, we instituted an annual Veterans Day service.

Each and every year, until he could no longer, the president was involved and supportive and helped recruit outstanding keynoters, including former Vietnam POW turned Episcopal priest, Colonel Robert Certain; former chairman of the Joint Chiefs of Staff Richard Myers; his successor, General Peter Pace; former chief of staff of the army General George Casey; Afghanistan veteran Lieutenant General Rick Lynch; astronaut Captain Jim Lovell; the last man on the moon, Captain Gene Cernan; actor and humanitarian Gary Sinise; and so on. Every single year, as well, Secretary and Mrs. Baker would participate, as they do to this day. The annual event not only gathered military veterans, but it has raised tens of thousands of dollars over the years for the USO and for the Gary Sinise Foundation.

The Twentieth Anniversary of the Liberation of Kuwait

As noted earlier, the thought, theological underpinnings, and prayer that went into the decision to launch Desert Storm was foundational to President Bush and his secretary of state, James Baker. They sought the counsel and prayer of numerous religious leaders, despite Saddam Hussein's accusation that President Bush was an "enemy of God." The war began on January 16, 1991, and ended six weeks later with the liberation of Kuwait on February 28.

Twenty years later, the president and officials with the presidential library in College Station decided to mark the anniversary with a series of gatherings, discussions, and presentations.

A large group gathered at the library for an extraordinary panel discussion. Guests included a number of folks from 41's cabinet, including General Brent Scowcroft, former national security advisor; General Colin Powell, former chairman of the Joint Chiefs of Staff and the sixty-fifth secretary of state; Vice President Dick Cheney, who was secretary of defense at the time of Desert Storm; Vice President Dan Quayle; and, of course, the president and Secretary Baker. But there were also a number of Kuwaiti officials, including His Royal Highness

Sheikh Sabah Al-Ahmed Al-Jaber Al-Sabah, the emir of the State of Kuwait; and the deputy prime minister and minister of foreign affairs of the State of Kuwait, His Excellency Sheikh Dr. Mohammad Sabah Al-Salim Al-Sabah.

Needless to say, the presentation was riveting, and when it was over, we recessed to the solarium of the library for a meal together. Despite the diverse crowd, the president wanted to launch the event with prayer. So a few days before, I had gotten an email from Jean Becker, saying the president would like for me to give a "very short" blessing before the dinner. "Can you bless all the Christians, Jews, and Muslims in the room in 90 seconds?" she asked. Later that day, I emailed Jean back: "I can do the blessing in 73 seconds!"

I was invited to the podium by NBC correspondent Brian Williams, and I, in turn, invited those gathered to share in a traditional Episcopal invitation to prayer: "The Lord be with you," I said and then invited those gathered to say, "And also with you," as our common desire to invite the presence of God into our midst.

Almighty God, Father of Abraham and Sarah; Isaac and Rebekah; Jacob and Rachel; Father of the prophets of Old and the Apostles of New; of Joseph, Mary and Jesus...

We gather this night with thanksgiving in our hearts for those around our globe who made possible the words, "The liberation of Kuwait has begun," and who, in less than sixty days, through leadership, sacrifice and mutual cooperation turned these words into the reality of freedom for countless numbers of citizens of the shining jewel we know as Kuwait.

We thank You for calling all of us to tasks which demand our best efforts. Remind us of the precious price and delicate existence of freedom. This I ask in the name of our Lord. Amen.

Laura and I happened to be sitting with two Kuwaiti citizens who were in the nation during the Iraqi invasion, the war, and the subsequent liberation. It did not go unnoticed that they seemed very young, and with a measure of sensitivity I said, "You must have been barely more than children when all of this happened."

Then a look of incredible softness came across both of their faces. We talked for a bit about what they did remember—and they recalled a lot for two so young. But then, almost welling up in tears, one of them said, "I thank God every day for George Bush..." and as he spoke, the other young man began to nod his head. "I was a teenager during those days, but I still remember how afraid I was. Tonight was very emotional for me. I thank God every day for the United States."

Really, what more needed to be said?

Knowing the president and Bar would be at church the following Sunday, I got up early and wrote him a letter, which I handed him when he came to worship.

Dear President Bush:

It is early Sunday morning, before the big day begins. I have spent much of the weekend watching clips and reading articles about the gathering in College Station. Laura and I were moved and inspired by the panel discussion and deeply honored to be included in the dinner afterward...

Laura and I were seated with two young men from Kuwait. We spent a good bit of time talking with them. One of them said, "I was a teenager during those days, but I still remember how afraid I was. Tonight was very emotional for me. I thank God every day for the United States." Mr. President, thank you for leading our nation and world in the difficult path of a just war to help liberate others and set on a hill, once again, an example of what freedom can mean.

Laura and I count it as a great gift to know you and Barbara, and perhaps even more to have you as friends, and *mentors as we creep ever more deeply into this season of middle age!*

With admiration and love,

Russ+

A few days later, I received a letter in response:

January 24, 2011

Dear Russ,

Your letter of 23 January was so thoughtful, but it is I who should have written first to thank you for coming to our Desert Storm anniversary celebration and offering that poignant blessing at dinner. We loved having you and Laura with us.

Thanks again for that wonderful letter.

Warmest regards,

G.B.

Some might have been surprised that the president invited his Christian pastor to pray over this diverse crowd, but here we see—yet again—how his faith was intimately connected to his life, and vice versa. This was not the first time for such an opportunity, and it would not be the last, as he asked St. Martin's, and his rector, to play a unique role in the twenty-fifth anniversary of the Points of Light Foundation.

More Than a Blessing

If you pull up the website of the Points of Light Foundation, one of the first things you will read is an inspiring quote from 41:

The solution to each problem that confronts us begins with an individual who steps forward and who says, "I can help."

How did the president want to begin the twenty-fifth anniversary of this extraordinary organization that has grown to be one of the largest service initiatives in the world? *With a worship service . . .*

Think of George H. W. Bush and one will quickly think of the words "thousand points of light" from his 1989 inaugural address. At that moment, he invited the nation to take action through service of one's fellow men and women. In 1990, the president established the Points of Light Foundation as an independent, nonpartisan, nonprofit organization to encourage and empower the spirit of service. The heart-beat of the foundation's mission is simple—"What government alone can do is limited, but the potential of the American people knows no limits"—but it was inspired by one of 41's most memorable quotes: "Any definition of a successful life must include service to others."

The foundation's chair is the president's son Neil. We were just get-ting to know one another better when Neil reached out with 41's idea to begin the 2015 gathering with a service of prayer, song, and inspira-tional readings and words.

Think back to when the president invited to St. Martin's those who attended the 1990 G7 summit. He loved his church and he loved to share it with others, so when this poignant anniversary of this founda-tion came around, he wanted people from around the US to experience his worship home, which served as an inspiration for so many of the things he had done in the service of others. So he asked Neil and me to sit down and think it through.

Again, because this would be a diverse and eclectic group, I knew the gathering would have to reflect the broad spectrum of religious perspectives and traditions in Houston. As of this writing, Houston is recognized as the most diverse city in the United States—over one hun-dred different languages are spoken in the school systems here, and there are nearly two thousand houses of worship. Any gathering that did not attempt to reach beyond the St. Martin's grounds, beyond the Christian faith, would likely have been a missed opportunity.

I reached out to my friends Rabbi David Lyon and Imam Wazir Ali. I had known David and Wazir for years already, and we pulled together a tapestry of faith leaders—Baptist, Methodist, Presbyterian, Roman Catholic, Orthodox, Armenian, Jewish, Muslim, and Buddhist. We agreed: no one would proselytize, and we would each offer a prayer from our own tradition that spoke of love and service—full stop. We called the gathering "One Prayer: Many Faiths, Marking the Beginning of the 25th Anniversary of the Points of Light." Our subtext was "A Time for Peace, a Time for Unity, a Time for Service, a Time for Prayer."

With the president's help, I invited author, historian, and Episcopalian Jon Meacham to offer a keynote address. Afterward, we shared a common meal, making special provisions for those who had dietary restrictions.

It remains, to this day, one of the most inspirational gatherings that has ever been held at St. Martin's. I would have, frankly, never thought of it myself—and none of this would have happened—were it not for the president, and it would birth friendships.

The Fruit of Good Living

Every now and then, when someone is making a speech, preaching a sermon, or writing an article or book—like the one you are reading now—the author might say or write something like, "Not to belabor the point," meaning they are about to do just that. I am, frankly, doing my best to belabor a specific point throughout this book: George and Barbara Bush were, in fact, two of the most godly people I have ever met. They were so, not because they were trying to prove a point, gain attention, strengthen their reputations, bolster their biographies. They were so, because they knew God, loved God, and were strengthened by that love—so that the service they rendered was a natural outgrowing of that umbilical cord–like connection they had to the Source of all Love.

There is a beautiful passage of Scripture from the pen of the beloved Apostle John:

Dear friends, let us love one another, for love comes from God. Everyone who loves has been born of God...Dear friends, since God so loved us, we also ought to love one another. No one has ever seen God; but if we love one another, God lives in us and his love is made complete in us.[1]

In the last decade-plus of their lives, there were plenty of opportunities to be busy: recognitions, award dinners, well-deserved honors; but the daily barrage that comes with public office had faded away. So what this priest witnessed was an increasing commitment to grow in their love of God—so church, prayer, service within the church became more and more of a priority as their years increased. They came because they hungered to go even deeper.

The generous sacrifice of their lives, in so many ways, cannot be fully logged, because much of it was done without any attention, without notice—especially in a large city like Houston. But it was easier to spot when fewer folks were around, in a small fishing village on the southeast coast of Maine called Kennebunkport. Let me take you back there for a bit.

---

1. 1 John 4:7, 4:11–12.

CHAPTER EIGHT

"SHANGRI-LA"

Hospitality is a test for godliness because those who are selfish do not like strangers, especially needy ones, to intrude upon their private lives. They prefer their own friends who share their lifestyle. Only the humble have the necessary resources to give of themselves to those who could never give of themselves in return.

Pastor Erwin W. Lutzer

We are in very cold Maine as I type and happy to be in our own special Shangri La. Love to all, G.B.

Letter from President Bush to Russ Levenson,

May 10, 2010

It was at that dinner with the Bushes and Lord and Lady Carey before my institution that Barbara leaned over and began talking about Kennebunkport. "You all must come next summer...come and bring your kids." To this day, I hope my double take was not obvious.

On the way home, I said to Laura, "Did you hear that invitation to Kennebunkport?"

"Yes," Laura said, and then I suspect about the same time, we both said something like, "They are probably just being nice..."

They were, but they made good on the invitation. As you know from pages past, we were fortunate to travel to this beautiful town more than half a dozen times at the invitation of the president and Bar— and once we again got over our "What are we doing here?" feelings, it became like a second home.

Founded on July 5, 1653, Kennebunkport remains small with its fewer than four thousand full-time residents. But it is visited by tens of thousands each year, many of whom purposely drive over the small bridge from Kennebunk into Kennebunkport, through town, past the simple and sophisticated shops, the galleries, and array of restaurants toward scenic Ocean Avenue—on their way to Walker's Point, the Bushes' "family home" since the late nineteenth century.

The perimeter of Walker's Point is called Rock Ledge and juts out into the waters of the North Atlantic. The property was purchased by President Bush's great-grandfather David Davis Walker and his son, the St. Louis banker George Herbert "Bert" Walker. Now only one of the two homes they built remains—the "Big House," as we came to call it.

When Bert died in 1953, his son, George Herbert ("Herbie"), did not inherit the property, so Herbie purchased it from his father's estate. When Herbie died in 1977, the property went up for sale and the future president purchased it.

To the world beyond its grounds, it has been a gathering place for the two presidents, who have spent their summers there, and leaders from around the globe, including British prime ministers Margaret Thatcher and John Major, Russian leaders Mikhail Gorbachev and Vladimir Putin, Canadian prime minister Brian Mulroney, and Israeli prime minister Yitzhak Rabin.

The president and Bar pushed back against calling it the "summer White House" and actually refused certain security measures like chain-link fencing and bulletproof glass. It is well protected, of course, by Secret Service members, who have both offices and private quarters on the property, but this was, and is, a "home," and far be it from Russ and Laura to ever think we would have been guests there on several occasions. But in time, it became a beautiful respite, a vacation spot for our entire family, a memory maker, a counseling center, a prayer retreat—and, in many ways, a place of reflection and worship.

It was clearly where the president felt very much alive. He loved to play tennis and horseshoes there, and he loved to fish and push *Fidelity* (the fifth of five of his boats christened *Fidelity*), a Fountain 38 with three 300-horsepower Mercury Verado outboards, to its upper limits—seventy-five miles per hour at full throttle.

Bar loved to garden there, both flowers and vegetables. She loved to walk the nearby beaches with friends, family, and her pups.

When in Kennebunkport, the Bushes were as faithful in their worship as they were in Houston, attending week to week at nearby St. Ann's Episcopal Church. The beautiful structure was built in the late 1800s and, much like Walker's Point, offers impressive views of the rocks and waves of the Atlantic.

In my experience, true hospitality is a gift of God's Spirit. There are those who, by virtue of this gift, open their homes, their dinner tables, and their playgrounds to virtually anyone who comes their way. It comes easy for some—it seemed to come easy for the president and Bar. Which we observed every time we visited.

The First of Many Visits

There has to be a first time for everything. When Bar issued that invitation, neither Laura nor I thought they were completely serious. How wrong we were. They pressed the point almost up until the day they left in early May 2008.

By then, I was quickly learning that correspondence of every kind was important to the president and Barbara, and it was one of the ways our friendship grew over the years. My hunch is, if you had ever met the president or Bar, you likely received some sort of correspondence as a follow-up. They were both masters at staying in touch—and taking the time to reach out through handwritten cards and letters, for this kind of contact was their preferred methodology.

Anyone who knows anything about President Bush also knows how very close he was to his mother, Dorothy Walker Bush, who died in 1992. In early July 2008, the Southern Maine Health Care system named its emergency care pavilion in honor of the late Mrs. Bush, and I dropped the president a note expressing my good wishes on the move.

In no time, he wrote back:

> *July 31, 2008*
> *Dear Russ,*
>
> *Thanks for your recent note.*
>
> *My mother was a very special woman, and having the pavilion here at Southern Maine Medical Center named in her honor means an awful lot to me and to my entire family.*
>
> *We're looking forward to seeing you up here. I guarantee you that it will not be 100 degree weather.*
>
> *Hastily, but with warmest regards,*
> *George Bush*

The die was cast and we pulled our young ones together, booked flights to Boston, and beat it out of town, not knowing as I wrote before that a hurricane would be in our taillights.

We landed at Boston Logan International Airport, rented a car, and then began what became a family tradition on the two-hour drive from Boston to Kennebunkport: "the lecture." Our kids did not go with us every time, but on this first trip they did. Our youngest, Luke, had just turned fourteen; his older brother, Jones, was nineteen; and older sister Evie was twenty-one. The lecture consisted of reminders about "no, ma'am / yes, ma'am," "no, sir / yes, sir." Other rules included basic table manners, not interrupting—especially Barbara—listening more than talking, and doing their best to refrain from the kinds of noises teen boys take delight in making.

Pulling into Kennebunkport was, actually, magical. You can hardly look left or right and not see beauty in every direction. No billboards, no tall buildings, no pollution, no horn honking. A traffic jam here, it was quickly deduced, was about three cars deep—and most of the time, it was due to the politeness of drivers letting pedestrians cross one of the narrow streets.

Then after the lecture, the driver, your narrator here, had broken a cardinal rule of etiquette. We were running late. My cell phone began to ring and when I picked up, it was Barbara: "Russ, are you all on the way?"

We had just crested the hill on Ocean Avenue that looked directly across to Walker's Point, and while the view took our breath away, I was stupefied that we were getting a call from the First Lady that was prompted, by all things, by our truancy. "Um, yes. I am so sorry...We ran into a bit of traffic. I am looking at the house right now. We should be there in just a few minutes!"

A second later, we turned onto the property, and as we rolled up to the Secret Service checkpoint, I whispered to Laura, "Can you believe this?"

We were welcomed, a pause, "The Levensons are here..." Another pause, "Drive straight ahead to the main house. Mrs. Bush will meet you there."

I have already shared a bit about that first visit in the opening of this book, but allow me to dig a bit deeper, if I may. As we parked, Bar was already standing outside waiting for us. She gave us big hugs, cheek kisses. She had met the kids before, but they had a bit of a reintroduction in this new paradise we had just entered.

The "Bungalow," as it was called, was built in 1921 as a wedding gift for Dorothy, the president's mother, and it was where Doro and her husband, Bobby, usually stayed with their children, but Bar was turning it over to us for our stay.

I can only assume that most of you reading think as I thought— that Walker's Point would be over-the-top—pristinely decorated, with beautiful furniture that was not made for child's play, exquisite wood-work, and stone flooring. This was not the case. Yes, it sits on what is arguably one of the most beautiful pieces of property in the United States, but the homes are built and decorated simply—perhaps *modestly* is a better word. This is not a showplace, and it is not a museum. This is a home, a beating heart for the Bush family. Walking through the doors of the main house or any of the other bungalows on the property is, actually, like walking into the open arms of hospitality.

Bar walked us around, opened closets, pointed to dressers, took us into the kitchen where we were told to make ourselves at home. "Drinks are at six p.m.; dinner is at seven p.m. Just come over to the house when you are ready." She made her way out the screen door, and I think the five Levensons all sighed a bit in relief—we had not blown the first five minutes; now we had to see if we could make it through the first few hours!

We got unpacked, and as I noted earlier, the president came over to check on us. He had recently acquired three new battery-powered Segways, replacing some of the old ones made famous by the forty-third president, who wiped out on one in front of the cameras in June 2003. The president told us that his aide, Jim Appleby, would be happy to give us classes in the morning after breakfast. "We're in!" I responded (whether that was a truthful statement or not, I cannot now honestly say . . . When the president issues an invitation, you say, "We're in").

As the sun set, we were changing for dinner, and Bar knocked on the door. I was wearing khaki pants and a white button-down. I opened up and she said, "You all okay? You need anything?"

"No, ma'am; we're fine. We'll see you in just a bit."

She turned and began to walk away but then turned back around, looked me in the eye, and said, "You do have a dinner jacket, don't you?"

"Yes, ma'am." (When the First Lady asks if you have a dinner jacket, you say yes—fortunately, I had one!)

Walking between the Bungalow and the main house was, in and of itself, moving. The wind was whipping, and even fifty yards away, the waves crashing against the large boulders offered a resounding repetitive beat, like that of a heart—it was hard to dismiss the metaphor.

We were welcomed into the main house, where the president was already sitting by the fire in the living room. The Bushes' newly acquired Maltipoo puppy, Bibi, barked at all of us like a protective Doberman as Bar came out of the master bedroom. "Hush, Bibi," she said. "Now, hush!"

Vodka and tonics for the president, Laura, and Russ; bourbon and water for Bar; sodas for the kids. Cocktails or wine were always served and enjoyed but never to excess—one drink, perhaps two, but never more than that.

Much to my surprise, there was plenty to talk about all the way up to dinner. I could not have been prouder of my children (perhaps that should have been a footnote here...but I was!).

We sat down, and the president nodded at me and said with a smile, "Offer a prayer, Pastor." Which I did. Lord only knows what I said. I was still trying to figure all of this out. Sitting there was not like slipping on house shoes one has worn for a lifetime, but more like squeezing on dress shoes that, at least in that moment, felt three sizes too small.

But at some point during dinner, it struck me that our children, though they knew they were sitting with a former president and first lady, had absolutely no full understanding of the weight of the moment, because, just to be honest, the president and Barbara were being George and Bar—doting, funny, warm grandparents to three children they had just met. Before long, our kids, all of whom knew at least to say "Mr. President" and "Mrs. Bush," were easily laughing, telling stories, asking questions.

It was hard not to notice the large photos on the wall of the forty-third president and Vladimir Putin, or the forty-first president with Gorbachev—how could this ragtag group fit into this picture? They fit because the president and Bar had the "gift" of hospitality.

After dinner came dessert and then something we later came to expect and cherish. When all the conversations were winding down and our bellies were full, the president leaned back in his chair and smiled and said, "Now it is time to see who will win."

"Win what?" one of my kids said.

"The falling-asleep-first contest!"

It was clearly his way of saying, *The night is done, and we are too!* But it was much nicer and softer than that.

"Whoever falls asleep first, wins!" We had finished dinner and it was time to head back to our bungalow, but not without instructions first.

Bar said, "Now, coffee is on at seven, hot breakfast at eight... Sleep in if you want, but after nine, it's cereal and milk!" Seriously, would we *even* sleep that night?

We did... soundly. There was something about the pure, clean sea air, the pounding of those waves, the rhythmic movements of winds outside, and we were all—every one of us—out like a candle.

The next morning, Laura and I were not going to miss breakfast with the president. We walked up to the house shortly after 7:00 a.m.

Now, here is the thing... Honestly, a guest at Walker's Point does not know who will be there on any given day. Another expression of the Bushes' extraordinary hospitality—there was almost always a guest for dinner, a meal. And as we rounded the back of the house, the president was already sitting out on the back porch, which overlooks the Atlantic. With him were a few guests, and they were all reading the paper.

As Laura and I approached, the president said, "Good morning!" And then he introduced us to the breakfast crowd—his brother William "Bucky" Bush; his former national security advisor, Brent Scowcroft; and a diplomat from China. Laura and I shook hands, and Laura said, "I'll go in the kitchen and see if I can help," which was her way of saying, *Good luck keeping up with the conversation out here, Hubby!*

I sat down, and the president tossed a section of the paper in my direction. "Russ, here's the sports." We all sat there reading, and I found myself, once again, thinking, *What am I doing here?*

The president treated his guests the same—like old friends around a poker table. There was a bit of chatter here and there until a hot breakfast was served in the main room. His brother, Secretary Scowcroft, and the visiting diplomat did not stay for breakfast, and all left with kind greetings of farewell to this interloper that no one knew!

The president and I retired to the dining area to join Laura and Bar, who by now had been joined by our three children. As the president had the night before, Bar turned to me and asked me to pray, but this time she held out her hands—and we, the seven of us, held hands and prayed. And, well, it felt like family.

The president was almost pulsating with excitement to get out on the ocean. He was dead set on all of us fishing. We loaded up but not without first having one of the most awkward moments in our Bush years' history. We had been snapping photos with our phones every chance we got, and as we climbed aboard *Fidelity*, I foolishly asked a member of the Secret Service team if they would mind taking our photo. The response was a firm but patient "No," which was another way of saying, *I am here to protect the president, not be an amateur photographer.* As our years increased, those same Secret Service officers who, perhaps on that day, thought we were bumbling tourists became close friends with whom we would spend more hours than we ever could have imagined.

We climbed aboard and had a ball. From time to time we would pass another boat, and the president would call out and wave. If it happened to be a lobster fisherman—and there were several along the way—the president would slow down the boat and visit. He would ask if they had caught anything and wish them well before pushing the throttle.

After a full morning of fishing, we headed back and experienced what can only be described as a thrill ride. There is a small cove right near Walker's Point between the main house and Ocean Avenue where *Fidelity* rests when she is not at sea. As we came into the cove, the president sped up...not a little...not a lot...but full speed ahead. I looked over at the Secret Service officer, and he was holding tight. He smiled at me, then rolled his eyes as if to say, *Here we go again.* There were some Bush-watchers on the bluff, and as the president dropped the throttle from full to zero, he whipped the boat in at about a 270-degree angle right up next to the dock. The crowd on Ocean Avenue broke out in applause. The president turned, waved, and smiled. I was hoping none of us needed CPR!

This first trip, as noted earlier, changed trajectory when Ike moved into the Gulf of Mexico and set its sights on Galveston. There would be no quick trip back, and so the president and Bar made it clear we could stay on until any danger of flying into Houston had passed.

This meant that our stay overlapped with that of First Lady Laura Bush, who came for a few days of R & R after the GOP convention in Minneapolis. This meant an extra measure of Secret Service was added to the Point. Margaret Bush, son Marvin's wife, also came in for a few days, so the population for meals and outings grew in number.

By now, not only were the young ones comfortable walking the grounds, swimming in the pool, playing tennis, putting on a small putting green near the Secret Service outpost, riding on the Segways, and tossing the horseshoes (one of the president's favorite pastimes on the property), but they had become very comfortable around the president and Barbara.

They came and went into the main house. They joined us each night for drinks (honoring local beverage laws, of course), and the addition of another first lady did not seem to rattle them much.

One evening the president struck up a conversation with Jones over the well-known phrase *You the man!* The president told Jones that he was responsible for crafting the phrase. When Jones cocked his head with a *What?*, the president pulled out an old VHS tape, popped it in the player, and pushed play.

Evidently, the Houston Astros stuck by the assertion and pulled together a fun video about how the phrase (which actually began appearing in the 1950s American jazz scene) could be attributed to the president.

First Lady Laura (who by now had asked all the adults to please call her Laura) was standing nearby smiling. As the video came to a close, Jones gleefully exclaimed, "Mr. President, me and my friends say that all the time!"

Keep in mind that Laura had been an elementary school teacher and librarian in Texas, so you can imagine the horror of Jones's parents when the second first lady we had ever met said, "Now, Jones ... I know your teachers did not teach you to say 'me and my friends' but 'my friends and I.'" There was an internal eye roll of parents, who both took their English lessons seriously! We survived.

As we were preparing for dinner, two more moments were worthy of a smile. The first was when Barbara looked at our youngest and said, "Luke...take Bibi out and let her do her business." He did not hesitate; he picked up Bibi—who by now had uncharacteristically taken to Luke—and carried her out into the yard.

In the meantime, the president had gone back to his bedroom and then came out sporting a red, white, and blue sequined jacket (as he evidently often did on nights when guests were first-timers at the Point). It was a gift of his good friends the Oak Ridge Boys, and he knew the kids would get a kick out of it—they did, and we did too.

About that time—the second smile-worthy moment—Luke burst in the door, raised Bibi up above his head, and said, "Mission accomplished." The irony was lost on him, but not on the rest of us. Before dinner, we all assembled in front of the fireplace for a photo.

After offering the blessing several nights in a row now, I turned the mantle over to my Laura, who handled it marvelously. A lot of conversation followed, and as things wound down, Evie said, "I wonder who will win tonight."

The president smiled as one of the other kids said, "Win what?"

"You know," she said. "The sleeping contest!" The president smiled at Evie—and she smiled back. Bar was smiling too. Evie had caught on quick.

My children were made to feel like this was their home—and though it was not, the hospitality of the president and Bar certainly made them, and us, feel that way.

The next morning, Barbara, Margaret, and Laura Bush had set aside some time to go shopping in various antiques stores in town. As we finished up breakfast, Barbara turned to my Laura and said, "Will you come with us?"

Laura said, "I don't want to horn in..."

Bar was quick to respond. "You would not be." But then she looked at me. "What will you do?" (as if to say, *You know you are not invited to this party*).

"The kids and I will find something to do," I said, and we did. I cannot adequately express to you how odd it felt to see my wife, Margaret, and two first ladies of the United States hop in Secret Service vehicles and drive away.

Beach Walks, Important Talks, and New Friends Along the Way

This first trip occurred in the summer of 2008, and so it was long before seasons where there would be ample visits back in Houston at the Bush home, so this was the first time Laura and I had long, uninterrupted walks with Barbara on the beach. Here is where our friendship really began to take root as we unpacked stories of her family and friends, and she pulled out of us stories of our own. She would listen as much as she talked, and vice versa.

It was heartwarming to see how many people would come up to her on the beach for a quick meet and greet. It seemed like an unspoken rule, or perhaps just the practice of good manners among the great people of Kennebunkport, but no one asked for an autograph or (God forbid) a *selfie*, and no one overstayed their welcome. But I suspect if they did, Bar would not have said a word.

I still recall one day when she and I had a long walk together, just the two of us (though of course Secret Service was there, but at a distance). We were finishing up and when we got up onto the boardwalk, Bar leaned on me with one hand while she washed off the bottom of her shoes, holding a nearby garden hose with the other. As we stood there, an older fellow came up and said, "You know...you look just like Barbara Bush."

Without missing a beat, she said, "Yes, I hear that a lot."

It only took a moment before he figured out his error, apologized, and self-corrected, but Bar quickly put him at ease.

In many ways, the citizens of Kennebunkport were a tight-knit family. Because of weather, the winter months drove a lot of the villagers away, including the Bushes, but come late spring, the town came back to life, and a large part of that life was the connectedness so many there felt for George, Barbara, and the rest of the Bush family.

When one thinks of Maine, one often thinks of lobster, and on that first trip we set out to find our fill. There are a lot of great lobster places in the area, but just as you cross that small bridge over the Kennebunk River coming into town, you would likely see a long line of folk waiting their turn to place an order at the Clam Shack. In 2000, Steve Kingston opened the Shack, and it deserves all the praise it has gotten from food critics around the country.

We would not let the line dissuade us, so we took our place. Steve was actually working behind the counter that day taking orders. As we placed ours, he said, "You look familiar to me."

Laura was good about coaching her preacher husband to resist the temptation to say, *I am the president's pastor*, and so I held back, but finally Steve said, "I know... You are the Bushes' pastor. I saw you at the tenth anniversary of the library."

He had me pegged, but I was immediately struck by the fact that the Bushes were friends to everyone they met—and those friendships compelled an amazing loyalty. It was not just high-profile Houston and DC folk who attended that library event in the fall of 2007, but also part of that huge circle of loving and supportive citizens from their second home in Maine. And over time, we found this to be true of any and every person we encountered—in shops, restaurants, parks. Conversation almost always, somehow, got around to the president and Bar, and nary a negative word was spoken; the locals had only admiration and affection for them. One cannot manufacture that kind of bond—it comes as the fruit of life shared together.

In her remarks at Barbara Bush's funeral, Susan Baker quoted Bar and then added her own take:

About Friendship Bar said, "The most important yardstick of your success will be how you treat other people—your family, friends, coworkers, and even strangers you meet along the way." She was the gold standard of what it meant to be a friend, because she was motivated by the desire to show God's love to each and every one of His children she met.[1]

The president and Bar were living proof of that.

As I have already shared, you never knew who was going to be at Walker's Point when you arrived. One summer as we arrived, presidential advisor Karl Rove had already arrived and settled in at the main house. He had brought along a lovely woman, Karen Johnson, whom he had known for years but had only started dating in the previous year.

We had never met Karl but had followed his career and some of his ups and downs living in the public eye. But it was late summer 2011 as President Obama geared up to run for a second term, and there was political conversation aplenty.

Though we were there for several days together, for us, it was in part a "work trip." Our daugher had gotten married earlier that summer, and many of the invited guests who wanted to be with us couldn't come either because of the date or the locale. Thus, Laura was intent on getting a very large stack of announcements out in the mail for those friends and family members as soon as we finished working on them.

We had rented a car and were headed into town to the post office, when Karl and Karen invited us to go into town with them to visit some of the art galleries. On the way to the post office, the sky opened up and a deluge began just as we pulled up to the post. So, I suggested we come back later, but Karl said, "Not a problem," and before we could nix the idea, he grabbed all the announcements, covered his head with his jacket, and ran them up to the mail drop.

We spent the afternoon together walking through town, and at some point, Karl asked if I had read Laura Hillenbrand's new bestseller

---

1. Susan Garrett Baker, remarks at Barbara P. Bush's memorial service, April 22, 2018.

Unbroken, about the life of Olympic runner and World War II POW Louis Zamperini. I had not and he said, "You've got to read it…You'd love it!"

He went on to say I would love it, not just because of Zamperini's incredible story of survival, but because (spoiler alert here) of the end of the book, when Zamperini comes to terms with his deteriorating emotional, mental, and nonexistent spiritual health, until he gives his life to Jesus at a Billy Graham crusade in 1949. Zamperini spent the rest of his days not only regaling audiences about his Olympic achievements, his harrowing days adrift at sea, his imprisonment and torture in Japanese prison camps, but also, and most importantly, sharing how all of this and more was redeemed when he encountered and embraced the love of a God who had long ago embraced him.

I would later learn that Zamperini's public talks, which he gave well into his nineties until just shortly before his death, were said to be electrifying. Karl and I talked about the book some more, and he said, "Don't buy it—I'll send you a copy!"

Well, this kicked open the door for Karl and me to have a number of conversations about our faith, church, and prayer. I learned that Karl was Episcopalian and that his first wedding ceremony was performed by an Episcopal priest in Houston. When that marriage began to fall apart, Karl returned to that same priest and parish with the hope that he and his wife could rebuild their love for one another, but it was not to be.

Over the days we were together, the president, Karl, and I went out on *Fidelity*, where lively discussions dominated the sound of the waves lapping up against the hull.

Karen Johnson was a bright, lively, and warm lobbyist. She shared Karl's wit and humor, and so after a day or so, I began to jokingly say to Karl, "You know, we could take care of all of this while we are here."

He seemed to appreciate and not appreciate the humor at the same time, but in a strange way, we quickly hit it off, and our connecting points about faith and church made the connection go deeper.

We agreed to stay in touch, and when I returned home to Houston, within days, a copy of *Unbroken* was waiting for me in my mail pile. As developments in the elections (local and national) unfolded, I would check in with Karl from time to time. Then early in 2012, Karl called and left a voicemail asking me what I was doing in June.

I called him back, and he told me he had proposed to Karen and wanted to know if I would officiate. I told him I would, but since he had been married and divorced, he would have to agree to go to premarital counseling, and I would have to receive a letter from the clergyperson who performed it, stating their readiness for marriage.

We set the date for June 28. I still have a message from Karl on my phone from the evening of June 25. He called to say he sensed that Karen was a bit nervous and edgy about everything, and he wanted to know if "that is normal!" I said it was and that I would probably be concerned if she was not a bit out of sorts!

In the end, everything came together. I knew how much Karl and Karen loved each other, knew all would be well, and was deeply touched to have been asked to officiate. It was a private service, with only Karl, Karen, Karl's son Andrew, and my wife, Laura, who offered the readings from Scripture before the exchange of vows and rings and inviting God to inaugurate this marriage.

Karl and Karen honeymooned in Ravello, Italy. A few weeks later, I received a postcard upon which Karl had done a little watercolor painting of a house in the nearby hills:

10 July—2012

Dear Laura and Russ—

   Many, many thanks for your pivotal role in the June 28 festivities. Karen and I are so grateful you were part of this important day for the Roves.

                                        All the best,
                                        Karen and Karl
                                (and who says 43 is the only painter?)

I guess you might wonder why I have included this little vignette about Karl and Karen. For me, at least, it is another layer of seeing the hand of God at work in the most unexpected places.

I only knew (as I suppose most do) Karl Rove as a skilled political strategist, a television commentator, and a regular columnist for the *Wall Street Journal*. I came to know him as a man who was firmly committed to staying connected to his Lord, his church, and his faith. He was a student of the Bible, worshipped regularly, and reflected on his Christian duty to the world. He, like most of us, was and still is working out his faith with fear and trembling, as the Apostle Paul counseled the Christians in Philippi to do.

Because of what I came to know and appreciate about Karl and Karen, I asked if he would be willing to come to St. Martin's and speak to our men's group on an early morning—not about politics or elections, but about his own faith journey and a time when he needed and felt closest to God. He did so with humor, brazen honesty, and heartfelt humility. Many left that day seeing Karl Rove in a completely different light.

Here, one of the many things I love about the Episcopal Church is its wide aisle—it has been the church of liberals and conservatives, progressives and evangelicals, traditionalists and charismatics—with clergypersons standing all across the spectrum but bound together by their common beliefs about the love and grace of God and its manifestation in the world about us. The Episcopal Church has been home to George Washington and George H. W. Bush and Gerald Ford, to Jon Meacham and Brian Williams, to Colin Powell and John Dalton, to George Patton and Sandra Day O'Connor, to Tom Hanks and Robin Williams, to Charlton Heston, Fred Astaire, to Julie Andrews, Van Morrison, Sam Waterston, Reese Witherspoon, Emmylou Harris— and, well, yes, Karl Rove. That is pretty much the Body of Christ, whether one likes it or not—we are all playing for the same team, even if we come at it from different sides of the field.

A Life Lesson on Parenting: "What Are We Going to Do about the Girl?"

In the early fall of 2011, we had, perhaps, one of the most interesting and memorable trips to the Point. It was in late September, shortly after Neil Bush's daughter Lauren married David Lauren, the son of American fashion executive Ralph Lauren and also an executive within the family business. It was a relaxed visit because another big family wedding was behind the Bushes.

Though, to be honest, we were surprised that they would even be entertaining guests, for surely they needed a rest. We were even more surprised when Bar encouraged our kids to come and bring any friends they might want to bring.

Only one of our children, Jones, took her up on the offer and brought his girlfriend at the time. As usual, on the drive from Boston to Walker's Point, I gave "the lecture" about manners and listening more than talking, especially when it came to Barbara. The guidance was lost on the guest along for the ride.

Once we got settled in, we dressed as we usually did and headed to the house for drinks. Much to our surprise, the girlfriend sat down next to Barbara and talked more than listened, and then, worse, we caught on that she was entering a disagreement with Bar about—of all things—how to pronounce "Ralph *Lauren*."

Bar was amazingly kind about the whole thing, gently reminding the young lady that her granddaughter had just married into that family and Barbara had been with a bevy of Laurens only days before. I suspect the look on my face was a giveaway. It was all I could do to keep from tackling the young lady to the floor.

She let up for a bit but then started up this argumentative and opinionated behavior at dinner. The kids were all staying in a different bungalow from ours, and as Laura and I attempted to drift off to sleep later that evening, we agreed this would likely be our last invite to Walker's Point (for the record, it was not).

The next morning, the antics continued a bit as we all prepared for our morning beach walk in casual clothes. Bar was actually in sweats, the rest of us were in beachwear, and the girlfriend had donned a semi-formal dress and string of white pearls. We did what we could to try and keep this young lady away from Bar to head off any more problems. Things got worse before they got better—actually, they only got better when we finally departed Walker's Point days later.

But by the evening of the second day, after dinner, after everyone was sent off to try and win the sleeping contest, the president headed off to the bedroom and Bar turned and looked at us and said, "Why don't you two take a look at the wedding photos from the wedding?" There were some already pulled together in a little photo book sitting on a table between some comfortable chairs in the nearby living room. It was an unusual request, but we always accepted those invitations. The lights began to go out, and Bar headed off to bed. As we flipped through the book, Paula came out of the kitchen and we visited a bit. Then she left as Bar came back into the room, now dressed in her nightgown and robe with slippers.

I suspect Laura and I had some idea of what was coming as she stood in front of us both, bent over, and whispered clearly, "Now, what are we going to do about the girl?"

In part, we were relieved that the cat was out of the bag—we were all thinking the same thing; we just did not know how to bring it up, which was never a problem for Barbara, so she just put it out there.

Laura and I both said, "Yeah, right...What *are* we going to do?"

Bar gave us some motherly advice at that moment. "Well, you can't say anything. You just need to be who you are and let her see that...and let it play out. If you say anything, it will likely backfire."

She went on to assess that the young lady was just that—young—and that while we had become accustomed to being around the Bushes, this was her first time, so she was probably nervous.

"But, but, but..." we said in several ways, several times.

"You can't say anything" was the overriding counsel. "Your boy will figure it out. Anyway, whatever he decides, you all will need to support him." She was right, of course—as she always was.

Then we talked for a bit about how bringing up children is wonderful but can be very hard at times, particularly as they get older and begin making their own decisions.

Only days later, as we got back to Houston, a handwritten letter dated September 11 arrived:

> *Dear Russ and Laura—*
>
> *I have thought about* [name redacted] *a lot. First of all—I should not have mentioned it—secondly, coming to visit the former President would be daunting. Your precious son probably did not put her at ease about how relaxed we were…*
>
> *Fall has finally arrived here. We are so lucky to be here and have each other. Do not answer, but I wanted you to know that I have thought about that lovely child and <u>no</u> "buts"…*
>
> *Bar*

Suffice it to say, the end of that story was more about Bar than it was about "the girl." Jones's girlfriend was nice, and she was likely nervous, and Laura and I were doing our best to grow comfortably to try and find our way from parenting adults to being parents of adults—without continuing to parent! Bar was right about a lot of things, and in time, our boy made the right decision about the girl. And, as Robert Frost wrote, "that has made all the difference."

Paints and Pinstripes and Heartstrings

By now, you can tell that I could go on and on about Kennebunkport. It is a beautiful town with wonderful people who count among their closest friends the late patriarch and matriarch of the Bush brigade and all those they brought into this world together, including yet another president and first lady.

On our last visit, just a year or so before the health of George and Barbara began to steeply decline, the summer pastor of nearby St. Ann's, the Reverend Peter Cheney, had invited me to preach at morning services. The president was not feeling up to attending church that Sunday, but the rest of us worshipped together: Bar, along with Doro, and the forty-third president and his first lady, Laura, who were in town. After church, the Cheneys, other Bush family members, Laura, and I gathered together on the great back porch for a family tradition: "Taco Sunday."

Hospitality reigned at these gatherings. We had attended when there were a handful of people and when there were more people than there were chairs to hold them. As the crowd slipped away, the forty-third president invited my Laura and me to his new painting studio on the upper floor of one of the new bungalows. Laura rode in a golf cart with 43, and I rode with Barbara in another.

Bar was not able to make the steps up to the studio, but the president wanted her to see some of his new work. Laura and I got the full tour and saw several of his oil pieces—flags, paintings of veterans he had met and with whom he had formed fast friendships. He talked a bit about how much he enjoyed painting. When I asked if he listened to music while he worked, he said, "Not usually... I like the silence."

"I want Mother to see some of these," he said. He pointed to two and asked me to grab them, and he grabbed a few as well. We took them down the steps to an admiring mom... then back up, and we bid farewell.

Not until we got back to our room did Laura point to my pants leg and say, "What's that?" I looked down, and evidently one of the paintings had not been dry, so I had a long, dark streak of oil paint on a relatively new pinstripe suit! "Well, that's not going to come out!" Laura said. We joked briefly about selling it on eBay—I never told the president. If one has to get paint on one's pinstripes, I suppose a president's is the best to have.

On this last visit, the forty-first president was not feeling well most of the time. He welcomed visitors into the master bedroom to join him as he sat in his reclining chair, watching sports, or just to visit. We did not know at the time that we would not be returning to Kennebunkport, but we suspected a page was turning. There was a bit of melancholy in Barbara's voice when we walked on the beach or around the property. She said to us more than once that she wanted to stay later that year than they normally did to "watch the leaves change color," adding, "I do not know if we will be coming back."

I loved it when Laura and Bar would walk ahead of me—they really had become close friends, and I was fortunate to see how much Barbara actually admired Laura. She never missed an opportunity to tell me how I had "married up."

She knew, as did I, that Laura was a wonderful mother, grand-mother, wife, and that she had accomplished something that is hard for some spouses of clergy—filling the unspoken, yet expected, role of "the pastor's wife" (or husband, as the case may be). One evening over dinner, Bar looked at Laura with that admiration and said, "You know, you never say anything wrong..." Bar meant it as a tremendous compliment. But later when Laura told me the story, she said, "I thought, *Barbara...you have no idea what hard work that is!*"

We took in a lot of Kennebunkport that summer. As with previous trips, we were encouraged to roam liberally together or on our own around the Point, to visit and borrow from the bookshelves, make ourselves at home in the kitchen or at the bar, and walk the beautiful and inspiring grounds.

One evening, as everyone else was getting ready for dinner, I walked to the easternmost edge of the house, which is surrounded by a porch that overlooks a promontory jutting out into what was almost always a raging North Atlantic. The wind was just extraordinary. The sun was beginning to set and there was just enough of a cold snap to awaken the senses.

I turned to look back at the house, and just below the window in the main sitting area, I saw, as I had seen on that first visit back in 2008, the small bronze plaque that read CAVU.

CAVU was an acronym used by navy fliers during World War II to describe the perfect conditions for flight—"ceiling and visibility unlimited." It was a motto for the former navy pilot and retired president of the United States, but it also was the way in which he looked at life—with faith and courage and the strength of family and friends, anything was possible. And he lived that motto until his very last day.

Before we left, Laura and I paid a trip to Ganny's Garden near the edge of town. Friends and family established the garden in 2011 as a gift of appreciation and affection for Barbara. The well-situated space is laced with a number of remembrances of Bar, including a sculpted version of her iconic straw hat, a pair of Keds tennis shoes, and an open copy of her favorite book, *Pride and Prejudice.*

As I stood in front of that little bench, in that moment, a sadness came over me. I knew someday—perhaps someday soon—Barbara would no longer be on this side of the great veil, and it also occurred to me that I would likely be called into that moment. My heartstrings were being pulled, and I could feel a tightness in my chest and tears welling up and spilling gently out onto my cheeks. Laura came up beside me and we placed our arms around each other and just stood there, once again, taking in what an incredible blessing and privilege it was to have been taken into the circle of this incredible family. Standing there, in "her" garden, I knew that if I was asked to offer words at her funeral, I would have to take those hearing my words to this special place, and when the time came, I did.

A Standing Ovation to Remember

The president never ceased to enjoy the fullness of Walker's Point. Every time we went, he would challenge the kids to jump fully into the cold waters of the North Atlantic—which they usually did. At one point, he said they should feel free to take one of the smaller motorboats out. Mercifully, I dissuaded my inexperienced children from accepting that invitation. But they eagerly used the Bushes' home gym, kayaks, and bikes, often taking those into town on their own.

One afternoon, Laura and I were a bit horrified to look out and see Bar leaning over and saying something to our youngest, Luke. Apparently, he had done something a bit displeasing to the First Lady. When he came in, we asked him what on earth he had done.

"Oh, nothing," he said. "I had left one of the bikes out and she just asked me to return it where I found it…no big deal." Such are the words of an "adopted" grandchild.

On another afternoon, the president and Bar had made early reservations at a seafood restaurant just outside of town. They wanted to beat the crowds and also have a little privacy, so we were seated upstairs and out of the way of the larger dining room.

The opportunity gave the president and Bar a good, long visit with the kids, and as usual, we were not leaving the table until each one had ordered a hearty dessert. By then, we could hear that the crowd downstairs had really increased as the dinner hour approached. We had successfully avoided the rush.

As we got up to leave, the president and Bar led the way, and I quickly noticed several of the patrons looking in our direction. I tugged on Laura's arm so that the kids would follow the president and Bar, and then sensing what was about to happen, I said to Laura, "Let's wait here—I want the kids to see this."

It began with a few, then more, with no cause other than being in the presence of two great American leaders—patrons around the room began to applaud, and then one by one, two by two, they stood, until every single person in the restaurant was offering a standing ovation to our forty-first president and his first lady.

If there was ever a doubt in our children's minds how privileged they were to be taken under the pair of such grand wings, I suspect it was wiped away on that evening. It did not diminish the familiarity our children had come to share with the president and Bar, but I am confident it deepened their respect—a respect that Laura and I, as well as all those who were, and are, fortunate to know the "Shangri-La" of Kennebunkport, already had.

A Pastor's Recommendation

Before we leave this lovely fishing village, allow me to recommend that you visit Kennebunkport if time and geography allow you to do so. You may not make it beyond the Secret Service station, but you can stop on Ocean Avenue, call yourself a "Bush-watcher," and take in the view.

In 2009, in gratitude for all the Bush family had done as chief cogs in the wheel of the Kennebunkport area, the community pulled together and made possible a monument in honor of the forty-first president: a six thousand–pound anchor from a naval destroyer set upon the stone on a bluff that looks out toward Walker's Point.

The plaque there reads FOR OUR FRIEND AND 41ST PRESIDENT GEORGE H.W. BUSH. AS HE WAS FOR OUR NATION AND WORLD DURING FOUR YEARS OF TUMULTUOUS AND HISTORIC CHANGE, SO, TOO, HAS KENNEBUNKPORT SERVED IN THE WORDS OF ST. PAUL, "AS AN ANCHOR OF THE SOUL, BOTH SURE AND STEADFAST"[2] TO HIM. PRESENTED BY THOSE WHO LOVE HIM AS MUCH AS HE LOVES THIS SPECIAL PLACE.

Indeed.

---

2. Hebrews 6:19. Though allow this pastor to point out that while the Letter to the Hebrews has traditionally been attributed to Paul, the actual author is unknown—and yet the verse is certainly well chosen!

CHAPTER NINE

A TIME TO LAUGH

There is a time for everything, and a season for every activity under the heavens . . . A time to laugh . . .

Ecclesiastes 3:1, 4

Mirth is the sweet wine of human life. It should be offered sparkling with zestful life unto God.

Henry Ward Beecher[1]

If you're not allowed to laugh in heaven, I don't want to go there.

Martin Luther[2]

Almost anyone who spent any time around the president and Barbara will tell you how impressed they were by their humility. Neither of them had any innate desire to be showy, and as I have already said time and time again, Laura and I witnessed their ability to connect and make conversation with anyone anywhere. That Bush rule about the "big I" took root early on.

---

1. D. March 8, 1887.

2. D. February 18, 1546.

A few years before his death, when the president and Bar were still entertaining in their home on a fairly regular basis, I happened to be talking with Jean Becker late one day. She smiled as she told me that earlier that day, some protective agents who were to accompany several royal officials from the Middle East on a trip to Houston and to a lunch at the Bushes' home made several stops at various checkpoints, including the Bushes' home on West Oak.

As they finished up, the agents said, "But where does the president *live*?"

"Here," the responding staff members said.

"No … This is a nice place to meet, to have a meal, but where does he actually *live*?"

"The president and Mrs. Bush live *here*."

The visiting agents could not imagine the forty-first president living in such modest digs.

But humility is not something one can "achieve." The moment one tries to be humble, that person has lost the point altogether. Humility, like many of the other traits we are witnessing in this reflection together, is in its truest sense a gift of God's Spirit.

But interestingly enough, *humility* comes from the root word in Latin for *humanity*—*humus*, which literally translated means "the lowly earth." In Genesis 2:7, the creation story tells its reader that "the LORD God formed a man from the dust of the ground and breathed into his nostrils the breath of life, and the man became a living being."[3]

---

3. It has always been interesting to me that this passage actually confirms something that evolutionists Charles Darwin (d. 1882) and Alfred Russel Wallace (d. 1913) would later explain through the discipline of science. Both the creation story and the theory of evolution confirm that humans emerged from the primordial dust of the earth. For Jews, Christians, and Muslims, as well as many other faiths, if one extricates the literal interpretations of time, creation narratives actually allow for the presence of evolution—divine though it is—while evolution closes the door to any divine initiative. For the record, your author can live with the tension of both, but I will not abandon the hand of God in creation.

Another word that also finds its origins in *humus* is *humor*. Authentic humor, like humility, requires that one is comfortable getting oneself out of the way. Many who wish to be taken seriously feel a constant state of seriousness is a must. Mercifully, for those who knew and loved the Bushes, that natural God-given humility gave birth to a wonderful sense of humor.

Pastor Rick Warren once said, "We take ourselves way too seriously, and we don't take God seriously enough. It is not by accident that human and humility come from the same root word. If you can laugh at yourself, you'll always have plenty of good material."

Well, if anyone had the capacity to heal and connect through humor, it was George and Barbara Bush.

So before we travel to the more serious and perhaps somber moments of this journey, I thought I would share just a few moments where we saw and experienced that humor come shining through.

Bibi Takes a Bite

The president and Bar loved their dogs. For many years, including those in Washington, their "go-to" breed was an English springer spaniel. Known for their energy, wit, and hunting ability, the springer spaniels became a regular fixture on the White House lawn. Millie became one of the most famous of the Bush spaniel clan when Barbara wrote the book *Millie's Book: As Dictated to Barbara Bush*, which became a bestseller in 1992.

When the last of the Bush spaniels, Sadie, went on to her heavenly reward in September 2008, the president was pretty blue. I wrote both him and Bar, expressing our heartfelt thoughts, which they appreciated, but the Bushes were dog people, and I suspected that there would not be a long wait before the patter of four feet would be added back into the mix.

There was much discussion in the Bush home as to what breed would be the next in line. The president naturally thought another springer spaniel, but Bar had something else in mind—a Maltese/poodle mix known as a "Maltipoo." The president was not too keen on having a lapdog—or as he liked to say, "a little fur ball"—take the place of such a regal lineage of presidential pups. But, as with most discussions, Barbara made her case convincingly.

When we came on the scene, Bibi was just a pup—so small you could almost put her in your jacket pocket. As a youngster, she took to many visitors, and Laura and I loved the chance to pick her up, scratch her tummy, or play fetch with any number of her toys.

But as time marched on and Bibi got older, she became much more protective of her two "parents." When we came through the front door, sometimes after ringing the doorbell, or sometimes unannounced, Bibi would begin barking, then charging. We had never seen her in attack mode, but that would soon change.

As was seen in the last chapter, as our years increased, Laura and I made more and more visits to the Bush home. We would come to share a drink, conversation, a prayer, and on most visits, Holy Communion. Bibi was usually sitting on a small dog bed between the president and Barbara. If one of us made a sudden move toward one of our hosts, Bibi would issue a low growl, which quickly put us in our places or on our guard.

One day, as we finished up our visit, Laura leaned over, as she almost always did, to kiss the president on the cheek. As she did, Bibi, as fast as lightning, jumped toward Laura's ankle, decided she could not contain herself, and gave Laura a chomp. Laura jumped a bit but did not give a hint as to the real impact of the bite, which went through her pantsuit before piercing the flesh!

Bar apologized and then began to walk us toward the door. Laura was not limping, but her gait was a bit slower, and Bar said, "Let me see what Bibi did." Laura responded repeatedly, "I am fine," and we walked a few more steps, when Bar said again, "No, really—I am not going to let you leave until you let me see." Laura paused and pulled up her pant leg, only to reveal a big round bite, with blood streaming down toward her ankle.

Bar gasped, and yet Laura, who has the pain threshold of a hardened field soldier, said, "Oh, it's nothing...I'm fine." As soon as we got out the door, beyond the Secret Service and outside of earshot, Laura said, "Can you believe that?"

We both started laughing as I said, "Well...you got bit by the First Dog..." We started laughing and laughed all the way home.

Laura did recover, but she still has the scar to prove it. However, the very next day, Laura was returning home in her car from a three-mile walk at our nearby Memorial Park. As she drove up to our house, she saw someone getting in a car and driving away. When she opened the front door, she found a beautiful white orchid with a note attached: *Dear Laura, I am so sorry about the bite, you just looked good enough to eat... Love, Bibi.*

It took a while, but suffice it to say that Bibi, and her added side-kick, another Maltipoo whom the Bushes named Mini-Me, eased to our presence. I knew I had passed the Rubicon when one of the pups would lie at my feet and I could scratch their tummy while talking to the president and Bar. That said, I do not think Laura ever returned to the house without wearing a thick pair of boots!

In the years that followed, we learned that Laura was a new member of the club of Bibi's victims—including Secret Service members and the president himself!

Oh...and Then There Was Lady Carnarvon

In the fall of 2015, St. Martin's issued an invitation to Fiona Herbert, the Countess of Carnarvon and the person whom many call the "real countess of Downton Abbey." Lady Carnarvon and her husband, George "Geordie" Herbert, the eighth Earl of Carnarvon, to this day own, live in, and manage Highclere Castle in Newbury, England, which became the chief filming location for the wildly popular period drama *Downton Abbey.*

Much to the delight of the members of St. Martin's, she readily accepted our invitation to speak, and it took a lot of elbow grease on behalf of our staff to find a venue that would hold the many people who would show up.

Just as I had not spent any amount of time around presidents and first ladies until our friendship with the Bushes blossomed, I also had not spent much time around countesses or earls prior to Lady Carnarvon's visit.

This was going to be a limited engagement (or so I thought), but when the Bushes caught wind that Lady Carnarvon was coming to town, Bar, who was an avid *Downton Abbey* watcher, reached out to me to see if I could bring the countess by for tea with her and the president at their house. Lady Carnarvon was more than happy to accept the invitation and asked me to come pick her up.

I had to put my starstruck response aside but did the best a Houston-by-way-of-Alabama boy could do in the way of manners. On the way to the Bushes' house, I must have called her "Lady Fiona" a half dozen times as she asked a few questions about what to expect, how to address them, and how the president was recovering (this was a few months after his neck break in Maine).

We made our way from her hotel and pulled off onto Post Oak Boulevard near the gate to their neighborhood. I punched the first security button. Secret Service answered and I felt a bit pretentious saying, "Russ Levenson here with Lady Fiona Carnarvon..."

On the short drive from this spot to the house, I felt it necessary to say, "Now, Lady Fiona, there is one more thing...The Bushes have this dog Bibi."

"Yes?" she said, with the lilt of a question in her voice.

"Bibi bites," I continued.

"Oh goodness," she said in a tone that did not sound like she was that convinced.

"No—I am serious. She may get near you. She may sit near the president or Barbara, but do not reach out toward them or make any sudden movements...or Bibi will bite you."

Another "Oh goodness."

As we reached the large security gate, it pulled back, allowing us to come through. Barbara was already out on the front porch, and Bibi, making her usual noises, started to run toward us, but by now, she had been (rather unsuccessfully, as you will see) to "discipline school," and when Bar called her down, she went from bark to low growl and returned to Bar's feet, clearly irritated at the tug on her personality.

We went into the large living room and enjoyed some tea, cookies, and conversation. The president came in later. The four of us sat for a bit talking (take note—once again, this pastor was very much out of place in this crowd, but as usual, I just sucked it up and did my best!). I was in a decorative chair to the left of a large sofa, with Lady Carnarvon to my immediate right. About two or three feet from her sat Bar, and the president was sitting across from us. Lying comfortably up against Bar's left leg was—you guessed it—Bibi.

The president and I had more in common in that moment than perhaps we ever had—neither of us had much to offer in the way of conversation about Victorian England. So we pleasantly listened, and then... oh goodness, then. As with all who visit with Bar, Lady Carnarvon quickly grew comfortable, and I saw that softness growing in Lady Carnarvon. But with it came a kind of physical shifting more and more toward Barbara.

Uh-oh, I thought. Bibi raised her head as the countess grew closer and closer. *Don't do it!* I thought. Then she did it. The Countess of Carnarvon reached out to affectionately touch the First Lady, and the First Dog sprang into action with a good old Bibi bite. Much like my dear Laura, Lady Carnarvon pulled back her hand with a bit of an "ouch," then covered the unseen wound with her other hand.

By then, well, this had become par for the course. Bar said something along the lines of "Oh, I'm sorry. Are you okay?"

I suspect we had a royal fib at that moment as Lady Carnarvon continued to cover her hand and said, "Oh, yes."

The rest of the visit went quite well—photos, an exchange of some presents, and some more small talk. Then we finished up, hugs all around, and said our good-byes.

And once the door closed behind us, on the way back to the car, Lady Carnarvon turned to me and said, "What was that?!"

Up to that point, it had been "Lady this" and "Countess that." But that moment broke the ice, and I said, "Well, Fiona, I told you she would bite you if you reached out toward her!"

"Bloody hell!" she said, which gave way to laughter—which often allows everyone to let down their guard. From then on, in private, I referred to her as Fiona, and she to Laura and me as Laura and Russ.

By the end of Lady Carnarvon's time in Houston, Bibi and the Bushes (perhaps in that order) had helped turn strangers into friends. The next summer, Laura and I were invited as guests of Lord and Lady Carnarvon to get our own behind-the-scenes tour of Highclere Castle and its beautiful gardens and grounds, enjoy a huge community picnic, and share tea and biscuits—sans the presence of canines or puncture wounds.

"It Still Wiggles"

Later that fall, St. Martin's had its annual Veterans Day service. Our special guest was someone who had become a friend over the years, Lieutenant General Rick Lynch, who had served in Afghanistan, and since his retirement, he had given a great deal of his time to inspirational speaking and working for the care, health, and well-being of wounded veterans.

It was our practice to typically hold a reception at our home after the service each year for all the participants—including representatives from every branch of the military. While we had invited the Bushes several times, they had declined, but in the fall of 2015, they accepted.

They had never been to our home, so the day before, Secret Service came to check out the house and the neighborhood. By now, the president was using a wheelchair most of the time, so we had a temporary ramp placed in the front yard.

I am not sure I had ever received a longer list of "honey dos" in my life, as Laura wanted the house to be in perfect order.

The service was inspirational and uplifting and then everyone began to arrive. The house was full of guests. As the president and Bar settled into our small library, I asked him if he wanted anything. "Vodka and tonic would be great," he said. Off I went, mixed it up, and returned to find, not to my surprise, most of the guests circled around the Bushes as they entertained and regaled with stories aplenty, most of them generating a laughter that spread around the room like a brush fire.

After dinner, as the conversation continued, the minutes were turning into hours, and no one, including the Bushes, gave any sign that they were interested in leaving. Knowing the president's limit was two drinks, I asked 41 if he wanted anything else. "Another one of these," he said, holding up his empty glass.

"Coming right up," I said, and made my way into the kitchen.

A second or two later an aide came in and said, "Perhaps a little less vodka this time." I had no idea I might have overserved the president!

The stories and laughter continued as eventually guests began to leave. My vice rector, the Reverend Marty Bastian, was sitting right next to the president when Bar said, "Well, it is probably time to head home." She got up off the sofa and began to walk away from the president and Marty, when 41 turned to Marty and said, "Check it out."

Marty was not sure what the president was referring to until he raised his hand, smiled, pointed at Bar as she walked away, and whispered, "It still wiggles..."

To this day, I would have loved to have heard what he had said if perhaps I made his drink a little stronger and we had sat together longer!

Thank You, But...

Clergy have a variety of habits. Over the years, I have made rather amateur attempts at painting. There is no Van Gogh or Rembrandt hidden within, but I can put paintbrush to canvas and from time to time produce something that is not altogether embarrassing.

In the summer of 2015, I painted some water lilies. At the time, I did not think much of the work, but the few who saw it complimented it. I am not sure what possessed me to presume it might be something Barbara would appreciate as a Christmas gift, but I made a run to a local craft store, bought a frame that fit my budget, and wrapped it up.

Before we left town for Thanksgiving that year, we went by the Bushes' house and had a great visit. I handed Bar our gift bag—which included some soap, some Grey Goose (which became the standard gift for 41), and the oil-on-canvas painting. Bar stuck it under their Christmas tree in the foyer, and we went on with our visit.

A few weeks later, Bar sent a wonderful email:

December 5, 2015
Russ and Laura,

While trimming the Christmas tree, I found your bag. George and I are overcome with the generosity of your gift. We love the water lilies. I know Laura told me they were her favorite. I hate to accept such a fabulous present, but will! I have the perfect place. Many many thanks. Bar and GB...

When we got back to town in early January 2016, the president and Bar invited us over to the house for a postholiday catch-up. Almost as soon as I walked in the door, she pointed to the hall right next to the entrance of the house. "Look what I have there!" she said. It was the painting of the water lilies, in a new frame.

"I love it," she said, "but I had it reframed. I thought it looked better 'floated' on a dark background."

Humbled and somewhat stymied, I thanked her, and then as we made our way toward the sitting room to join 41, she opened a closet door beneath the entry stairs. Subtlety was never Bar's strong suit. She dug around a bit until I heard her say, "Here it is." She pulled out the frame that I had used in my gift making, and in a "Thank you, but..." moment, she handed it to me. "Here...you can keep this cheap old frame for something else..."

I filed that away as a lesson for future gift giving.

Laughter Is the Best Medicine

The source of the proverb "Laughter is the best medicine" cannot be tracked down, but clearly it has been held as a wide truth since the dawn of time, for as the author of Ecclesiastes suggests, there is a time for laughter, and 41 and Bar seemed to be masters at the craft without trying.

I wish I had as glowing of a record, but in over ten years of being together, I only saw Bar irritated at the president one time. I had arrived at the house for one of our regular visits. When I got there, Bar welcomed me in and said that the president was still sleeping.

"He was up late watching some trash!" she said.

I found that a bit hard to believe but could not resist asking, "What was he watching?"

"Something horrible—*The 40-Year-Old Virgin*. Can you imagine?" And then she asked a question that she often asked. "What do you think about that?" Normally, I did not mind when she asked me this, because the best answer to that question was usually to agree, but I was not about to put myself between the president and first lady, or vice versa, for that matter. So I think I came to his defense, telling her it was a bit of a raunchy comedy, but there were far more worse things he could be watching that would not sit well.

But that was it. I never heard about the scandalous late-night television watching again. I suspect that was a one-off, because by and large all they had for one another were words of affection and tenderness, and they were not just going through the motions—they so loved one another. Laura nor I ever witnessed a cross word between them. When she talked, he listened; and when he talked, she returned the favor. They left space for one another in their conversation, such that you knew the mutual respect was not perfunctory but from the heart. And they did, in fact, love to make each other laugh.

Age did not seem to have any impact on the affection they had for one another. Not long after I began my ministry at St. Martin's, the president had been hospitalized for a minor procedure, and Laura and I went to visit. When we came in, Bar held up the president's CPAP breathing device that he sometimes had to use to sleep through the night. She cocked her head, smiled, and said, "Well, the romance is over." If it was, we never saw it. If anything, the older they got, the more affectionate they seemed to become. There were times I arrived at the house by invitation for prayers or Communion, and I would find one or both of them had dozed off watching the television but holding hands as well.

On occasions, especially on days when the president was fighting off an illness or recovering from a medical or even surgical procedure, I would find Bar stroking his head, talking to her "boy." In those moments—which in many ways were holy to me—I almost felt like an intruder, an interloper. I did not belong there—or did I, if only to hear him whisper to Bar with that broad smile, "I do love the sound of your voice"?

The touches, the smiles, the laughter, and even the quiet moments between them—all of them were healing moments—a potent medicine injected at just the right time.

Humor to the End

As I will share later, in the spring of 2018, I do not think any of us who knew and loved Barbara thought she only had months left in this life. She had some serious medical issues, and there were a number of trips to the doctor and some hospital stays, but her spirit and spunk were never dampened.

On March 31, I paid her a visit at the hospital. She was alone and welcomed me in with a strong, hardy voice. But she had her reading glasses on and was fiddling with a new cell phone.

"Neely just picked this up for me . . . and I can't read the letters. They are too small."[4] She tinkered with it just a bit more, then lowered her

---

4. Neely Brunette was Barbara's personal aide at the time, beginning in April 2017.

glasses, held out the phone in my direction, and said, "Here…can you make the letters bigger?"

Despite our close friendship to Bar at the time, I felt like I should not take this on. "I bet Neely can do it when she gets here. Bar, I don't think your priest should be fiddling around with the First Lady's phone."

She handed it to me anyway and said, "Well, give it a try."

I am no handyman when it comes to technology, but I accomplished the assigned task and returned the phone, much to Bar's delight. We had a good visit and prayer, and I left.

I had Bar's cell phone number in my contacts but rarely took advantage of it. But in this case, I thought it worth checking in, so at 7:34 p.m., I texted her:

> Bar! Are you texting yet! This is your rector praying for two of the most wonderful people I know. Laura and I will see you tomorrow after the services…hope and pray you and the President rest well tonight…Russ+

Within a minute, Bar texted back: *P*

Which, if you know your "letter emojis," represents someone sticking their tongue out at you!

It was the last electronic communication Bar sent to me, as she would die less than three weeks later. But as she often did, Bar had the last word on whether I should have mended her phone, and fortunately, for me anyway, she also had the last laugh.

CHAPTER TEN

HOLY MOMENTS AND HOLY SPACES

Do any human beings ever realize life while they live it—every, every minute?

Emily Webb, Our Town

The LORD is good, a refuge in times of trouble. He cares for those who trust in him.

Nahum 1:7

D o any human beings ever realize life while they live it—every, every minute?" Emily, a young woman in Thornton Wilder's play *Our Town*, asks.

In the play, Emily dies in childbirth but is granted a unique experience: the stage manager allows her to return from death and live one day of her life with her family. Although Emily has high hopes for that one day, she is disappointed. Just before she returns to her place in the cemetery, she cries in frustration to the stage manager: "It goes so fast. We don't have time to look at one another...Do any human beings realize life while they live it—every, every minute?"

The stage manager speaks a word of truth to Emily and the audience: "No. The saints and poets, maybe—they do some."[1]

I think in all my years of ministry, I have seen few people more fully live "every, every minute" than George and Barbara Bush.

I hope, by now at least, you are beginning to understand why I felt so compelled to write this book, to share these insights with you. From their youngest days to their last days, as you will see, I suspect it never really occurred to the president or Barbara that they should not take each and every moment as an incredible gift. How many times had I heard them say, "God is good," "Life is wonderful," "We are blessed"?

Some might be quick to say, "Well, it is easier to say that when you have wealth, success, and power." But I think their lives attest to the fact that George and Barbara did not bank on that when it came to feeling blessed.

Like the apostle Paul, Bar and the president knew what it was to be in need, and knew what it was to have plenty, and yet they, also like Paul, had learned the secret of contentment, which was, in fact, to draw on the strength of the Lord to live in whatever the circumstance.[2]

The most precious treasures our forty-first president and his wife possessed were not tucked away in a secret vault but were firmly knitted into their hearts—friends, family, and faith. And so for them, each moment given, in whatever matter or circumstance, was to be cherished and enjoyed to the fullest.

It is said that one day, a rather stern monk came upon Francis of Assisi as he was doing one of the things he loved to do best—working in his little vegetable garden. The monk thought this was a waste of time and that Francis should be investing these minutes more wisely by praying

---

1. Thornton Wilder, *Our Town* (New York: Coward McCann, Inc., 1938), act 3, final scene.

2. Cf., "[12] I know what it is to be in need, and I know what it is to have plenty. I have learned the secret of being content in any and every situation, whether well fed or hungry, whether living in plenty or in want. [13] I can do all this through him who gives me strength," Philippians 4:12–13.

The Bush family leaving Sunday services, circa 1965. When I asked the family if we could use this photo in Barbara's burial booklet, everyone said yes, but we noticed Jeb was blocked by his siblings, which prompted his comment, "Story of my life!" *c/o The Bush Family*

Before heading to Washington, the future president served on the vestry as an usher and was happy to serve coffee to fellow church members. *c/o St. Martin's Photo Files*

President-elect Bush speaks at a Thanksgiving service he requested to be held the morning after Election Day, November 4, 1988. His request— win or lose—we gather with friends and family to pray and give thanks. *c/o St. Martin's Photo Files*

First Lady Barbara Bush stayed connected to her St. Martin's "Saintly Stitchers." In this photo, she shares a Nativity scene set up in the White House populated by hand-stitched figures provided by the St. Martin's needleworkers. Barbara invited her "Sister Stitchers" to the White House during Advent of 1991. *c/o Merchant Logo, George H. W. Bush Presidential Library and Museum, White House Photo*

On Sunday, July 8, 1990, the president and first lady brought British prime minister Margaret Thatcher and her husband, Sir Denis Thatcher, as well as Canadian prime minister Brian Mulroney and his wife, Milica, to St. Martin's on "Bring a Friend to Church Day," instituted by St. Martin's third rector, the Reverend Claude Payne. The dignitaries had gathered for the sixteenth G7 summit held on the campus of Rice University in Houston. *c/o White House Photo/St. Martin's Photo Files*

The president and Bar spent their sixty-third wedding anniversary celebrating the institution of the fourth rector of St. Martin's on January 6, 2008. Pictured to my left is Laura's late mother, Evelyn; and to Bar's right are our son Luke; daughter, Evie; son Jones; my late mother, Lynne; and my father, Russell Levenson Sr. *c/o St. Martin's Photo Files*

Early in my tenure at St. Martin's, our staff photographer snapped this photo after a morning worship service just outside the doors of St. Martin's. We were all a bit younger then, but the friendships grew more deeply with each passing day. *c/o St. Martin's Photo Files*

Our first trip to Kennebunkport in the summer of 2008 provided some lasting memories. First Lady Laura, and Marvin Bush's wife, Margaret, were wonderful additions to what quickly felt like a family gathering at Walker's Point. *c/o Merchant Logo, The Bush Family*

Laura snapped this photo of Bar and me on Gooch's Beach, Kennebunkport, where we walked and talked together dozens of times over the years. Loved the time a passing fellow said, "You look a lot like Barbara Bush," and without missing a beat, Bar said, "Yes, I hear that a lot." *c/o Author's Personal Photo Collection*

In January 2008, I chose the president and Bar to receive the Star Award, recognizing them for their extraordinary years of service to St. Martin's, our state, nation, and world. By the time I finished reading all they had done for so many, there was not a dry eye in the house, including the Bushes'. A few days later, 41 wrote me a note . . . *"I am sorry I choked up. I find I cry more at 84 than I did before and I feel badly . . . Life is so good and I am grateful to you and to our Church."* *c/o St. Martin's Photo Files*

The president and Bar, along with active St. Martin's members the Honorable James A. Baker III and his wife, Susan Garrett Baker, have served in various leadership roles for every major campaign of St. Martin's. Here they are part of the groundbreaking for a new youth center, scout center, and the Hope and Healing Center, all made possible by the $25 million Building for the Ages campaign. *c/o St. Martin's Photo Files*

This remains my all-time favorite photo of 41 and me. We were gathering for our annual "Parish Photo" outside of the church on St. Martin's Day. *c/o St. Martin's Photo Files*

Our trips to Kennebunkport provided loads of memories. This photo was taken outside of the main house on our last visit before Barbara's death. You can see Bibi keeping guard on our heels! *c/o Author's Personal Photo Collection*

In October 2015, St. Martin's was invited by President Bush and his son Neil to host an ecumenical and interfaith prayer service to launch the festivities for the twenty-fifth anniversary of the Points of Light Foundation. Jon Meacham was our "preacher," which allowed the large circle of religious leaders in Houston to listen, and to pray. *c/o St. Martin's Photo Files*

On Sunday, May 10, 2015, Barbara was officially confirmed by a longtime friend to St. Martin's, the 103rd Archbishop of Canterbury, Lord George L. Carey. His wife, Lady Eileen; Neil Bush; and Laura (Levenson) were the only guests at the private service. *c/o St. Martin's Photo Files*

Before the funeral service for Barbara, and prior to the entrance of dozens of dignitaries, the Presidents Bush came into Bagby Parish Hall at St. Martin's holding hands. The omnipresent and fiercely loyal medical aide Evan Sisley, guiding the chair, is, as he always was, close at hand. *c/o The Bush Family—photo by Paul Morse*

There were a number of moments that allowed for smiles prior to the funeral, one of which was when I told a room full of presidents, first ladies, and guests that we were in Texas now—so we were going to hold hands and pray. And we did! *c/o The Bush Family—photo by Paul Morse*

This iconic photo was taken moments before Barbara's service began on Saturday, April 21, 2018. *c/o The Bush Family— photo by Paul Morse*

After the service, as our motorcade made its way to College Station, Texas, for Barbara's burial on the grounds of the George H. W. Bush Presidential Library, tens of thousands of well-wishers lined the roads, streets, highways, and overpasses to say farewell to their beloved Barbara. *c/o The Bush Family—photo by Paul Morse*

Of all the moments around the state funeral, this is one that endures. As we were flying to DC aboard Air Force One, Secretary Baker came for a good long visit. Here, he sat across from Laura, going over the memorial service bulletin. The conversation that began at the end of the discussion was about how the "way things were" and the "way things are now" in the world of politics was a reason for grief, prayers, and hope. *c/o Author's Personal Photo Collection*

Evan Sisley took this photo aboard Air Force One with friends who would become very close over my eleven-year relationship with the Bushes. Pictured: communications director Jim McGrath; one of President Bush's longtime aides, Jim Appleby; and the president's chief of staff, Jean Becker. *c/o The Bush Family—Evan Sisley*

The nave of Washington's National Cathedral was filled to the brim for the president's state funeral on the morning of December 5, 2018. More than three thousand people attended, and approximately 17.5 million people viewed the broadcast of the service. *c/o Photo Courtesy of the National Cathedral*

When the service in DC was over, the president offered his father's priest a little fist bump with First Lady Laura smiling on. *c/o The Bush Family—photo by Paul Morse*

There were thirteen moments when musical honors were rendered, consisting of four ruffles and flourishes and the playing of "Hail to the Chief." This was near the end of our journey, after we returned to Houston from DC. *c/o The Bush Family*

As with Barbara's service, hundreds of members of the Texas A&M University Corps of Cadets lined the motorcade along Barbara Bush Drive approaching the library complex as the president's funeral procession neared the final resting spot. By then, not a word was being spoken. *c/o The Bush Family—photo by Eric Draper*

Here, the Reverend Peter Cheney from St. Ann's in Kennebunkport and I lead the last funeral procession. On a drizzly afternoon, December 6, 2018, President George H. W. Bush was finally laid to rest, only steps away from his beloved Barbara and Robin. *c/o The Bush Family— photo by Eric Draper*

The small bronze plaque on the northeast wall facing the Atlantic Ocean at Walker's Point says, CAVU—"ceiling and visibility unlimited." *c/o Author's Personal Photo Collection*

or reading Scripture or serving others. The hard-hearted ascetic raised his voice and snapped at Francis. "What would you do if you knew Jesus was coming back any minute?!"

Francis is said to have paused, put his chin on the end of his wooden hoe, and, with a sigh, replied, "Well, I suppose I would be working in my little vegetable garden."

Francis had learned the secret of contentment in life: that not one moment but all moments were holy—not one place but all places were holy. He had laid hold of Jesus's offering not just of life but abundant life.[3]

The same is true, I think, of George and Barbara Bush—something I witnessed every time I was with them.

Saintly Stitchers

Bar was a faithful member of the self-named St. Martin's guild "Saintly Stitchers." The group has been around almost since the birth of the church and is responsible for hand stitching kneelers and pew cushions for the holy spaces of the parish.

From the get-go, Barbara joined. While there has always been a leader of the group, this was not something to which Bar aspired. She was just a part of it. And when an election took the Bushes from Texas to DC, Barbara stayed stitched to her group.

Once, Barbara actually invited her fellow Stitchers to a White House luncheon. Many of those particular Stitchers are still with us today and remember well how they were welcomed into the home of their long-time friend as if they were visiting diplomats.

When the primary location for worship at St. Martin's moved from the original 1950s-era church to the new, stunningly beautiful neo-Gothic-style space, Barbara was recruited by longtime member Lee Hunnel to stitch one kneeler, and then another and another.

On two different Christmases, once in 2012 and again in 2014, the

---

3. John 10:10.

president's health demanded a hospital stay. On both occasions, after the unveiling of presents and opening of stockings had wound down at the Levenson house, I donned my collar and collected my Communion kit to head down to the hospital.

By the time I arrived, family had already come and gone. By 2012, the regular "check-ins" with the Secret Service had been waived—at that point, many of them were more like friends than security agents. I would usually stop and ask how they and their families were doing.

But Christmas Day at the hospital is different—it is subdued, quiet. No one really wants to be there on the Feast of the Incarnation, but there you have it.

On the second of those two Christmas visits, I came in without either of the Bushes noticing at first. The president was watching whatever Christmas Day game happened to be on, and Bar was sitting near the window where the light was good, wearing her reading glasses, and...carefully stitching. Whenever I would find her like this—which was often, whether at the hospital or at home—she would quickly say, "I did not start doing this because I knew you were coming!" And if she finished one kneeler, she would start another.

I think one of the things that surprised me about her relationship with her band of sisters (and there was one brother as well!) was her transparency with them. On occasion, she would share something with me that I felt to be confidential, personal—a word not to be shared beyond Laura—only to learn from the Stitchers that they knew about the matter, whatever it was, far before the priest!

I suppose some might look on a woman in her late eighties creeping toward ninety and wonder if she should spend her time more prudently, but no—this moment, like all others, it seems, was holy to her.

Other Moments and Spaces

Here is something I want to share with you with such emphasis that I should put it in bold or italics. I have been ordained for more than three decades and have been in the presence of those suffering all kinds of conceivable emotional, mental, and physical anguish. These types of experiences can make cowards of us all. Worse yet, suffering can cause one to become angry, impatient, harsh—mean, for lack of a better word. And for honesty's sake, I can see any and all such reactions justifiable.

Not once on any occasion—never—did I see the president or Bar allow the circumstances of their physical condition to dampen their innate ability to be gentle, kind, caring, and considerate. They struck up conversations with every person who entered the room, whether they were a physician or an orderly, or whether it was someone administering medication, serving dinner, or cleaning out the trash cans— everyone was treated as if they were part of "Team Bush," and for lack of a better analysis, they were!

Surely it weighed them down from time to time, but the president and Barbara seemed to know exactly where to turn when the dark night of the soul would visit: not only to friends and family but also to their Lord.

It is no secret that there were times, especially in Barbara's life, when the shadow of depression seemed overwhelming—in particular after Robin's death and at times during the unrelenting pressure of the White House years. My mentor, John Claypool, used to say to me as he aged, "Life gets better and better, and harder and harder." And I think for the Bushes, that was true.

They had emerged from deep caverns of pain—the death of a child, the bruising defeat of a presidential election—only to begin years of struggle against an untold number of physical ailments. But as the number of those grew, so did their faith, and so did their need and desire to turn to our Lord as a refuge, a source for healing.

In the early years of my time at St. Martin's, the calls to come to the hospital or to the house were infrequent. I think when they happened the visitations were appreciated, but as time marched on, there would be no question that the hospital room and the sitting room became chapels of refuge against the scourges of illness and the challenges of recovery.

When I visit people in the hospital, I typically carry a pyx—a small silver container that contains a bit of fiber with absorbed consecrated oil. The first time I took it out, the president pointed and said, "What is that?"

"It is called a pyx, sir. It has a bit of consecrated oil, and I'd like to anoint your head with a cross of oil and pray for you." After that, I was never asked again, and with few exceptions, every visit in whatever place had the potential to be holy. Over time, we would share these holy spaces and moments with others—Neil, Jeb, Doro, Marvin, and our forty-third president. If he came, I usually took it upon myself to scram, but I was often there when he would call in, and occasionally, he would join us in prayer.

That said, Laura and I hated to see the president or Bar in distress of any kind—in want of any kind. One afternoon, the president, Bar, Laura, and I were all together in the president's hospital room, watching a football game. The orderly came in to take his order and finished up by asking if the president wanted any dessert. Coffee ice cream was his favorite, but when he asked for that flavor, he was told they only had strawberry, chocolate, or vanilla. With a little downturned smile, he said, "I'll take chocolate."

On my visit the next day, I was sure to bring along coffee ice cream, and as I was leaving, after having anointed his head with oil and praying together, I heard him ask an aide to find a bowl and spoon!

An Incredible Reminder

I think it is fair to say that these visits were, in many ways, routine. They were like almost any other visit I would have with any other member of St. Martin's, with the exception of the ones who were being visited. That exception, however, was something not to be missed or overlooked, and I was reminded of this in December 2012.

As I shared earlier, the president and Bar, along with Secretary James Baker and his wife, Susan, had agreed to serve as honorary co-chairs for the Building for the Ages campaign. When our vestry—our governing board—felt confident we were well on our way to our $25 million goal, in April 2011 we broke ground on buildings and ground improvements that would pave the way for expanding ministry to teens, young adults, and the needy in our community by building a Hope and Healing Center to provide behavioral, emotional, and mental health services to Houston and beyond. Construction wrapped up in less than two years and a grand blessing-and-dedication service was planned.

Among the many guests were our returning friends, the 103rd archbishop of Canterbury, Lord George Carey, and his wife, Lady Eileen Carey; sculptor Chas Fagan, who had crafted a beautiful bas-relief of 41 and Bar in thanksgiving for their many contributions to St. Martin's over the years; the president and Bar's son Neil and his wife, Maria; and the actor Sam Waterston.

I had thought of inviting Sam to participate that weekend for several reasons. I knew he was a faithful Episcopalian who found great strength in his own faith. Sam had previously met the Bushes many years before when he performed Abraham Lincoln scholar Harold Holzer's program *Lincoln Seen and Heard* at an event benefitting the George H. W. Bush Presidential Library.

I had long admired Sam's work since his starring role as *New York Times* reporter Sydney Schanberg in the 1984 Academy Award–winning Vietnam-era film *The Killing Fields*. And just to be honest, both the president and I were big fans of the crime drama *Law & Order* and its various spin-offs. Among those, his favorite was *Law & Order: Special Victims Unit*. One afternoon, I arrived at the house to visit the president just as the famous "dun-dun" from the *Law &Order* theme was sounding from the television. I shouted out, "*Law & Order,*" and the president smiled, lifted up his remote, and said in return, "SVU!" Which inspired one of my birthday gifts to the president one year to be two DVD boxed sets of *Law & Order: Special Victims Unit* seasons and a bottle of Grey Goose vodka—something that Bar did not quite fully appreciate. She wrote me a note of thanks but included *Imagine . . . your priest giving you two seasons of a crime drama and a bottle of Vodka!* When she brought it up again during my next visit, I told her, "It's his favorite show! And mine too!"

After multiple invitations, Sam agreed to come to St. Martin's for the weekend. After he arrived, I met him at the hotel. He could not have been more generous with his time. He came with no expectation of being paid—as a "gift" to the church and, I think, out of his admiration for the Bushes.

Hours after he arrived in Houston, and prior to the dedication, we sat down for lunch. I was talking him through the schedule of the weekend—adding one thank-you after another, until I finally asked him why he agreed to come. Sam smiled and said, "Well, you would not leave me alone!" Persistence had paid off!

In addition to the dedication, Sam agreed to be a reader earlier in the day at an Advent worship "lessons and carols" service, wherein he read the various appointed lessons from Scripture, and Archbishop Carey preached.

The service was jam-packed, and we then moved to the facilities to be blessed and dedicated. Unfortunately, the president was in the hospital again, but I checked with Jean Becker and Bar and asked if they would be comfortable with my bringing Sam down to the hospital for a visit—there were yeses across the board.

When the morning's events were all over and the crowds had scattered, Sam and I hopped into my car. He had not been to Houston in years and wanted a quick tour, so we drove around some of the notable points of interest on the way to the medical center downtown.

We had good conversation on the way, but he said something that has stuck with me to this day and that clearly meant he was, as was the president and Bar, keenly aware of the preciousness of each moment.

I asked Sam how, in a business that seemed to be littered with stories of disaster and self-destruction, he had managed to maintain a successful career that spanned decades and venues—film, television, and stage—without a hint of scandal. He smiled and said, "Well, first you have to marry the right woman, which I did...eventually" (Sam's beloved Lynn was his second wife, but by then they had been married for almost forty years). "And I was very fortunate. To be in over three hundred and fifty episodes for over sixteen years in the same drama is basically unheard of. This can be a very cruel business, so I know how lucky I am." And then he said, "And I learned a really important lesson from Robert Redford."

"That being?" I asked.

"When I was playing Nick Carraway in *The Great Gatsby*, I thought it just could not get any better. I was in my early thirties, and here I was in a movie with Redford, and Mia Farrow, being in Fitzgerald's most famous story that had been adapted by Coppola. And one day Redford calls me over and says, 'So...what do you think about all of this?'

"And I said, 'This is incredible. This is great.' And he said, 'Well, enjoy it, but don't be fooled; it's not about you.'"

Sam went on to say, "So I took that to heart. Actors are looking for approval, obviously—it comes with the job—and you can't expect it from the business, because the business is tough. But it's full of good people, there's a lot of love inside it, and I've just tried to keep in mind how fortunate I was, and am. Plus, I lived in New York for almost twenty years, but we raised our kids on a farm in Connecticut, and I think it helped us keep our feet on the ground, and Lynn and I still live there now."[4]

About that time, we arrived at the hospital, and Sam and I made our way up to the twelfth floor. We arrived and got the wave by the Secret Service agents. I popped my head in the door, and said, "Mr. President?"

"Hello, Russ."

"I brought a special guest with me." Sam was at my side, but Bar had clued the president in ahead of time.

"Sam! How are you!" the president said.

---

4. Lynn Louisa Woodruff has been Sam's wife since 1976.

"Just fine, Mr. President. And how are you?"

By now, I had learned how important it was to step back and keep my mouth shut and observe. Most people did not get this kind of time with the forty-first president of the United States, and there was no need for the priest to butt in. So the president and Sam had a great visit. He asked Sam about his family and his work. How he felt about the church and the expansion. When they finished up, I said to the president, "Let's pray and we'll be on our way."

I turned to Sam and said, "After I anoint his head with oil, we'll hold hands and pray." Sam smiled and took to it like an old pro.

It was really a great visit—a great moment. But I noticed Sam was quiet as we left. We stepped on the elevator by ourselves and he dropped his head and said, "What an amazing moment. What an incredible opportunity." He asked me, "Do you do that a lot?"

"More and more," I said.

"Do you ever get used to it? Used to being around the president?"

"In some ways," I said, "but there are lots of days when I ask myself, *What is a guy like me doing in the midst of moments like this?*"

We spent most of the rest of our trip back to his hotel reflecting on 41's incredible contributions to the well-being of the world.

And I suppose to this day it is a reminder that each encounter like that was, in its own way, a precious once-in-a-lifetime moment—a holy moment indeed.

Bar Seals the Deal

Over the years, one of my closest friends and colleagues in ministry has been the Very Reverend Dr. Ian Markham, dean and president of Virginia Theological Seminary, my alma mater. Ian and I came to our differing posts about the same time, and while we have had some differences on some of the larger issues in the Episcopal Church, we know we are, in every way, blood brothers through our shared commitment to know Christ and make him known.

In early 2015, Ian reached out to me and asked what I thought about giving Barbara Bush the seminary's highest recognition, the Dean's Cross Award. I fully supported the idea but told Ian I did not speak for the First Lady and would be happy to ask—which I did on our next visit together.

A few days later, Bar emailed me:

January 10, 2015
Russ,

You are kind. I have written you a note about your request. Doro and Marvin were here. She voted yes. He is on their financial board. Speaking of a small world. I could not travel, [to the seminary], but if it can be done here, I would be honored. Thank you Russ.

A few days later, I got a handwritten letter from Bar, which recapped some of what was in her email but added a few things...

Dear Russ—

I have tossed and debated over the Virginia Theological Seminary great honor. I truly don't deserve it—I can think of many others who do more and have done more...

...We have prayed over it and if it would work out here in Texas—I will accept. I am certainly <u>not</u> remarkable, but I confess to having a remarkable husband, children and grandchildren—all giving, caring and loving.

Love to you and Laura—

Bar

Bar had accepted, and Ian and I were so pleased. She was remarkable, she had done so much, and she was deserving—I did not tell her all of those things, but that was the truth and it was an important and appropriate recognition.

We toyed around with dates for a while and finally decided it would be great to grant the recognition later that year on Mother's Day, during the morning church service.

Now, in many ways, this was a year like many others. There had been some real ups and downs and lots of visits to the house. By now, Bibi was learning, for the most part, to behave around me.

Some days the visits were just with the president, some just with Bar, some with both, most often with Laura. But one day, Bar said she wanted me to come over by myself, just to talk about something.

Keep in mind from earlier in this book that Bar had made a decision many years ago not to be confirmed at St. Martin's. She loved all of her clergy, but she and the first rector did have a small falling out. Bar was a believer, was a disciple of Jesus. She was born into a family of Presbyterians, but during her adult years, had grown to love the Episcopal Church, and found her faith nurtured in its liturgies, traditions, and its commitment to Scripture and the centrality of loving both God and neighbors.

But she knew, officially, the deal was not done until she was "confirmed" as a member of the Episcopal Church. So she went through confirmation classes—one of her classmates being their good friend, James A. Baker III.

At a meeting the day before the service was to take place, Dr. Bagby said to those adults gathered, almost all of whom were coming from other Christian denominations, "Well, now those of you who have been flying coach all these years are about to know what it is like to fly first-class."

When Bar told me this story more than once many years later, she would always say that at that moment, she thought to herself, *Nope, not going to do that.* It did not sit well with her at all. She called James Baker that night and told him she would not be going through with the service.

I knew in an instant that was not the thing to say in Barbara's presence, but as a priest who has said perhaps a thousand thoughtless things in my life, I could only sympathize with the late Dr. Bagby.

Bar did not hold grudges, and in some ways, it was just a page that was turned for her. By the time I came on the scene, St. Martin's had been her worshipping community for over fifty years.

In the eight short years between 2007 and 2015, we had been through a lot together. We had laughed and traveled and shared meals. We had talked endless hours, worshipped together, prayed together, and wept together.

In March 2015, my hunch was she had been thinking a great deal about her long history with St. Martin's, the many and deepening discussions we had had, and her decision to accept the Dean's Cross from VTS, and uncharacteristically, through an email, she said she wanted to meet with me personally. Initially, I was concerned, perhaps especially when she emailed, "If it would help I could come to the church. Bar."[5]

I came over, and she was alone. We talked for a bit, and somehow the story about Dr. Bagby came up again. As we revisited that memory, she paused and said, "Now, I need to tell you something."

I leaned in.

"I do believe..." There was a strong emphasis on *do*.

I think I was a bit mystified.

"I believe in Jesus...I believe..."

The thought that she might not never crossed my mind. "Well, of course you do. I know you do!"

"Well, don't you think I should get confirmed?" she said.

"Bar, it is not necessary. You are a member, but if you feel like that is something you want to do, we can make that happen."

She asked whether or not she had to "take a class." As someone who had taught Sunday school and had been one of two to lead the United States—and had never missed an opportunity to attend church—I told her there was no class that could teach her anything she did not already know.

She smiled and said, "That's what I want to do."

---

5. Email from March 17, 2015.

★   ★   ★

By design, I had again invited Lord George Carey and Lady Eileen to visit St. Martin's the same weekend that Ian Markham would be visiting to award Barbara the Dean's Cross.

I do not think I ever saw Bar enter into something with quite as much gentleness and thoughtfulness. She did not want any special treatment and wanted to make sure she was doing everything that I felt was necessary.

I told her I thought this was a very special moment and so as not to turn it into a "story," I would be prepared to arrange for the service to be in private. Many might ask why she waited until now to be confirmed, and few knew the reason, so why make more of it than necessary?

I went over to her house, and the two of us went over what would happen at the service.

A few days later, on Saturday morning, the president and Barbara, ++George and Eileen, Neil Bush, Laura, and I gathered in our small chapel at St. Martin's.

++George, on behalf of the bishop of Texas, looked at me and said, "The candidate will now be presented."

And I responded, "I present Barbara Pierce Bush for confirmation."

++George stepped close to Barbara and said, "Do you reaffirm your renunciation of evil?"

"I do," Barbara replied.

"Do you renew your commitment to Jesus Christ?"

"I do, and with God's grace I will follow him as my Savior and Lord," Barbara responded. At this point, I could see tears in everyone's eyes. What a lovely moment; what a special and holy moment.

++George asked all of us, "Will you who witness these vows do all in your power to support Barbara in her life in Christ?"

We all offered a hearty "We will."

Then, after some additional prayers, ++George placed his hands upon Barbara's head and prayed, "Defend, O Lord, your servant Barbara with your heavenly grace, that she may continue yours forever and daily increase in your Holy Spirit more and more, until she comes to your everlasting kingdom. Amen."

There were smiles and tears all around—there was not a dry eye in the place. After a final prayer, there were hugs and kisses—Barbara had sealed the deal.

The next day at our morning service, the chair of the board of Virginia Theological Seminary, Bishop Bud Shand, along with Ian, presented Barbara Bush with the Dean's Cross. After recognizing many of her civic achievements and specifically her work to promote and further literacy around the world, Dean Markham spoke of her faith:

It is an honor to confer on Mrs. Barbara Bush the Dean's Cross for Servant Leadership. The temptation is to be faithful for advantage in this world. This was never true of Barbara Bush. Her faith was never a means to an end. She prayed; she attended church; she grounded a commitment to service in her faith; and she worried about those close to her and those further away and offered her concerns to God in prayer...

On this mothering Sunday...she is an example to us all. We should all live our lives for God; we should find time to create initiatives that can change the lives of others; and we should exercise a discipline in our prayer life and in our church participation. Mrs. Barbara Bush is not simply a mother of her children, but in her example and disposition, she is truly a mother to this remarkable nation of ours.

A long standing ovation followed, and there were more tears and more hugs.

Not too long after, I received one of Bar's wonderful handwritten notes:

Dear Russ. Many thanks for the VTS news. I still can't believe I received the Dean's Cross...a huge honor...

Thanks again.

Bar

To the end, I think Bar still believed she was undeserving—she was the only one who thought that, for sure.

When What Is to Come Begins to Sink In

I hope you have enjoyed this journey so far. I think it tells us so much about the president and Barbara—their kindness, gentleness, integrity; their humor; their genuine devotion to friends, to family, and to faith; and of course, their joie de vivre.

But as 2016 gave way to 2017, it became clearer and clearer to those of us close to the president that this incredible story would someday come to its natural end. And so, my patient readers, let us turn the page and begin our journey toward the end that would end with a beginning.

CHAPTER ELEVEN

TUNING UP THE HARPS

Don't get out the harps just yet.
　　President Bush to his staff when gathering for funeral planning

Does it have to be a big thing? Who will come?
　　Barbara Bush to Levenson when they first discussed
　　Barbara's funeral

O come, let us worship and bow down, let us kneel before the LORD, our Maker! For he is our God, and we are the people of his pasture, and the sheep of his hand.
　　Psalm 95:6–7 (NRSV)

If not you, then who?
　　Email from Michael D. Wagner, chief of National
　　Events Planning, Joint Task Force–National
　　Capital Region, to Levenson

A s I shared early in the book, when Laura and I came to St. Martin's, while we knew that the Bushes attended the church, we had no idea how often we would see them; nor did we even presume that we would share the kinds of experiences or spend the amount of time with them that we ultimately did.

Before we go on, I think it is important to note that plans about the president's funeral and, in particular, the state funeral in Washington had been discussed for years before I was brought into the conversation. Jean Becker; Jim McGrath, President Bush's communications director; and the Bushes' wider staff were all well along in the planning stages of major and, frankly, indescribably intricate details around what happens when a president and/or a first lady dies. Much was way above my pay grade, and a great deal was out of my hands—but I was soon to find out that a great deal was also in my hands, and toward that end, I had to quickly adapt. This was on-the-job training.

"Don't Get Out the Harps Just Yet"

I had not been at St. Martin's more than a few months before Jean Becker called and said, "We want to have a meeting about the funeral here at the office, and we want you to come." At this stage of the game, the president still kept a very busy calendar, but needless to say, this was a priority. Jean said I should come early to get a look around the president's office, which was on the ninth floor of a beautiful office building on 10000 Memorial Drive.

After signing in with the Secret Service for the first time, I was buzzed into the president's office. As I opened the door, I was immediately welcomed by "the voice of the president's office," his receptionist, Mary Sage, who had been at the job for years and welcomed me as if I were a visiting dignitary. "Dr. Levenson, can I get you anything to drink?"

"Nothing. And you can call me Russ."

It took a while for Mary to get used to that.

Next up was Linda Casey Poepsel, who had worked with the president in Washington from his vice presidential years onward and, at this point, oversaw his correspondence. Linda gave me a quick tour. To the left of the entry were other staff offices and an office for the legion of volunteers who came and went on demand—many of whom were St.

Martin's members who would help with a myriad of things from stuffing envelopes to orchestrating details around visitors to the president's office. All along the walls were ubiquitous reminders of the achievements of the president in the form of framed photos and letters, and awards, medals, and scripted recognitions from various heads of state around the globe.

To the right was Linda's office, across from Nancy Lisenby, a key aide in the president's office; next was Jean's office, and then the president's. He was at his desk but stood to greet me when I entered—with that great smile and outstretched hand. He welcomed me and then jokingly said, "Are you here to talk about the big funeral?"

I think I tried to say something like, "Well, that is also on the agenda." It was, frankly, an incredible treat to visit. He took a bit of time to show me around his office, including pointing out a few favorite things like some of the chairs from his White House cabinet room, and a bronze cast of Abraham Lincoln's hand. Of course, there were photos aplenty of Barbara, the children, and grandchildren.

When we finished up, Linda ushered me into the conference room, which, among other things, had a photo of one of the president's most cherished memories—the day he got to be with Joe DiMaggio and Ted Williams.

Lunch was provided—this was going to be a long meeting. Around the table were people I would work with for the next eleven years, and when the health of both Bar and the president declined, our occasional meetings would increase to weekly, and then daily. Among those in the room were Jean Becker, Jim McGrath, Linda Casey Poepsel, Nancy Lisenby, David Jones, Laura Pears, Melinda Lamoreaux, and Mary Sage. We went around the room and introduced ourselves, and then Jean said, "Well, it seems appropriate that Russ should pray." And as she was about everything, Jean was right, and I did.

We had been meeting for about thirty minutes when the president entered from a door that connected to his office. "So, you are all here discussing my funeral…Well, don't get out the harps just yet. I am not planning on heading out anytime soon!"

We all laughed, but he meant it. He greeted a few folk and then left for his next meeting.

What quickly began to emerge was something I would see in small meetings and large and everything in between—these people, around this table, so loved and respected this man that they would have, had they been given the chance, laid down their lives for him. Even though, "God willing" many were saying, this event would be many years away, they—each of them—wanted to be ready and they wanted everything associated with the death of the president and the memorial services that went with those deaths to be done with dignity and honor. Everyone was on the same page—full stop. Their respect for 41 literally permeated the room.

But the second thing that I observed was that no one expected the president, or Barbara, for that matter, to die anytime soon. Even though they were in their eighties, they were in remarkable health at the time. Both were still very active in every way, and along with health of body, their minds and wit were sharp as a razor's edge. This planning was only "just in case" planning. For all I knew, I would be long gone by the time this even rolled around. I paid attention, had my legal pad at the ready, but did not have much to contribute until we got to the end of the meeting and Jean said, "Now, Russ, what do you need from us?"

I am confident the look on my face gave away my ignorance, if not naivete, about the plans being slowly constructed. I felt a bit like Schultz in the old *Hogan's Heroes* series—"I know nothing"—because, really, I did not know anything... with, mercifully, one saving exception...

A Worship Service in the Making

For those of us in the Episcopal Church, the worship service is key. All parts of the life of the church and all of its duties are important—but the worship service is our widest door; it is usually the moment that long-time Episcopalians feel most engaged and new members are introduced to the "Episcopal way."

And for Episcopalians, memorial services, burial services, and funerals are, in fact, also "worship services." We have a playbook and it is our Book of Common Prayer.

So when Jean asked what I needed, I think the only thing I had to say in response was, "Do they want a standard Episcopal memorial service?" If the answer was yes, then much of my work was done, but if the answer was no, then I would likely be even more clueless than I was when that meeting began. There were nods and yeses around the room, but only a few of those present were Episcopalian, and none had even broached real details of the service with the president.

Once I got a clear signal that the answer was yes, I said, "Well, then all we have to do for the service is fill in the pieces—lessons, music, speakers, and so on."

Jean said, "Well, then you better set up that meeting." And I did not. It was only a short season after the launch of my ministry, and I did not want to turn over the applecart by starting my first conversation with 41 by saying, "So, when you die…" Thus, this remained constantly on the agenda, but the specifics about whatever role I would play would not be discussed for years.

That did not mean that a great deal of planning—and I stress: a *great deal*—continued. I decided to keep every single note, email, text message—everything—related to the president's funeral in binders at my office with the title "CAVU."

Over the years, the few binders became many as we met, planned, revised, prepared drafts to review, made more changes, and on and on it went.

But not long after that first meeting at the president's office I had my first of what would be dozens of meetings in the years to come with Michael D. Wagner, the chief of National Events Planning with the Joint Task Force–National Capital Region. Mike, as I came to know him, had orchestrated a number of state funerals—including the state funerals of Presidents Reagan and Ford, as well as the funerals of First Ladies Betty Ford and Nancy Reagan, and he also served as the military lead planner for the inaugurations of President Obama in 2013, President Trump in 2017, and President Biden in 2021.

Mike was extraordinarily respectful. He never called me out for what I did not know (and there was plenty at the beginning), and he was a constant encourager—reminding me that when it came to the religious and spiritual aspects of the events before us, I was the final say for anything that happened in and through St. Martin's. When that day came, Mike, like the members of the president's team, wanted things to go off without a hitch, and he worked tirelessly to do everything he could to accomplish that goal.

Not too long after that first meeting at the president's office, Mike called together a large circle of folk, including Secret Service agents, members of the local law and traffic enforcement, and representatives from Houston's George Lewis funeral home. Mike had asked me before this first meeting if I was comfortable opening with prayer, and I told him, in this crowd, that was one of the very few things I was capable of doing.

There were numerous security matters to handle, of course, but Mike also knew—as he had seen many times before—that this was, again, going to be a worship service, so why not begin it with prayer?

With Much Regularity

One of the many things I did not know was how often members of Mike's team would be visiting the church campus. Sometimes it was merely to introduce others to the campus, and at other times it was to get the full scope of security needs. On occasion, I would meet with the team, and other times, my vice rector, Marty Bastian, and/or my executive assistant, Carol Gallion, would meet with them. St. Martin's executive director of facilities, Bruce Smith, who was a former personal investigator and had some experience in security, as well as our plant superintendent, Dennis Davis, usually toured with whichever group was on campus.

One day I was just beginning a staff meeting, when Carol called and said a group from Secret Service would be on campus. I asked her if I needed to go and greet them, and she said, "No." When I said, "What are they doing today?" she responded, "They are measuring the thickness of the church walls to determine bomb blast protection capabilities." I think I mentioned before that there are a number of things I did not learn in seminary that I had to put into practice at St. Martin's—add this one to the list.

But as the months turned into years, the groups came more often and they grew larger with the need to widen the circle of preparation. St. Martin's is not tucked away in the suburbs but rests right on a main drag en route to some of the most commonly traveled roads in the city.

If the president, or Barbara, for that matter, had a serious health issue or had to spend the night in the hospital, Jim McGrath was always efficiently putting out a statement so that the city was aware and could be in prayer for their beloved friends. But at the same time, I had to caution Mike and his visitors to use discretion when making these kinds of visits especially at times like these.

One day, when the president was in the hospital recovering from one of his bronchial bouts, I found Mike and about twenty-five other men and women, all dressed in very dark suits with sunglasses, standing out in front of the church. It looked like they were about to shoot another *Matrix* movie, and I suggested they might "move it along" so we did not start getting calls from the community and members of the press, which, by the way, we did by day's end.

In any case, we all knew we had a job to do, and Mike, Jean, Jim, and others were going to lead the St. Martin's team carefully through the years ahead.

Over time, it became clear to me that the discussion I was to have with the president was crucial. Keep in mind that at this point, none of us were really assuming or considering that Barbara would precede the president in death. Occasionally, I would ask Mike if she did predecease the president whether we would have the same resources and attention to detail as we had in working with him. The official answer was "No," but the unofficial answer was "Of course." Mike was not going to leave us hanging.

So slowly, methodically, Mike began to build a schedule for the events following the president's death, which many of us started calling "The Dreaded Day."

Of course, the president spent most of the year in Houston but part of the year in Kennebunkport. If he were to die while in Maine, the various scenarios we were considering were far different than the ones we were planning in Houston. Either way, by 2010 things were beginning to come together.

Mike's responsibilities were clear. As the chief, Mike also served as the designated representative of the president and was responsible to plan, coordinate, and conduct all ceremonial arrangements for the state funeral in Washington DC and any other funeral services throughout the United States (Kennebunkport, Houston, College Station), subject to the desires of the family members and any restrictions of St. Martin's, St. Ann's, or the George H. W. Bush Presidential Library. This included incorporating all of the historical traditions of a state funeral.

The Bush team was charged with just as many, and just as important, responsibilities. The Bushes not only had family members and friends aplenty, but the president still maintained relationships with politicians from around the state and the nation and kept tight his ties with many former and current world leaders. Every arrangement for each and every person who would attend or participate had to be precisely planned for flawless execution.

While I was kept abreast of these matters, I had little, if any, say in them, but as these plans became increasingly concrete, it also became clear to Jean and me that "the talk" would have to happen, or at least begin.

Finally, with Jean's prodding and blessing, it was time.

The Talk That Went Much Easier Than I Thought It Would…and Some Helpful Advice

If I wrote exactly how it all came together, I would get some of it wrong, but suffice it to say, I eventually had to bring it up—and I decided to talk to both the president and Bar about their funerals.

We had some discussion about all of the things that had to happen in and through Mike's office and the city.

For the president's service, there would be either a small service at St. Ann's in Maine, then possibly straight to DC, then on to Houston; or Houston, then DC, back to Houston, and then on to College Station for burial.

For Barbara, there would be one service—at St. Martin's—followed by a burial at College Station. Then, of all things, Barbara began questioning whether or not there really needed to be a large funeral. "I know it will be huge for him, but for me? Does it have to be a big thing? Who will come?"

When she asked, I honestly do not think she was joking; nor was she feigning humility. I assured her it would be a "big thing." When I brought up a public visitation, she said, "Can't you just place my casket in the chapel and people could just come by if they want?"

I rarely said no to Barbara, but I told her, "That would not work. There are going to be a lot of people!"

Then I confirmed with them both that they wanted a standard Episcopal service (with the obvious exception that these were funerals for the president and first lady). We actually have "funeral planning guides" that suggest lessons, anthems, and hymns. I suggested they take some time to read through them and we could eventually come up with services that would lift up those gathered. That seemed to sit well, and over time, we began to slowly, rather methodically, put together our mutual ideas for each of the services.

I kept in regular touch with Jean and Mike and would get their feedback. Over time, Jean had the primary responsibility of deciding who would get invitations because there was only room for so many in any of the worship spaces—St. Ann's, the National Cathedral, and St. Martin's. The problem—in Houston, at least—was that anyone who had met the president or Bar probably thought they were already close friends.

In my years that followed, I would run into people who had conversations with one or both of them in pizza joints, fine restaurants, or one of their favorite haunts (Christie's on Westheimer, Masraff's near the church, Post Oak Grill near the Galleria, Molina's Tex-Mex, or Fuzzy's Pizza!). Barbara did her own grocery shopping, so it was not uncommon at all for her to be pushing her buggy through Walgreens, pull a medicine or lotion off the shelf, stop a passing patron, and ask, "Have you tried this?" Within minutes, the patron thought she was a best friend of the First Lady, because she was treated as such! But when choosing who would be invited to the actual services, that herculean task was left to Jean Becker and her able crew.

While the president and Bar were, no doubt, reviewing the material I had left with them, they told me they were certainly open to suggestions. "I just don't want 'Amazing Grace'—everyone has that!" Bar said to me at some point. I pushed back gently and suggested she rethink that, as most people know the words and can sing along. "I'll think about it," she finally agreed.

Fortunately, the Episcopal Church, for all of its large and stately buildings, is a relatively small church family, and through various circumstances, I knew the priest who officiated and preached at President Gerald Ford's service—the Reverend Robert (Bob) Certain, who served in the Vietnam War, was shot down, and became a POW in the "Hanoi Hilton" with John McCain. After his liberation, he responded to a call to ministry, studied in seminary, and was ordained as an Episcopal priest. He was, as noted earlier, a speaker at one of our first Veterans Day services at St. Martin's.

I also was fortunate to be introduced to the former senator from Missouri and the twenty-fourth ambassador to the United Nations, John (Jack) Danforth, who also happened to be an ordained Episcopal priest and who officiated and preached at the funeral service for President Ronald Reagan.

I reached out to both of them with a plea for any guidance and counsel they could offer. Bob was still humbled by having participated in President Ford's service, and he counseled me to "take it all in" because of its historic implications. Ambassador Danforth had similar guidance but reminded me to carefully secure the confidential matters around the family and services.

He told me to keep my guard up with the press because they would want to know anything and everything, and not to say a word without permission from the family. And then he added, "And just remember: it is an opportunity to honor the president and our faith," adding, "so it's not about you." I came home from that personal meeting and wrote those notes down.

Of course, my predecessors in this role assumed I would be preaching at these services, and I had to say, "I am not sure that I will be. There has been no formal invitation. They know everybody, so they may have someone else in mind!"

So the stage was being set in every way. Jean and Mike felt like it was time to pull the entire team together—national, state, and local officials: Secret Service; officials and assigned officers with the Houston Police Department; the Houston Fire Department; various medical support team members; limited press; the president's staff; and St. Martin's staff. Bob Boetticher Sr. was the senior director of the ceremonial funeral detail, and I was told that when the president did die, aside from Jean and Mike, Bob would be one of the key folk with whom I would deal. As you will read, he was there at one of the most poignant moments in the story I am sharing with you. The crowd of well over one hundred met for half a day at the Federal Reserve Building in Houston.

Then a small group of us broke off and traveled to Spring, Texas, from whence the president's body would be transported to College Station, and finally we met at each of the staging areas for the burial, with the last stop being the burial site.

Then it was time to have a discussion with the National Cathedral. Fortunately for me, I knew the cathedral's dean, the Very Reverend Dr. Sam Lloyd. Sam had actually been my first "boss" out of seminary. Sam was serving as the chaplain at the University of the South in Sewanee, Tennessee, after my ordination and invited me to serve alongside him as his assistant. So we knew one another and approaching the discussion about the service was not a task so much as it was a reunion. Sam, as any good dean or priest should, was keen to meet the needs of this historic family, but also—as we both knew—the needs of our nation.

So when I told Sam that the president, aside from all the important matters associated with a state funeral, wanted a basic, traditional Episcopal service, it was not a matter up for discussion—just pastoral accommodation. We would work well together on this project and I was looking forward to the opportunity to be with a former mentor—indeed, history continues to turn on slim hinges.

This, of course, began to bring it all home. I was to have a more direct discussion with the president and Bar on a Labor Day weekend trip to Kennebunkport in September 2010. Before that visit, I got an email from Mike:

> July 19, 2010
> Russ,
>
> I believe you are planning to meet with the Bushes in the Labor Day timeframe to discuss liturgy, readings, etc. for the services in DC and Houston. It will be great to start to get answers to all your questions about the orders of worship.
>
> I'm going to be in Kennebunkport, ME for the next few days, meeting with Jean Becker and her staff, USSS, etc. regarding funeral planning. If there is anything I can do, any subject I can broach for their consideration before your visit, I'd be happy to do so—just let me know how I can help!
>
> All the best!

In response, I sent Mike the drafts of bulletins and thoughts I had been working on with this email:

> July 19, 2010
> Mike...that would be great...I am on the road...I prepared drafts of bulletins for the President for St. Martin's and National Cathedral including most music, readings...left out speakers, but I think Jean knows most of those. I have also prepared a bulletin for Barbara. Would love it if you could

review and make any necessary changes/revisions. I have not prepared a draft for graveside. Is that necessary? I think the only major unfinished pieces for liturgy are pallbearers at both and final speakers at both. Again many thanks for any counsel you can give. Russell+

Ten days later, Mike responded:

Russ,

Thank you for the opportunity to review the draft bulletins Carol sent me. Though I've yet to go over them with a fine-tooth comb, I have given them a preliminary read-through and have some thoughts to share. First, though, I would say that I find all the recommended Scripture readings to be "spot-on"— absolutely appropriate to both the setting and the individual, sometimes a little surprising, and definitely thought-provoking.[1]

In terms of specifics of the Washington Cathedral program…

Homilist. If not you, then who? (I think you are the right person to do it, by the way.)…

I hope this helps a bit. More to follow.

Mike

Seven Days for the Ages

It was hard to believe, but we began putting things in "ink" (always subject to be changed) many years before the actual death of the president.

We learned that on the day of the president's death—regardless of where he was at the time—in Houston, all traffic along the roads abutting the church would be closed and monitored for seven days. Additionally, any building near or overlooking St. Martin's would be secured by Secret

---

1. I should note here that while I had landed on some specific Scripture references, we did not confirm that until some years later, closer to the actual funeral services.

Service. Armed agents would be placed on, within, and around these buildings, and several more would be on our campus for days at a time.

Fortunately, we have plenty of space at St. Martin's, along with a restaurant, a chef, and a full cooking staff, along with an activity center with showers, locker room, and workout facilities. So, when I was asked if we could provide food, lodging, and large spaces for the entire security team, I was able to say with confidence that we could roll that into our plans. In a sense, our campus, and the surrounding areas, while maintaining our Christian identity, would also essentially be federal property from the time of the president's death until the time the final motorcade left our campus.

We also learned that the president had been working on a plan for quite some time to have his body transported from St. Martin's to a train station in Spring, Texas. There, the president's coffin, close friends, and family would board a specially modified train that would travel the ninety miles to College Station. Then the president's body would be transported by motorcade one last time to the final resting place near the presidential library on the campus of Texas A&M, where there already rested a stone marked ROBIN BUSH, as if to welcome her parents to join her in her heavenly rest.

With those matters handled, Mike actually handed out a formal sequence of events that would serve as our operational guidebook those historic seven days. There were multiple versions of this document over the years, with some minor details that shifted in the last few days, but the essential elements of the schedule remained the same.

Sequence of Events for President George H. W. Bush

D-2 (DAY 1)

DEMISE. (Assumes demise in city of residence prior to noon.)
Remains to Funeral Home.
Family Makes Travel Arrangements

D-1 (DAY 2)

All Day   Family Travels. No Ceremonies

D-DAY (DAY 3)

9:00 a.m. Family Motorcade departs The Houstonian Hotel en route to George H. Lewis Funeral Home

9:30 a.m. George H. Lewis Funeral Home Departure Ceremony

9:45 a.m. Motorcade departs George H. Lewis Funeral Home en route to Ellington Field.

10:30 a.m. Ellington Field DEPARTURE CEREMONY

Note: This is the first official ceremony.

11:00 a.m. CST – 3:30 p.m. EST Flight from Ellington Field, Houston TX to Joint Base Andrews, MD.

3:30 p.m. – 4:00 p.m. Joint Base Andrews **ARRIVAL CEREMONY**

4:00 p.m. Motorcade Departs for US Capitol

4:45 p.m. ARRIVAL CEREMONY: US CAPITOL

5:00 p.m. ROTUNDA SERVICE AND LYING IN STATE

7:30 p.m. Lying in State open to public

D+1 (DAY 4)

LYING IN STATE continues, U.S. Capitol

Family receives groups of callers at specified times through-out the day; Blair House

D+2 (DAY 5)

9:30 a.m. Motorcade Departs Blair House

9:45 a.m. DEPARTURE CEREMONY: U.S. CAPITOL

10:00 a.m. Motorcade Departs

10:30 a.m. Motorcade arrives at Washington National Cathedral

11:00 a.m. ARRIVAL CEREMONY AND FUNERAL SERVICE

12:00 p.m. DEPARTURE CEREMONY: Washington National Cathedral

12:15 p.m. Motorcade Departs

12:45 p.m. DEPARTURE CEREMONY: Joint Base Andrews, MD

1:15 p.m. Aircraft Departs

3:45 p.m. ARRIVAL CEREMONY: Ellington Field, Houston, TX

4:15 p.m. Motorcade Departs

5:00 p.m. ARRIVAL CEREMONY AND REPOSE: St. Martin's Episcopal Church

D+3 (DAY 6)

6:00 a.m. Public repose at St. Martin's Episcopal Church concludes

9:30 a.m. Family Arrives at St. Martin's Episcopal Church, TX

10:00 a.m. – 11:15 a.m. FUNERAL SERVICE

11:15 a.m. DEPARTURE CEREMONY: St. Martin's Episcopal Church

11:30 a.m. Motorcade Departs en route Union Pacific Auto Facility

12:30 p.m. – 12:55 p.m. Train DEPARTURE CEREMONY: Union Pacific Auto Facility

1:00 p.m. – 3:25 p.m. Train from Spring, TX, to College Station, TX (Lunch provided)

3:45 p.m. – 3:55 p.m. Train ARRIVAL CEREMONY at Texas A&M University

4:00 p.m. Motorcade departs Texas A&M University en route to George Bush Presidential Library Center

4:20 p.m. – 5:00 p.m. ARRIVAL AND INTERMENT: The Committal Service at the George Bush Presidential Library Center, College Station, TX

5:15 p.m. Motorcade departs College Station, TX, en route— Houston, TX. ARRIVAL AND INTERMENT, George Bush Presidential Library Center, College Station, TX

Interment Complete 5:00 p.m.

Motorcade returns to Houston

And the Assignment of a Lifetime…

As noted in the exchanges with Mike Wagner, there was a great deal of discussion about who would offer remarks at the president's services in Washington and in Houston. In some Episcopal funerals, remarks, eulogies, or homilies are not offered at all. As I will touch on a bit later, the service itself is, in fact, a sermon. But no one would think of bidding farewell to a United States president without one or more people offering remarks.

Several names were being discussed, and outside of Secretary Baker, no final decision had been made. In addition, being that both the services in Washington and in Houston were to be Episcopal services, it was traditional for a clergyperson to offer the final homily. Without going into deep details, the Bushes made it clear that responsibility fell to me.

I knew, in that moment, I was being offered a unique, once-in-a-lifetime opportunity—not to take center stage but to celebrate the president's life and faith and to invite everyone who heard to experience the hope the Christian faith offered, in the same way it sustained the president.

From the day that decision was shared with me, I began to pray about it. Of course, the president could certainly outlive me, and there was no certainty that I would still be in this post at the time of the president's funeral, but I knew, in any case, I needed to pray, think, and prepare.

After the president suffered a series of serious bouts with illnesses in the fall and winter of 2012, I thought it best to try and put some thoughts together, and I created my first draft.

I prepared as carefully as I knew how, using the words of Scripture that we had, at least at that point, chosen for the service. By then, I had a deepening relationship with our member James Baker. The former secretary of state and perhaps closest friend to George H. W. Bush was becoming a mentor. He had accepted my invitation to be appointed as special counsel to the vestry, and I had turned to him a number of times for matters around leadership and policy within the church he also so faithfully attended and supported. We had met numerous times, traveled together, hunted together.

So, since he was the only other person of certainty to speak and was someone who knew a lot more about public speaking in settings like this than any clergyperson on planet earth, let alone me, why not ask him to read my remarks and give me some honest feedback? I am so glad I did.

What follows is the letter he wrote in response.

PERSONAL AND CONFIDENTIAL

January 4, 2013
Russ

Here are my thoughts about the two homilies that you asked me to review. I know you want me to be as frank and honest about this as I would want you to be with me.

First, I think both of them are very well done and there is so much to be said about 41. However, it appears to me that both are longer than 30 minutes (or more than 3000 words apiece). That is way too long—twice as long as the 15 ½ minute eulogy that George W. Bush gave at Ronald Reagan's funeral, almost three times longer than Maggie Thatcher's eulogy for Reagan and four times longer than George H.W. Bush's 7 ½ minute eulogy at the Reagan funeral.

When I compared with other recent homilies, the one that John Danforth gave at Ronald Reagan's funeral was about 9 ½ minutes (939 words). And the homily that Robert

Certain gave at Gerald Ford's funeral was about 9 ½ minutes long (829 words).

It is important to remember that at the funerals of Presidents it is not unusual for three or four people to speak. The length of one speaker's homily or eulogy should not overwhelm any of the others. This is particularly true given your position as 41's home church rector. It would not be appropriate if your homily were vastly longer than the eulogy of a head of state or a former head of state.

So as tough as it may be to do, I think you should shorten them. For what it's worth, I'm trying hard to keep mine for him to no more than 1200 words.

JAB, III

After I got up off the floor and licked my wounds a bit, I wrote the secretary back:

6 January 2013
Epiphany
Jim:

Thank you very, very much—of course your frankness was exactly what I needed. I have found over the years (though I have never had a project/assignment as important as this one) that I tend to "put it all down," and then cut back from there. Your counsel gives me the direction to move and I will spend some of this week honing it down to the length you directed.

Jim…God willing, neither of us will have to put our thoughts to work on 41 any time soon. Our visit yesterday was great…humor was with us every step of the way.

Please let me know how I can support you.

Faithfully,
Russ+

The next Sunday, Jim caught me at church before the service. He evidently thought his remarks might have stung a bit. And to be honest, they did not. They were what I needed to hear. But he pulled me aside before church and said, "Those were really good homilies—nothing in them was wrong. They were just too long!" He was right, of course.

I thanked him again and was grateful to have my internal compass recalibrated—this was not about impressing anyone; it was about lifting up the president and the faith.

The Most Memorable Conversation

Mercifully, the president emerged from his winter illnesses, and by early spring, he was returning to his old self. But the close calls, the funeral planning, and the formalizing of details were clearly, increasingly, on the president's mind. One day, Jean told me the president had been asking her some questions about life and death and life after death.

He asked Jean if she believed in hell. Jean said she did. And he then asked, "Well, who do you think goes there?"

She told me that she said, "Well, I think Saddam Hussein...and Adolf Hitler." And then Jean paused, smiled, and said, "Why? Are you worried?"

"No, just wondering."

"I think this is something you should be discussing with Russ."

Later that day, Jean called me and said, "I think you might want to make an appointment to visit him...He's talking about hell!" But then she got a bit more serious and said, "I just think he is thinking about a lot of things right now. It would be good to visit."

So I set up a meeting for the first week of April, which was a few days later. When I arrived, aside from the Secret Service posted outside the house, only the president was home, as Bar had gone out.

I came in and as usual the pups barked, then recognized me and began wagging their tails. I called out, "Mr. President?"

He responded from his sitting room, "Russ, is that you? I'm in here."

I came in, we shook hands, and I settled in a chair across from him.

We visited just a bit and then he just put it out there—"Russ, what do you think heaven is like?"

I paused for a minute and then gave my own point of view.

"Do you think I'll see Robin there?" he asked.

"Absolutely, Mr. President."

"How old will she be?" he asked with a kind of wonderful childlike innocence.

"That, Mr. President, I don't know, but I do know this—you will absolutely be reunited with Robin. And you will know her and she will know you."

We talked a bit more, but that seemed to be enough for the moment.

As I drove back to my office, the key questions he asked struck me to the core. He did not ask, "Do you think there is a heaven?" or "Do you think I will make it?" but "What do you think heaven is like?" and "Do you think I'll see Robin...?" Here was a man who was close to his God and who knew his God was close to him. I suspect he was thinking on all those things over the previous few months.

I thought about our chat for a few days. I think his frankness threw me a bit off guard; so I felt the need to follow up with a letter.

8 April 2013

Mr. President:

...I have been thinking a lot about your question the other day when we were at the house, "What do you think heaven is like?"

As you know there have been a lot of books in the last few years written about "near death" experiences, in which (thanks to modern medicine I guess!), people have actually "died" and had a wide variety of experiences... experiencing a feeling of peace and tranquility, seeing a "great and welcoming light," being greeted by loved ones who have "gone before," being greeted by Our Lord. All of these, of course, are encouraging to me...

The short version is that I believe the Gospels testify that life after death is real...not some kind of "mystical" netherworld where we get wings and play harps! But that we will be in the presence of our loved ones, one another, and where we will likely continue in some sort of service beyond ourselves in God's everlasting kingdom. I do not know "exactly" what that life will be like, but when I was in my mother's womb, I really did not know what this life was going to be like, and it turned out pretty good! I can only imagine when we pass from this one to the next, it will be more than we can now ask or imagine.

You asked whether or not you would see "Robin," and how old would she be. Good question! I really don't know an answer to the "age," question, but I do believe you will be greeted by her, by your mother and father, and friends and loved ones just waiting for you.

You know, because I have told you many times, what an honor it is to serve as your priest; and what a blessing it has been to grow as friends with you and Barbara for now—well, over half a decade. You have shown us more hospitality than I could have ever imagined; we have shared good laughs, good meals, good times here, in College Station and in Maine—and I hope and pray there are many more to come.

The last several months worried me so, but I am glad to see your health improving day by day. We have, at your request, "put away the harps!," and we have done so, I pray, for a long, long time.

It is my hope, and prayer, that the 41st President will outlive his priest, but if our dear Lord decides to call you to our eternal home before me, please know that I would like to be with you in prayer and presence. And, if He calls me first, I'll be there waiting for you with open arms, a fresh plate of oysters, and no broccoli!

… Thank you for being a friend, a mentor, and a counselor—
thank you, sir, for being my brother in Christ.

Love,
Russ✝

Just a Word of Honesty with You…

There are parts about what I will now share that I hope will be tremendously helpful and inspiring—not because of my words, but because of so many moments, so many people, so much in the way of life and love that bubbled up and out of those last days with Barbara, and with the president.

But there is a part of me that does not want to tread those paths again. As you will see, I miss the president and Bar very, very much. But I know it is time to turn the page, and if I do not finish what I have started here, I suspect the whole point will be lost. Up to now, there have been some moments that gave you a bit more insight into the marvels of George and Barbara Bush. But now, join me as we step even more fully into the deepest places of their days on this earth: their last ones.

CHAPTER TWELVE

"HOME..."

A capable wife who can find?
She is far more precious than jewels.

Proverbs 31:10 (NRSV)

For to your faithful people, O Lord, life is changed, not ended.

Book of Common Prayer[1]

Home...

Barbara Bush's last word

An Unexpected Journey

In the midst of all of the planning for the president's funerals, it was always in the back of our minds that we should consider the possibility that Barbara might predecease him. It was something we considered, but I am not sure any of us began to think seriously about the possibility until the winter of 2017 and 2018.

Despite increasing bouts of illness and hospitalization due to both congestive heart failure and chronic obstructive pulmonary disease,

---

1. Book of Common Prayer, 382.

Barbara continued to stay active. She regularly spoke with friends by phone, and when she was at home, visitors still streamed in on a fairly regular basis. Even during what became her last several months, it was not unusual at all to find her stitching on the pew kneeler she was doing her best to finish up.

We continued to discuss her funeral and begin to rather meticulously choose lessons, readers, and speakers.

Barbara, as the world knows, was in many ways a very practical woman. She dealt with life as it came, including her declining health. For that reason, I suggested the passage from Ecclesiastes 3:1–14, which begins, "For everything there is a season, and a time for every matter under heaven: a time to be born, and a time to die; a time to plant, and a time to pluck up what is planted..." (NRSV). Bar approved of this lesson, not only because of the way it spoke about the ups and downs of life, but she, as an avid gardener, did like the words "a time to plant."

We had one small challenge as we planned. She wanted *all* of the granddaughters to read—all six of them. Once we landed on the passage from Scripture on the "capable wife" from Proverbs 31, I made the suggestion that all the granddaughters would come up together, and each would take a small section. That seemed to suit, and we added that to the service.

Then, with honesty and frankness, which I knew Barbara would appreciate, I suggested the passage from 2 Corinthians 4:16–5:9, which begins, "So we do not lose heart. Even though our outer nature is wasting away, our inner nature is being renewed day by day..." (NRSV). Bar and I had talked about life beyond this life, and that the "wasting away" we all experience is merely preparing us for the life to come. Bar wanted the service to be uplifting—joyful, if possible—and what powerful words the apostle Paul wrote when he penned, "For we know that if the earthly tent we live in is destroyed, we have a building from God... eternal in the heavens... what is mortal may be swallowed up by life... for we walk by faith, not by sight." I followed her requests exactly and we added this into the draft.

Then, as we have seen again and again, Bar was not shy about her Christian faith. She wanted the broad and diverse audience who would attend to feel welcomed and embraced by a loving God, but she had no qualms about allowing her Christian faith to be proclaimed, so the beautiful passage from John's Gospel was chosen—6:37–40—in which Jesus says,

> And this is the will of him who sent me, that I should lose nothing of all that he has given me, but raise it up on the last day. This is indeed the will of my Father, that all who see the Son and believe in him may have eternal life; and I will raise them up on the last day (NRSV).

Then we turned to music. By now, I had talked Bar into including "Amazing Grace" (as we will see in the next chapter, she actually had the last word there). Given her role as First Lady, our music director, David Henning, found a special arrangement by Mack Wilberg of "My Country, 'Tis of Thee," originally written by the Baptist pastor Samuel Francis Smith.[2]

Other hymns were chosen—"Praise to the Lord" as an entrance hymn. Barbara loved "In the Garden," and also "The Holy City," and she wanted to know how best to include them.[3] After again consulting with Dr. Henning, he quickly laid his hands on the anthem versions of each, which would work perfectly with the St. Martin's choir. And finally, what better way to lift the spirits of those attending than a rousing congregational hymn, Henry van Dyke's "Joyful, Joyful, We Adore Thee," set to the melody of the final movement of Ludwig van Beethoven's final symphony, Symphony No. 9?

The clergy of St. Martin's would serve, including some that had

---

2. Smith died in 1895 and wrote the lyrics while he was in seminary. They were first performed at a children's Independence Day celebration in 1831. Mack Wilberg has been the music director of the Mormon Tabernacle Choir since 2008.

3. "In the Garden," C. Austin Miles, d. 1946; "The Holy City," Michael Maybrick, using the pseudonym Stephen Adams, d. 1913.

retired and moved on. I suggested that we also include the Reverend Peter Cheney from St. Ann's in Kennebunkport. The Bishop of the Diocese of Texas, the Right Reverend C. Andrew Doyle, as the primary ecclesiastical shepherd of the Diocese of Texas, would also be asked to participate, as would one of my predecessors at St. Martin's, the retired bishop of Texas, Claude Payne.

As it was coming together, Barbara shared who she wanted to make remarks—a close friend and confidant of the Bushes', historian and writer Jon Meacham; her dear friend, prayer partner, and sister in faith Susan Baker; and her beloved son Jeb. Each choice, of course, said much—and was an incarnation of the three essential Bush values—friends (Jon), faith (Susan), and family (Jeb). Each, in their own way, would bring to the tapestry that was Barbara Bush's life their own patch to weave into a day that we would long remember.

Once these assignments were made, these three took seriously their tasks. Some will recall that in June 2016, Barbara had been rushed to the hospital with an episode related to her congestive heart failure. That moment was sort of a wake-up call for those of us tasked with planning her funeral. She would later admit that angst around the election and some of the brutal attacks on Jeb were to blame. "The campaign is truly bothering me," Barbara wrote when we exchanged emails in September 2015. "George has faith, I worry about my boy." The next month after a primary debate, Barbara wrote in another email, "Can't read the reports. They will trash my precious son."

My wife and I were actually vacationing in Mexico in October 2016, when Governor Bush called. He left a voicemail: "Hey, Russ, this is Jeb Bush. I hope you're doing well. I need to speak to you about my mom and need your advice on something, if you could call me back anytime. Nothing urgent...but you can call me when you get back."

I had no intention of waiting until we returned. When we finally connected, it was just a very, for lack of a better word, "sweet" conversation that began with, "There are so many wonderful things to say. Where would I even begin?"

I love that he knew what this moment was about—celebrating his mother's life and her faith, full stop. He got to work, as we all did.

None of us wanted to be surprised, but it would have been a surprise if she were to die first. But we were to be surprised with that unexpected journey we would all soon be taking.

After the long bout with illness in March, Barbara began talking with those closest to her about how much one does to preserve life when life is beginning to slip away. I know she talked with the children, with Jean, with the president, and with me.

As a pastor, I have had that discussion many times with members over the years. I have seen people go to extraordinary measures to keep loved ones in this world, when the life that was being preserved looked nothing like the life they had lived. That said, I have been fortunate as well to see people brought back from the edge of death, through prayers and medical care, only to have many more years of life yet to live.

The considerations around end-of-life care, hospice care, and how far to go with regard to resuscitation or other potentially lifesaving measures are very, very serious—as they should be.

There is often a lot of talk about "God's will" in these conversations, but I am pressed to remind those I serve that we live in a time when the advancements of medicine have made possible the sustainability of physical life that at times may not be congruent with a vibrant emotional, mental, or even spiritual life. One hundred years ago, very few people who would have experienced the kinds of health crises we face today would have lived on. Medical advancement has been a blessing in so many ways, and at times, it has been a curse, as loving people are put in positions of trying to decide when to "pull the plug." To the point, "God's will" is much more difficult to determine in the twenty-first century than it was a hundred years ago.

These are things I discussed with family members, with Jean Becker, and with Barbara, but in the end, my counsel was that if the patient is able to make the decision, then it rests primarily with him or her.

Bar's March visit to the hospital slipped into April, but she was beginning to improve, but how long, or if, that would last was an unknown, and so our work continued.

Part of that work was touching base with each person offering remarks. As the homilist, I would be essentially "last up to bat," and there was no need for me to repeat or overlap with anything anyone else said (this process would be a bit different when it came to President Bush's funeral, which I will share a bit later).

Everyone was so gracious with one another. Like all things around this moment, everyone wanted to do their best for Barbara and, of course, for the president.

One thing did shift the discussion about both funerals. We all knew we were (and continue to be) living in a time when any gathering, especially ones like the funerals of national figures, could become less of a memorial service and more of a political rally. There was no question among the family that anything like that would be unacceptable. In addition, in this family, we had two presidents and two first ladies, and a former governor of Florida and his first lady—all of whom had been to funerals aplenty. Forty-One used to quip during his days as the vice president that he had attended so many state funerals around the world that his motto had become "You die, I fly."

While Barbara had appropriately earned her nickname, "The Enforcer," in the Bush family, it was clear that President Bush 43 would take those reins when it came to the full scope of the memorial services for his parents. He very wisely said that he wanted each service to be no longer than ninety minutes. This applied to Barbara's funeral and to the president's state funeral in Washington and his home parish funeral in Houston.

To be honest, as one of the architects of these services, along with Mike Wagner and Jean Becker and others charged to pull it all together, I was relieved. Whenever I sit with a family to plan a funeral, I often have to share that any funeral that runs much longer than an hour begins to lose its efficacy. The last thing that any family member wants is to have those attending looking down at their watches. Bush 43 was exactly right to make this decision, and this gave us not only a goal but some parameters. And as I will share a bit later, it even became a source of comedic relief when we needed it.

On April 2, 2018, I reached out to Susan Baker in an email, informing her that preparations for Barbara's service had been ongoing and her "decline has been somewhat steady." I asked Susan to send me her planned remarks when available, so I could review and make sure I didn't repeat what others were going to say. "I just want to go ahead and finish my homily so I can focus on pastoral care when the time comes."

Susan wrote back later that day, promising to share soon. "I'm working on my remarks again after being so pleased to put them away for months...Sadly, I know the time draws nigh." She added, "How I thank God for this wonderful mentor and her 92+ years..."

But as we got well into the first week of April, everyone felt that things were changing. We needed to begin putting together final plans.

Though the invitation list had long since been complete, there were last-minute additions. I lost count of how many times Jean would call and say, "Can we add two more?" My answer was always "Yes...We will find a way."

With the pieces of the service put together, we began to print various drafts of the bulletin. It seemed fitting that we include somewhere in the bulletin what had become a rather iconic photograph for the St. Martin's family—that of the Bush family outside the first church building.

But knowing that whatever we pulled together would become available to the press and the world at large, I felt I best clear it with the family—which, alone, allowed for a much-needed smile.

On April 6, 2021, at 5:44 p.m., I emailed three of the president's children and Jean:

Governor, Doro, Neil and Jean;

Attached is a photo we have in our files. Since 43 is coming in this weekend, I thought I would share with you. This is the family outside the old church many years ago…one of BPB's oft-mentioned quotes is "St. Martin's has been our Church for over 50 years…" Would it be appropriate to include this photo in the back of the bulletin we have been working on these last few weeks?

Doro and Neil, do you want to discuss with 43 this weekend? It is a nice photo…though I think Marvin is hidden…but nice, nonetheless. Let me know and we'll do what you want…

At this point, praying, certainly…hourly.

With love, prayers and admiration…

Russ+

At 6:20 p.m. (CST), the governor emailed the group:

I love the picture. Who is the kid behind the kid? ☺

At 7:46 p.m. (EST), Doro emailed the group:

Cute: Jeb is hidden.

At 6:52 p.m. (CST), the governor emailed the group:

Story of my life but it is a great picture and I say yes!

At 6:56 p.m. (CST), Neil chimed in:

I agree!

Though we were ready, we had a brief respite. On the afternoon of April 10, Jean Becker sent an email to Peter Cheney, Jon Meacham, and me:

With one fell swoop I will tell all 3 of you that BPB came home
today...so hope she will be okay...This is a huge step. Now
she needs to figure out how to stay home. But we have a lot
more people taking care of her this time. They are both happily watching TV together, with the dogs, the last time I had
an eye witness report.

And Then Came the Decision

Bar had obviously already been thinking about it, but she finally shared
it with her loved ones—her beloved George, the children, her staff, and
her priest. Whatever happened, now that she was home, she was not
going back to the hospital and she was not going to ask for anything
beyond comfort care. If she improved, all well and good; but if not, she
just wanted to be comfortable to the end.

This is something this small circle of folk knew, but we were keeping
it in this "extended" family. There were many things over the years that
the president and Barbara's family, staff, and priest knew that were not
shared until the timing was right.

In the early years of my ministry, no one in the public eye would know
me from the average man on the street (though the collar is somewhat of
a giveaway). However, as the Bushes' years increased, particularly when
there were long hospital stays, the press would camp outside of Methodist
Hospital in Houston. I had done some interviews with local and national
press at that point. So I had a modicum of recognition. If I visited during
the day, I tried to take more out-of-the-way paths into the hospital, or
better yet, I would visit at night. I knew if I were seen going in, I would
have a call from the press. This happened on a few occasions, and I was (as
noted earlier after the invocation I gave at the GOP convention in Tampa)
a "no comment" guy, unless there was something to comment on—and
then, and only then, with the permission of the president's staff.

So yes, several of us knew a few days before it became public that
Barbara had chosen comfort care.

Jim McGrath worked with Jean and the family to craft a statement, which was released on April 15.

> Following a recent series of hospitalizations, and after consulting her family and doctors, Mrs. Bush, now age 92, has decided not to seek additional medical treatment and will instead focus on comfort care. It will not surprise those who know her that Barbara Bush has been a rock in the face of her failing health, worrying not for herself—thanks to her abiding faith—but for others... She is surrounded by a family she adores, and appreciates the many kind messages and especially the prayers she is receiving.

And So, "Home..."

For quite some time over what would be the last weeks of her life, my last call in the evening and first call in the morning were to the outstanding medical aide Evan Sisley. Evan is more than a medical aide; he is part of the family and his constant care and concern for President Bush and Barbara Bush have been a thing to behold.

On the afternoon of Saturday, April 14, I got a call from Evan telling me that Barbara was showing signs of quickly declining. Without hesitation, I told him I would be right over. I called Laura, who was in Alabama tending to her own mother, who was ill at the time, and asked her to start praying.

When I got to the house, Marvin, Margaret, Jean, and Evan were all there with the president. Evidently, Bar had told the family as the day went on that she was "ready." She made calls to President Bush 43 and Laura, Jeb and Columba, and then said she wanted to go upstairs and go to bed—to "be alone." Every indication was that Bar felt like the end was near. Doro was upstairs with Bar.

When I came in, he held out his hand and greeted me. He was already in tears and I said, "I heard your girlfriend is very sick."

"She is," he said, and there were more tears, but as he always—always—did, he asked me, "How are you?"

We gathered in the small sitting area where we had shared conversations, laughs, prayers, and Communion for over ten years—more times than I can remember. Doro came down, also teary, and said, "Mom's in bed now."

"Does she want me to come up and pray with her?" I asked.

Doro said, "Let me go ask," and went upstairs. A few minutes later, she came down and said, "Mom wants you to stay with Dad—to pray with Dad." By then, Neil and Maria had arrived, shortly after Neil's son, Pierce, and his new bride, Sarahbeth.

I looked at the president and he said, "I want you to go pray with her!" I was not sure who had greater authority in the house at that moment, but I followed his directions.

I went upstairs and knocked on the door. "Bar...it's Russ."

She was lying with her eyes closed, but she said in a loud, clear voice, "I'm not checking out yet!"

I told her, "I understand, Bar, but your husband asked me to come pray with you."

"All right, then," she said. "Come on in."

We visited for a bit, I anointed her head with oil, and I prayed for her. I gave her a kiss on the forehead and said, "I love you."

"Love you too," she said.

I left the room, pulling the door all but closed and talked to two of the hospice care nurses in the next room—both of whom felt like Barbara's death was imminent. That is when I heard her call out, so I stepped back to the door, opened it, and asked "Bar, are you okay?"

She said, "Yes...just tell him I adore him."

I went downstairs and said, "Mr. President, she said two things: she said, 'I'm not checking out yet,' and 'Tell him I adore him.'" There were more tears, and then we circled up for dinner, and to wait. After dessert, the president was ready to go on to bed, and he bid us all good night.

Not knowing if this was it or not—but assuming it was—Neil said, "Maybe Russ should pray."

I looked around the table, looked everyone in the eyes—we were all in tears. Jean was on my left. We all held hands, we all wept, and then we prayed. Afterward, we shared hugs and "I love yous" all around. Since Bar's vitals were okay and I only lived a few blocks away, I decided to go on back home and, again, kept the phone by my bed.

When I woke up about 5:30 a.m., I called Evan and he quickly contacted me back—he said she made it through the night and was actually resting comfortably. I checked in during the morning in between services at St. Martin's, and Evan said she had actually had breakfast. I offered to come over and bring Communion and have prayers, which I did. When I arrived at the house, she was in the sitting room, along with, again, the president, Marvin, and Margaret. Her spirits were up, and she made a few jokes about "not believing what you read in the news." We shared Communion, prayers—and with a kiss on the cheek, we exchanged "I love yous." Unbeknownst to me, because she was clearly better than she had been the night before, that would be the last time we would talk together.

Sometime on Sunday, as has been widely reported, she and the president were alone and had a heart-to-heart. The president looked at his beloved wife of seventy-three years and said, "I'm not going to worry about you, Bar." And Barbara looked at her beloved George and said, "I'm not going to worry about you, George."

And then, they each had their favorite drink—a manhattan for her, and a vodka martini for the president.

In my work, I have often seen those close to death "rally" for a day or two after a serious dip. Barbara had a rally for the ages. She knew what was coming, so much of Sunday and Monday was spent on the phone, calling friends and loved ones.

On Tuesday morning, April 17, about 9:00 a.m., the phone rang. It was Evan: "We are there this time." I quickly made it over to the house. The president was already with Bar, holding her hand. Throughout the day, Evan, Neil and Maria, Pierce and Sarahbeth, and Marvin's daughter, Marshall, were constantly present. Bar's aide, Neely Brunette, was in and out—but mostly in—and though Jean Becker had to be with staff at the office (knowing what was ahead), Jean called me several times during the day, and when not talking by phone, we were texting throughout the morning.

Though Bar was not able to respond, President Bush 43 called and spoke to her over the speaker phone as did Jeb and Doro—they had all been back and forth over the last few weeks. My Laura was at our home, and as the hours marched on, she and I called and texted one another several times.

Then—well, we took turns reading to Barbara. I read her the first forty-eight psalms—and after a while, frankly, that got a bit tedious. On a break, I went downstairs and found a copy of *Little Women*, came up, and read her a few chapters of that. Neil, Pierce, Marshall, and I took turns reading from *Millie's Book*. The president was with her the entire day, holding her hand.

The only break he took was about 2:30 p.m. to get his daily massage on the third floor. Given his physical challenges with Parkinsonian syndrome, daily massages were absolutely essential—but this was his only time away. However, about 3:00 p.m., the power went out. The power almost never goes out in this area, but it did. There was a quick scramble for battery backup to make sure there was no break in Bar's oxygen. The power stayed out.

Bar was comfortable the entire day—she never called out or indicated she was in pain or discomfort. The only thing I heard her say during the day was, "Home...home," which she whispered once or twice. Since I did not leave her side during the day, especially over her last several hours, this was, in fact, the last word she spoke: "Home..." She was clearly, clearly ready.

★   ★   ★

We knew it was close but did not know when it would be. Jean Becker called and said she had been talking with 43 and felt like we all needed to pray that if this was Bar's time, now was the time also to pray even more for a peaceful and timely death—not one that lingered on for days.

So I went downstairs and went to the side garden of the house and prayed. I gave thanks for Bar's life and prayed that if this was the time, then let it be the time—a peaceful and painless death.

Neil came out and joined me. He had been such a constant presence in Barbara's life, especially in these last years, and I could only imagine what he was feeling. I told him I was praying for our Lord to gently receive his mom. Neil did not want to see her leave, but he agreed that was the prayer needed at the time. We talked a bit, and then I went back inside.

Given her steady decline, and not waiting on the local power company to set things right, Evan and company decided to bring the president back downstairs. It took a bevy of Secret Service agents to carry him down four flights of stairs on one side of the house and back up two so he could sit with Barbara until the end. If I heard it once, I heard it two dozen times—as he sat there, holding her hand throughout the day, he said, "Bar...I love you...I love you, Bar" with such brazen passion and tenderness it was palpable. At one point, when he, she, and I were together alone, he looked at me, gently smiled, pointed at her, and then pointed toward heaven. "Yes, sir," I said. "That's where she will be."

At 5:30 p.m. the power was still out. By then, Bar's physician had arrived and both he and Evan told everyone, "We are there...If there is anything you want to say, now is the time to say it." Neil asked me to pray again. I anointed her head with a cross of oil. The president was holding her hand, as he had been all day. Everyone in the room—all of us—then knelt by her bed—Neil and Maria, Pierce and Sarahbeth, Evan, Neely, Marshall, and I. We all put our hands on her—and again, prayed the prayers we had prayed only a few nights before.

Almighty God, look on this your servant, lying in great weakness, and comfort her with the promise of life everlasting, given in the resurrection of your Son Jesus Christ our Lord. Amen.

Depart, O Christian soul, out of this world;
In the Name of God the Father Almighty who created you;
In the Name of Jesus Christ who redeemed you;
In the Name of the Holy Spirit who sanctifies you.
May your rest be this day in peace,
And your dwelling place in the Paradise of God.

Into your hands, O merciful Savior, we commend your servant Barbara. Acknowledge, we humbly beseech you, a sheep of your own fold, a lamb of your own flock, a sinner of your own redeeming. Receive Barbara into the arms of your mercy, into the blessed rest of everlasting peace, and into the glorious company of the saints in light...

As we prayed, we wept, and we held on to one another, and we held Barbara. In my entire life, this was one of the few moments where the demonstrable presence of God was as real to me as the pages of the book you are now holding.

When I finished with "Amen," everyone was weeping and telling Bar, "I love you." The doctor was near, and Bar took her final breath. "She's gone," he whispered. The president asked him to repeat it. "She's gone to heaven, Mr. President."

The Celtic Christians teach about something they call "thin places." Thin places are those times and moments, people and experiences, that you have or encounter and for whatever reason—at that juncture, at that meeting point—the line between heaven and earth is so thin it is hardly detectable, if detectable at all. I will share a few of those "thin places" with you in this book, and here is one.

At the moment that Bar's physician said the second time, "She's gone to heaven, Mr. President," at that very moment, the lights—the power—came back on... in that instant.

We were still all kneeling, still all weeping. Maria lifted her head, looked at me, and whispered, "What does that mean?"

I said, "I don't know—but let's take it for what it is."

Now was a time for family, not for those of us who were not—so Evan, Neely, the doctor, and I left and the door closed. We were quietly standing in the hall outside the room. Pierce opened the door and said, "Russ, he wants you to come and pray again."

So I came in and knelt in front of the president and by Bar's body. I placed their hands together—his on top of hers—and put my hands around both of theirs. I gave thanks for her life. I prayed that God would welcome one of his own. I prayed that God would comfort the president and all Bar left behind. I thanked God for the love and witness of these two and this wonderful family. When I finished, the president and I both were in tears, but while I was still on my knees, I took his face in my hands and said, "Mr. President, she is at peace now. She is in heaven. She is with her parents and your parents, and she is with your dear Robin. And you will see her again.

"And you, sir, will be okay—we will take care of you. We love you; I love you."

"I love you," he said. I kissed him on the cheek and stepped back out of the room. It was, up to that point, the most intense moment in my ordained ministry. God was present and real and there—in that moment.

And Barbara? Barbara was home.

CHAPTER THIRTEEN

A FUNERAL THAT SPOKE AND INSPIRED

The seed dies into a new life, and so does each human.

George MacDonald

If worship does not change us, it has not been worship. To stand before the Holy One of eternity is to change: Worship begins in holy expectancy; it ends in holy obedience.

Richard Foster

A Kiss Good-Bye and Preparations Begin

After Barbara took her last breath, and after we said our prayers, those in the room began to offer their good-byes. One by one, there were hugs and kisses. One of the tasks of a priest is to offer a final farewell, in whatever fitting way.

I stepped out and called my dear wife, Laura. There is nothing like being in the presence of a husband and wife when one or the other dies to remind you of those who have captured your heart in the same way. My Laura was that person, and I knew she was about to be called upon to walk alongside me for several days in a way we had never before walked—and I also wanted her to know I loved her.

Then I called the church to put into motion all the pieces that we had so meticulously planned, especially over the last few weeks. Unlike the state funeral for the president, there would be no lying in state in the US Capitol, no service at the National Cathedral. This would be the only service, and there was much to begin.

Though most of the preparation for a "Bush funeral" over the last several years had been focused on the president, the president's staff and his legion of volunteers had been carrying out a gargantuan effort to honor this great woman in the best way possible. Not a few hands, but hundreds, would come together beginning on the evening of Tuesday, April 17, 2018. Once I got off the phone, I returned to the bedroom, where there was what I can only describe as "a holy quiet."

Maria Bush and I sat with Barbara's body for quite some time as the buzz of activity began outside the room. We talked in whispers for a bit. Bibi and Mini finally made their way in and up onto the bed where they lay quietly. When the time seemed right for me to leave, I stood up, kissed Barbara's forehead, and bid her good-bye with the words, "Bless you, Barbara; bless you, dear Bar."

Everyone in the house was quiet, was reverent. Secret Service agents were posted about the house, inside and out, and most had their hands folded in front of them, as if in prayer. They knew what America was about to know, that the much beloved Barbara Bush had left this life for the next.

The news began with Jim McGrath's tweet: "A former first lady of the United States of America and relentless proponent of family literacy, Barbara Pierce Bush passed away Tuesday, April 17, 2018 at the age of 92."

Moments later, the forty-third president put out a statement that not only sounded the right notes but proclaimed a deep truth:

My dear mother has passed on at age 92...Laura, Barbara, Jenna, and I are sad, but our souls are settled because we know hers was...Barbara Bush was a fabulous first lady and a woman unlike any other who brought levity, love, and literacy to millions. To us, she was so much more. Mom kept us on our toes and kept us laughing until the end. I'm a lucky man that Barbara Bush was my mother.

Her soul was indeed settled. She had lived her whole life through in such a way that the "peace of God, which surpasses all understanding," was not something elusive to her but a daily experience.[1] She was at peace, and now it was time to turn our attention to a full-on communal experience of honoring her and the faith that sustained her.

You will recall that Barbara Bush had quipped, "Who will come?" and suggested there was no need for any kind of visitation. Her suggestion to "just place my casket in the chapel" was not going to work.

Not only Houston wanted a chance to honor their First Lady, but the state, the nation, and the world.

I worked closely with the members of my extraordinary team to put into place massive plans, with four foci leading up to the funeral— transportation, accommodating the press, the visitation, and the reception prior to the service. All of these had the potential of being managerial and security nightmares, but keep in mind, as I have often shared with you now, everyone—and I mean everyone—wanted to honor this woman, and everywhere I looked, I couldn't find a soul unwilling to do everything they could to make that honor possible.

On transportation, the plan that we would eventually enact for the president could now be employed for those guests attending Barbara Bush's funeral. Second Baptist Church, the largest Baptist church in the US, headed by Pastor Ed Young, had graciously opened their campus for our aid. Because of security reasons, there was a lockdown on any unauthorized traffic in every direction within several blocks of St. Martin's.

Second Baptist was 1.8 miles from St. Martin's, and they would become the operational hub for those parking and being transported to St. Martin's both for the visitation and the funeral. Houston city buses,

---

1. Philippians 4:7 (NRSV).

various city officials, and loads of Houston Police Department officers joined the Secret Service in preparation for the coming days.

It will come as no surprise that the press attention was massive. In short order, we set aside our northeast parking lot as the "press pool." By the next morning, April 18, local affiliates were setting up shop, as were national press representatives from ABC, NBC, CBS, CNN, FOX, and PBS. All of them would have tents and "mini" outdoor sets from which to carry out their reporting.

I began getting calls for interviews within an hour after Barbara's death. So Karin Thornton, our communications director at the time, along with my executive assistant, Carol Gallion, would screen the calls through Jim McGrath, and if he gave the thumbs-up, I would agree. Karin attended every interview I did to keep me focused and to ward off any unwelcome questions, but her job was made easy. All the interviews took place prior to the funeral and each and every person with whom I interviewed could not have been more kind and respectful of the moment and of our campus. I interviewed with most local outlets and several national.

Particularly memorable was my interview with CBS's Bianna Golodryga in the church. At one point, as I was describing Barbara's last day, and then last moments, I looked over and she had tears in her eyes, which prompted my own. She was feeling what we were all feeling. Then she asked me, "Are you prepared?...Are you ready?"

And I answered honestly, "I am prepared because I think my task as priest and pastor to this home and its family is to honor her and to give thanks for her remarkable life and to celebrate her faith."[2]

As well, later that same day, my interview with Neil Cavuto from FOX News was memorable because it gave me an opportunity to do something that I hope this book is doing for you. Neil spent a good bit more time with his interview, and when he asked about the family and how they were doing, I was able to echo what 41 and other members of

2. CBS, April 21, 2018.

the family had already said aloud by now—that they were sustained by the prayers and support of others. I told Neil about the authentic affection I witnessed for over a decade in my time around all of the Bush family members. I stressed to Neil that "I love you" were three words often spoken and heard in the Bush home. Yes, this was the former First Lady, but this was, in fact, also a child of God who loved her Creator, her husband, her family, and virtually everyone God sent her way.

Sometime before the visitation, I thought it a good idea to check in with Neil and Doro, the two children of 41 and Barbara whom I knew the best. Neil was in as good spirits as one could expect. He, too, knew his mother was at peace, but he also missed her terribly. We did not hang up the phone (this time or any other, for that matter) without Neil thanking me and often adding "We love you." This is one of those persistent themes, albeit behaviors, that runs throughout the Bush DNA— "thank you . . . thank you . . . thank you." Gratitude is a way of life.

My conversation with Doro was very different only in that it revealed yet another one of those rare "thin places" in the days that followed Barbara's death. We talked a little bit about Bar's last day and the plans that were unfolding at St. Martin's even as we spoke, and then she said, "You are never going to believe what happened."

"What?"

"A friend of mine came from out of town and we decided to go shopping for a dress. You know, I wanted something simple . . . appropriate. Together we picked out this dress, and almost from the moment we left with it, I felt it was the wrong decision.

"Mom would not have liked it. It felt like it was too short, it had slits in the sleeves—it was black but looked like it was more for a dinner party than Mom's funeral.

"So I decided to try it on. I put it on in that room where Mom died, slipped into the bathroom to look in the full-length mirror.

"I was right, and I said out loud, 'Mom would just hate this,' and at that instant the full-length mirror just fell off the door and broke into a thousand pieces on the floor!"

She was right—I was astounded.

"What do you think that means?" Doro asked. "Do you think Mom did that?" Much like Maria's question about the power coming on at the moment of Barbara's death, I said, "I am not going to put anything past Barbara... I would just take it for what it's worth!"

Needless to say, Doro wore a different dress!

Then the visitation began. With the help of Second Baptist, beginning the evening before the funeral, people began to show up—dozens, then dozens more, then hundreds. They would park at Second Baptist, load onto city buses, ride down to St. Martin's, and wait for a chance to come in and pay their respects.

Even though this was to last all night, which it did, I had asked the St. Martin's family of clergy, staff, and volunteers to be present the entire time, from the moment the doors opened until they closed. Not surprisingly, no one declined—and everyone was more than willing to do more than was asked. The staff and volunteers of St. Martin's are simply remarkable people.

What followed was equally remarkable, as people of all ages, from seniors down to little ones; people of every color; people from varying Christian churches and other faith traditions stood in line to quietly come into our worship space and stand, or sometimes kneel, for a moment before Barbara's casket. Many of the women, and many of the young girls, donned blue dresses and a string of pearls to honor Bar's image.

As this was going on, I gave Evan a call to see how the president was doing, and if I should come by the house to see him. He paused, then said: "Hang on, let me check." After a moment or two, he said, "We are coming your way."

"What?" I asked, and he said, "Forty-One wants to go and greet people." And that is exactly what he did.

It began with a quiet moment—in what has become a rather iconic scene, the president and Doro took a moment near the altar. And then they turned him around in his wheelchair and he and Doro greeted people for a good long time. No one expected the president to be there, let alone greet anyone and everyone that came his way—but that was, in fact, "his way." He stayed for a bit before returning home. Doro stayed behind and she, Neil, Marvin, Pierce, and other family members along with the leadership crew of St. Martin's spent reverential hours in celebration and thanksgiving of Barbara Bush.

I suppose in one of the few times of her life, Bar was wrong about "who would come" to her visitation. By the time we were closing the doors in preparation for her funeral, over eight thousand people had made their way to the visitation at St. Martin's to pay their respects.

On Saturday morning, April 21, we were as ready as we could be. By now, we also had been informed that President Bush 43 had asked us to host a reception in our Bagby Parish Hall for his father and the many special guests that were coming—among them, President and Mrs. Barack Obama; President and Mrs. Bill Clinton; First Lady Melania Trump; former prime minister of England Sir John Major and his wife, Dame Norma Major; former prime minister of Canada Brian Mulroney; former vice president Dan Quayle and his wife, Marilyn; former vice president Dick Cheney and his wife, Lynne; former CIA director Bob Gates; Luci Baines Johnson; Caroline Kennedy; Tricia Nixon; the Honorable Condoleezza Rice; and a host of others.

We were prepared, but prepared all the better, when a few days before the gathering, local businessman and friend to the Bushes Jim McIngvale called my assistant, Carol Gallion. McIngvale, known to Houstonians as "Mattress Mack," owned and operated Gallery Furniture.

He knew St. Martin's would be host to a group we had never before hosted, and he called to offer to bring in some of his finest furniture: sofas, chairs, lighting—basically whatever we needed to make the gathering more special. Though it was a loan (we thought), it certainly made the event all the more meaningful. A few weeks after the funeral, Carol Gallion got back in touch with McIngvale's staff to set up a return of the borrowed furniture, and his response was, "Oh, just keep it as a gift."

Beginning about 10 a.m., one after another they came. The two Presidents Bush came in together with First Lady Laura Bush. Then, about every five minutes, the other presidents and first ladies came in order of service—President and Mrs. Clinton, followed by President and Mrs. Obama, and then, lastly, First Lady Melania Trump.

I have, as you have noticed by now, done my best to steer clear of the political climate through which we were all living in 2018, but let me make one observation. There were two other iconic moments leading up to the service. First, three former presidents and four first ladies present stood around the sitting president, 41, smiling, as if they were family. That represented the feeling throughout the parish hall—no anger, no tirades, no divisiveness, and a spirit of unity prevailed and launched what would be, for all the world to see, a few hours when everyone came together, when everyone got along.

The second moment occurred just before we prepared to enter the church. I gathered everyone present to offer final instructions, and then I said, "You all are in Texas now, and in Texas, we hold hands and pray in a moment like this." And so we did, heads bowed, eyes closed, holding hands—Republicans, Democrats, young, old, black, white. Barbara Bush had brought everyone together—really together. If anything spoke to our times, it was that moment and the hours that would follow.

The Worship Begins

As I shared a bit earlier, for Episcopalians, a funeral service is also a worship service. Episcopalians are not coming together to "worship" the deceased but to lift the souls of those present into the presence of God. The late archbishop of Canterbury William Temple wrote,

> To worship is to quicken the conscience by the holiness of God, to feed the mind with the truth of God, to purge the

imagination by the beauty of God, to open the heart to the
love of God, to devote the will to the purpose of God.

Yes, there were innumerable notable guests. And many more who
were just friends and volunteers. Secret Service team members who had
served as protective agents for the family over a period of forty years
came from around the nation on a pilgrimage to salute one they had so
nobly served. Outside the church, the press pool had swelled to dozens
with cameras perched on the bleachers we had placed in front of the
church. Pacing on buildings nearby in camouflage with binoculars were
armed active members of Secret Service. Motorcades, with an extra
hearse in case the primary hearse had any mechanical issues, waited outside with their engines running.

But inside...inside the holy space of St. Martin's people had gathered—
over fifteen hundred people—to sing and pray and remember...and to be
reminded of one who shared the love of God, and to be inspired by her life
to devote themselves to the purposes of God.

Before the service began, Barbara's coffin was brought into the narthex. My wife, Laura, and several other members of our altar guild, all
dressed in black with white gloves, carefully laid a pall over the coffin,
and I offered the words of reception:

> With faith in Jesus Christ, we receive the body of our sister
> Barbara for burial. Let us pray with confidence to God, the
> Giver of life, that he will raise her to perfection in the com-
> pany of the saints.[3]

And the worship began as we had planned it over the last few months.
The clergy of St. Martin's, joined by the Reverend Peter Cheney; the
Right Reverend Claude Payne, the seventh bishop of the Diocese of

---

3. Book of Common Prayer, 466.

Texas and the second rector of St. Martin's; and the sitting bishop of Texas, Andrew Doyle, all stepped into their various roles.

After the reading from Proverbs, Jon Meacham was the first to offer a tribute. He helped set the tone by opening with humor—something which Barbara would have appreciated, as did those who had gathered in her memory.

Jon told a story about being approached by an adoring fan only to find out later that she thought he was novelist John Grisham. When he had shared the story with Barbara, she had said, "Well, how do you think poor John Grisham would feel? You know he's a very handsome man." But Jon went on to wonderfully recount the incredible traits of one he called "the First Lady of the Greatest Generation."

He highlighted her commitment to literacy with a heartfelt story of a moment when she joined a son of a former sharecropper who had only recently become literate. He had been invited to read the preamble of the Constitution at part of a televised event commemorating the bicentennial. Bar sensed he was nervous and asked if it would help if she read along with him. He agreed and they stepped out together. As they did, Barbara slowly lowered her voice such that the man began to weep as he found his own voice with the help of the First Lady. Wonderful remarks they were.[4]

I wrote earlier that Bar got the last word on the selection of "Amazing Grace." Following the reading from 2 Corinthians by Bar's namesake, her granddaughter Barbara Pierce Bush, Susan Baker was to have offered her remarks. I confess that I was running on most gears but not all, and I promptly stood to announce the hymn before Susan had a chance to offer her comments.

Horrifyingly, I realized this faux pas I had made not just in front of those gathered, but in front of a television audience across the nation and around the world. I made my way over to my friend Susan and

---

4. Jon Meacham, "Remarks," Barbara Pierce Bush funeral, St. Martin's Episcopal Church, Houston, Texas, April 21, 2018.

suggested she begin after the Gospel reading from John that was offered by my vice rector, Marty Bastian.

Later, Susan eased my pain by saying, "It is okay; the hymn gave me time to pray and prepare." There you have it—a true friend and a devoted follower of Jesus.

Susan gently climbed into the St. Martin's pulpit, and with tender words just above a whisper, she began, "It's hard to think of life without the 'force of nature' that was our dear friend..." Susan also knew Bar would appreciate a bit of humor, and so she began offering adjectives— Barbara was strong, smart, fun, and feisty, "even sometimes making a headline she later regretted."

This was so hard for Susan. She and Barbara were sisters in service, in friendship, and in faith. But she mastered the moment, and the pure silence of the congregation professed that each one wanted to hear every word Susan spoke.

She closed by lifting our spirits through a reminder of the core belief of Christians, that when this life comes to its natural end, it merely changes into resurrected life, and then she thanked her dear Lord for bringing the "vibrantly beautiful human being into the world."[5] As she stepped out of the pulpit on her way back to her place in the pew, she smiled at the president, he smiled in return, and she blew him a kiss. And then—Bar's son Jeb. There is an old saying, "A son is a son until he takes a wife, but a daughter is a daughter all of your life." That was not true of any of the Bush sons—who so deeply loved their mother—and that came through with vibrant colors as the former governor of Florida spoke passionately about his mother.

He said his mom, in that moment, was thinking, "Keep it short... and don't get weepy... I've spent decades laughing and living a life with these people." And then he spoke that honest truth everyone listening knew: Bar filled "our lives with laughter and joy."

---

5. Susan Garrett Baker, "Remarks," Barbara Pierce Bush funeral, St. Martin's Episcopal Church, Houston, Texas, April 21, 2018.

He then shared, "Mom was our first and most important teacher," followed by a list of ways to walk through life, including "be kind... serve others...treat everyone as you would want to be treated...and love your God with your heart and soul."

Jeb went on to say how the Bush children were witnesses to the "most amazing love story," reading a bit from a letter the president wrote to Bar on their anniversary, January 6, 1994:

> *Will you marry me? Oops, I forgot, we did that 49 years ago! I was very happy on that day...but I am even happier today...I have climbed perhaps the highest mountain in the world, but even that cannot hold a candle to being Barbara's husband.*

And then, in a moment of beautifully crafted evangelism, the governor talked about the last time he was with his mom. He asked her about her death—was she "ready to go?" And Bar did not pause and told her son, "Jeb, I believe in Jesus and he is my Savior. I don't want to leave your dad, but I know I will be in a beautiful place."[6] The governor's honest, tender words were so genuine and sweet that I do not suspect there was a dry eye in the church by then.

My remarks followed, which you will find in an appendix at the end of this book, and then we continued with the burial liturgy. Father Peter Cheney offered the traditional prayers—nothing more, nothing less. The service was as we had planned, with one addition from Bar's beloved husband of seventy-three years. The president requested a reading that reminded him of her—and "them"—from Shakespeare. Doro told me about it days before the service and wondered where it might fit, and I suggested she read it and that it be the last reading before the commendation.

---

6. The Honorable John Ellis Bush, "Remarks," Barbara Pierce Bush funeral, St. Martin's Episcopal Church, Houston, Texas, April 21, 2018.

> And when she shall die
> Take her and cut her out in little stars,
> And she will make the face of heaven so fine
> That all the world will be in love with night
> And pay no worship to the garish sun.[7]

I looked over at the president and he was smiling and weeping at the same time.

We offered a commendation of Barbara into our Lord's hands, Bishop Doyle blessed the congregants, and then we left the church, as Barbara wanted, singing, "Joyful, joyful, we adore thee, God of glory, Lord of love..."

We had worshipped indeed.

What Followed—Laughter, Warmth, Inspiration, Tears, and Farewell...

A small behind-the-scenes moment here. We knew that all of us who were leaving the church after a service that had now stretched well beyond an hour would be getting into a motorcade and then taking nearly two more hours to drive to the campus of Texas A&M. We "held" everyone in the church, as we stood with Barbara's coffin in the narthex, until all the family members had a chance for a restroom break.

There was some measure of relief, even some whispered laughter. Some hugs and tears. I was standing next to the forty-third president, who had been very clear about the "ninety-minute rule." "Sir?" I said, and he looked at me, and I held up my watch and pointed and said, "Eighty-two minutes." He smiled and bobbed his head up and down.

I took my own break and was leaving just as Governor Bush was coming into the restroom. About that time, the forty-third president said in a clear, loud voice, "Russell! What the heck's taking so long?"

---

7. William Shakespeare, *Romeo and Juliet*, act 3, scene 2.

And I said, "Sir, your brother has just stepped into the restroom."

He made a beeline to the men's room. I was standing just a few feet away and heard him say, "Jeb! Let's go!" Once a big brother, always a big brother.

We all prepared to step out of the front of the church. I knew the press corps had been outside for hours, and as soon as the doors opened, the cameras began clicking away. Barbara's coffin was carried out as it was carried in—by her grandsons. Members of the Houston Police Department stood at attention, saluting the coffin, as it moved past the gathered family and clergy and was placed in the hearse.

Laura and I, along with Peter and Kiki Cheney, would be riding in one bus with the Bush staff, and the family would be in another bus and appropriate cars as we all pulled away from campus, thirteen vehicles in total with many more police motorcycles and vehicles before, beside, and behind us.

Within moments, all of our phones began to go off with calls and text messages. The singer Amy Grant, who had performed at St. Martin's just a few years before, texted, *That was such a beautiful service.* I texted back, *Did you watch it on television?* She responded, *No! I was here . . . !* She, along with the hundreds of others, began to leave as they came, loaded back onto buses, back to Second Baptist, and back to their cars.

But the respect among everyone in and around those moments was simply awe-inspiring, which is what we experienced all along the road on the seventy-eight-mile drive from St. Martin's to College Station.

The highways were, for obvious reasons, cleared of all traffic, but as we made our way northwest, with each mile we became increasingly awestruck. With American flags, WE LOVE YOU, BARBARA signs, and hands over hearts, hundreds of people—which turned into thousands, and then tens of thousands—lined the roads and highways, looking down from overpasses, standing atop fire engines, ambulances, and military vehicles, waving and weeping as we passed by.

We thought it could not get any more moving, and then at approximately 2:45 p.m., as we pulled onto the campus and then onto the long road leading from the campus entrance toward the library, all of our conversations stopped, and again, tears began to flow. Seven hundred military cadets, along with members of Aggie Band's Bugle Rank, lined the road on either side, saluting in complete silence. We later learned that they had been standing at the ready for hours.

It had long ago been decided that there would only be family, and no press, at the graveside. The graveside portion of an Episcopal service— what we call "the committal"—is brief, but it does close out the day.

I will say we were, again, somewhat concerned about the time. It was 3:00 p.m., and the day was wearing on. Some of us were concerned about the impact this might have on the president.

About that time, again, in the quiet, I heard the forty-third president say, "Russ, what the heck's taking so long?"

I smiled and said, "Sir, I am not in charge down here. That would be Mike Wagner."

"Mike," he said, "what's taking so long? Let's go!" No need to pause when a presidential directive is given!

We walked slowly, reverently from the library to the burial site. As we arrived, fifteen members of Texas A&M's Singing Cadets stood near the burial spot and sang "Eternal Father" and "How Great Thou Art."

Bar's coffin was put into place. Nearby was Robin's gravestone: ROBIN BUSH, DECEMBER 20, 1949–OCTOBER 11, 1953. As I saw her name, I could only think that now, they were, in fact, reunited.

This final moment was as it should have been—solemn. Peter Cheney and I divided the service. "In the sure and certain hope of the resurrection to eternal life through our Lord Jesus Christ, we commend to Almighty God our sister Barbara."

As I spread some sand across her coffin, I prayed,

Earth to earth, ashes to ashes, dust to dust. The Lord bless her and keep her, the Lord make his face to shine upon her and be gracious to her, the Lord lift up his countenance upon her and give her peace. Amen.[8]

We all said the Lord's Prayer together, and I offered a final blessing and then a dismissal. Peter and I stepped back, away, as we should at that moment. There were tears and hugs, whispered "I love yous" all around—especially showered upon 41.

Slowly, in groups of two, three, and four, the family slipped away. Laura and I stayed behind until everyone had gotten on the path headed back toward the library. Once they were well out of sight, one more time I knelt, put my hand on Bar's coffin, and prayed quietly. When I finished, I stood, kissed my palm, and tapped her coffin. "Farewell, Barbara."

A Small Epilogue

I think it is fair to say we were—all of us—exhausted. We got back up to the library, and I began to divest of my robes. Laura and I were preparing to get back on the bus to head to Houston, when Jean said, "The president wants you all to join us for a meal."

Honestly, I could not believe he had an ounce of energy left, but remaining behind were Pierce and Sarahbeth Bush, David Jones, Jean Becker, and other members of the president's staff.

There was a small dining area near the atrium of the library, and we circled up and shared simple sandwiches and wine. The weight of the moment was lightened with our conversation.

Laura and I were sitting next to Jean, who was sitting next to the president, when Jean's phone went off. She talked for a minute and then said to the president, "It's John Major. They want to get some Tex-Mex." Jean then named a restaurant, and the president said, "No...

---

8. Book of Common Prayer, 501.

don't send them there. They aren't as good as they used to be." He held out his hand for the phone and then began to talk with the former prime minister of England about the best Tex-Mex places in Houston.

And then, to the amazement of us all, he said, "Well, where are you?" He held for a moment and said, "We'll just come meet you and we can all go out for Tex-Mex." He then started inviting all of us at the table to join them. Amazing! The president, who had just had the most taxing day anyone could imagine, had more energy than any of us, and he was going out to dinner!

We politely declined, drove back with others on the bus, and made our way home. Before bed, as I said my prayers, I gave thanks to God for allowing Laura and me to not only be part of this day, but to have been deeply and richly blessed by our friendship with Barbara.

Here is what I observed in the hours of that long, historic, momentous day. Everyone—not just family and friends, not just Houstonians and Texans, but America—came together to honor a woman of honor. Full stop.

People spoke of her humility and her humor, her compassion and her courage, her life and her love. If we had forgotten, we were reminded of the deepest of qualities that not only make life worth living but make life worth something. Barbara Pierce Bush had been laid to rest and had, by God's grace and mercy, been raised to new life and reunited with her Robin and all the saints in light.

CHAPTER FOURTEEN

"LOVE YOU MORE"

Hey, Bake, where are we going today? —*President Bush*
Well, Jefe . . . we're going to heaven. —*Secretary James A. Baker III*
Good. That's where I want to go. —*President Bush*

I love you too.

Last words of President George H. W. Bush

That he may rest . . .

From "Prayers at the Time of Death"[1]

The Days That Followed

The president possessed a remarkable burst of energy in the hours that followed the long day that held within it the closing hours of Barbara Bush's visitation, a reception with presidents and first ladies and heads of state, a funeral, a two-hour procession, a burial, and finally a small reception with close friends, staff members, and family. No one would have expected him to do anything other than return home and fall deeply asleep. But that was not the president's style.

---

1. Book of Common Prayer, 466.

He made good on his promise to meet up with Prime Minister John Major and his wife, Dame Norma, along with others for Tex-Mex at a local restaurant. As I noted in the last chapter, the president had invited Laura and me to join him, and other family members, but honestly, I knew that this was not "our crowd" and that it was time for the president to finish out the day with some lifelong friends and loved ones.

I had planned for lots of things prior to Bar's death and her funeral, but I had not planned, nor anticipated, the hundreds and hundreds of letters and emails I would receive in the days and weeks that followed her service. Beginning the afternoon of her funeral, for nearly a month after the funeral, the volume of mail I received was almost unimaginable.

Watching the service for Barbara Bush. It was so beautifully done—readings, and music, and prayers…I have loved Mrs. Bush, wrote Kathryn of New Albany, Indiana.

Am writing in reflection of the memorial service today for Barbara Bush. I so wish I had known her better before now. I was so impressed also with the service—the words spoken, the songs sung, the flow of the service…Perhaps my favorite part was when [Governor Jeb Bush] told of Barbara's response to dying… "I'm not afraid of dying—I'm going to see Jesus"…Amazing, wrote Judith of Springfield, Missouri.

I want to "thank you" for a beautiful memorial service for our former First Lady Barbara Bush…My tears flowed freely as I remembered Mrs. Bush and all of her wonderful contributions to our country. Barbara Bush was a woman of grace and she chose how she wanted to end her life, at home with her loved ones, wrote Bob of Wall Township, New Jersey.

Many of those writing requested copies of the funeral bulletin; some wanted copies of the various remarks or my homily. But most of them were just notes revealing how the author was impacted by Bar's life, death, and funeral service.

Prior to Barbara's decline, Laura and I had already made plans to drive to the Florida Gulf Coast to be with our children and grandchildren for an early summer vacation. Those plans were delayed a bit, but we were able to shift them immediately to the day after Barbara's funeral.

Laura and I loaded up the car and decided to stop overnight in Biloxi, Mississippi, for a night of rest, good food, and some low-impact aerobics entertainment. Just as we settled in the hotel room, my cell phone rang. It was Doro.

"Doro...is everything okay?"

"Well, no. Dad's very sick. They've taken him to the hospital."

I was stunned. I could tell Doro was upset and terribly worried. The news had not, mercifully, hit the press just yet. "It's some sort of blood infection."

"We just got to Mississippi. Do you need me to come back?"

"No...not now. I just wanted you to know."

"Let's just stay in touch. I will call you later."

I hung up, looked at Laura, took a deep breath, and said, "He's in the hospital...does not sound good."

Evan Sisley would later share with me that his condition was quite critical. It was so serious that there was no time to wait on an ambulance. He was loaded into Secret Service vehicles and rushed to the hospital. When they arrived, the attending physician speculated that he was within an hour of dying, had Evan and the team not thought so quickly on their feet.

Amazingly, however, within about twenty-four hours, he, as he had so many times before, began to rally. We went on to meet up with our family but were in daily touch. God forbid, if something were to happen, at least we were ready.

The president emerged from the hospital, not in perfect health but in better health. As the end of May came along, there was a great deal of discussion as to whether or not he would return to Maine for the summer.

Over the last years, he had shared with many folk that he would like to die in Maine, not Houston. On the other hand, Jean Becker, the Bush office staff, his medical team, and his family felt that, for a variety of reasons, it would be better for his death to occur in Houston than

Maine. It was no slight on Maine. The fact that he had stated that Kennebunkport was where he wanted his last days to be said a great deal about that lovely beating heart of the family.

But he did improve and began to set his sights on returning to Kennebunkport. Between Bar's death and his departure for Maine, I would go by the house, often with Laura, once a week.

Since they were headed to Maine in mid-May, I scheduled our annual "last visit before heading north" get-together for the morning of Monday, May 14. I told the president that Laura and I would come by for good-bye prayers and Communion. Jim Baker found out we were going over, and he and Susan wanted to join us. To be honest, I think all of us were happy he was getting to go, but at the same time we were very concerned about the trip itself. How would he fare on that long journey? Only time would tell. But it was a good time to gather and pray and for him to be with his best friend, Jim, and Jim's wife, Susan.

The reason I mention the date here was that this also happened to be the day that the US opened an embassy in Jerusalem. Just a bit of history here: On October 23, 1995, the United States Senate and House of Representatives overwhelmingly passed the Jerusalem Embassy Act, which recognized Jerusalem as the capital of the State of Israel and proposed formally moving the United States Embassy from Tel Aviv to Jerusalem. Though the act had the strong backing of Congress, its pieces were not put into play by President Clinton or his successors, George W. Bush or Barack Obama. Many scholars believed rushing the move, without at the same time recognizing Palestinian statehood with a corresponding capital, would only heighten tensions in the ongoing Israeli-Palestinian conflict. The "two-state" solution was supported by Bush and Baker, but to establish one embassy within its corresponding state, without the other, would make a long-term path to peace even more challenging.

So Laura and I arrived shortly before the Bakers and visited with the president for a while as we waited for Jim and Susan to arrive. When they did, Laura and I felt we were witnessing a moment in history as Jim and the president discussed the embassy move and how it made the kind of lasting solution they both hoped for all the more difficult. Laura and I just listened in yet another in a moment of hundreds now, which prompted us to ask, *What are we doing here?* Needless to say, it was a history lesson for the books.

The president shared that he hoped we would make it up to Maine that summer, and we said that of course we would if we could, but we also knew we would have to run that by Jean Becker. The president was constantly inviting people up to the Point, and by now, we were keenly sensitive to the impact that kind of hospitality could have on him.

We shared Communion and prayers—including those for the Middle East—and said our good-byes. Laura was able to offer a kiss without a bite from Bibi or Mini.

By now, the president was saying something we had heard him say many times—but now, on the heels of Barbara's death, he would say it without fail almost every time.

As we parted, we said, "I love you," and he quickly said back, "Love you more."

As we walked to the car, I said to Laura, "Gosh, I hope he makes it back here in the fall."

Our Own Saint Departs

On December 23, 1925, the same year Barbara Pierce Bush was born, Evelyn Boehms was born into the loving arms of her parents, deep in the mountains of Middle Tennessee. The mother of my wife, Laura, and her three brothers and late sister, Evelyn was one of the kindest women I had ever known. She and her late husband, Jay, had traveled the Southeast until they opened a small family-owned carpet business in Randolph County, Alabama.

When I married Laura in August 1984, one of the many blessings was to have Evelyn as a second mother, a confidant, a friend. She did not have it within her to say a negative thing about anyone she met. She loved and reared her children and grandchildren. She was a wonderful

Christian and faithful churchwoman. She worked incredibly hard and was spunky to the end. She and Barbara had met on a few occasions and seemed, in many ways, connected—by their years and the generation in which they were born and reared. And they both had daughters who died—Robin of leukemia, and Jenny in a drowning accident.

But in the midst of all that we were doing between Barbara's decline and death, my mother-in-law, Evelyn, began her own steep decline. Laura was back and forth to Birmingham, Alabama, to tend to and eventually care for her mother.

On June 10, Laura alone was with her mother as she left this life for the next. We were, frankly, devastated. Evelyn was such a huge and important part of both of our lives, but on the heels of Barbara's death, in many ways, it added insult to injury. That is just the truth. It was hard, and it was exhausting. And yet, much like our desire to do our best for our first lady, we did all we could to do our best for the first lady of Laura's family.

The day after Evelyn's death, I flew to Alabama and we dug in as a family. Evelyn's funeral was on June 13 at First United Methodist in Roanoke, Alabama. It was, much like Barbara's, a reminder that life is a gift—each and every precious moment; and sometimes God sends incredibly special people into this world to remind us what a life of goodness and grace is all about. Barbara was that sort of person, as was Evelyn, and now we began the summer without these two saints on this side of the veil of life.

The Last Summer in Kennebunkport

I stayed in regular touch with Jean in the early days of the summer, and the president began to improve. The fresh sea air was a real gift, and while he obviously could not be as active as he wanted, he could still enjoy the ocean breeze, and time with family, which grew with an important addition thanks to Evan Sisley and America's VetDogs. America's VetDogs is an organization that supplies disability assistance dogs for veterans as well as facility dogs for Walter Reed National Military Medical Center. Evan, working closely with America's VetDogs, was able to recruit a beautiful golden Labrador retriever, Sully, to be at the president's side, day and night. The president was thrilled, and as the nation was slowly exposed to the newest "First Dog," they came to love Sully as well.

With everything moving in the right direction, Laura and I decided to go forward with long-arranged plans to travel to England and Scotland for some continuing education and also to support our St. Martin's choir, which was singing in Edinburgh and some of the surrounding areas. Needless to say, we made arrangements to be back in the US within twenty-four hours if the president's condition were to change in any way.

While overseas, I stayed in touch with Jean, Neil, and Doro. The president had improved, but he was indeed much weaker. There was some concern that he might, in fact, not make it back to Houston. Laura and I began to think that a trip to Kennebunkport would not be a lift as much as it would be a burden. Barbara was typically our hostess, and we were not sure to whom that role would fall if we just showed up.

In August, we got our direction. Jean Becker wrote,

Russ,

I've been tasked to writing and suggesting to you that you don't come visit Maine this fall. The kids really want to lock the front gate and throw away the key.

I think that is going a tad too far...but, in their defense, it has been a struggle this summer with so much family in town, both immediate and extended.

Anyway, they really want to cut down on the traffic. We'll be back in about 2 months. Yes, we think we might be bringing him home.

Jean

I wrote Jean back later that day, telling her I completely understood and asking her to keep me updated on the president's condition.

Jean,

I pray daily for our favorite President. I know his journey from this life to the next will be extraordinarily tough…on so many…part of me believes he'd like to be in Maine for that… but that is not in our hands is it? So I just pray…

That said…if for some reason it looks like we could head toward that…I'd like to be with him…whether there or here; if you all think that is appropriate…but let's just hope and pray his summer days are filled with good memories…restful sleep…fresh air…

Russ

Before the day was out, I heard from Jean once more.

Russ,

Thank you for your graciousness, as always.

If we can give you a heads up that the end is near, we will. We are not sure it will go down that way.

We aren't sure of anything at this point, to be honest.

Keep praying for us.

Jean

As the rest of August played on, the president improved. Given this news, and given the emotional and physical challenges Laura and I had faced with Barbara's death and funeral, followed by Laura's mother's death and funeral, we moved forward with a sabbatical to Greece and Turkey. But needless to say, we felt it necessary to run it all by Jean.

She supported the trip and wrote a nice note on September 11:

Russ…

Evan is fairly confident we will be getting President Bush back to Houston…I am confident you will be able to hold his hand again.

Go have a wonderful trip. I think it will be fine.

Jean

We got things in order but not without some final preparations for the president's funeral—whenever that would be.

Getting the Final Pieces Together

By now, my friend and mentor, Sam Lloyd, had stepped down as dean of the National Cathedral to return to his previous post as rector of Trinity Church in Boston. The new dean, the Very Reverend Randy Hollerith, took the post in 2016, and we began to build a necessary relationship in the preparation of the state funeral. Randy; his provost, the Reverend Jan Naylor Cope; and the canon (director) for worship, the Reverend Dr. Rose Duncan, quickly became fast friends.

It is important to add here that the cathedral team under Randy's leadership was 100 percent accommodating. I attribute a lot of that to Randy's hospitality, to the great, broad umbrella that is the Episcopal Church, but also to President Bush. St. Martin's is well-known as a parish that plants itself in a more conservative, orthodox, and traditionally evangelical wing of the church, whereas the National Cathedral has typically been guided by more liberal and progressive initiatives. Neither the cathedral nor St. Martin's was going to get in the way of a moment to give witness to Christian charity and unity.

It may seem like a little matter to a wider audience than Episcopalians, but it was important to the Bushes that the liturgy reflect their theological bent—which meant traditional language in the readings from Scripture, the prayers, and the other pieces of liturgy. Randy's basic approach was "We will do whatever you need and want." Why? I think Randy and I both knew we had an opportunity to show the world what authentic Christian diversity, inclusiveness, and unity looked like—and we wanted to honor this great man in the best way we could.

So in the remaining weeks leading up to our trip overseas, we essentially nailed down all the details for the services in Washington, Houston, and in College Station. Of course, there were a myriad of other pieces around the state funeral aspects—and for those, we stood aside and let Mike Wagner and his team take the lead.

Jean Becker was once again tasked with reviewing, editing, and constantly revising the guest lists for Washington and Houston, as well as making arrangements for who would travel on Air Force One to Washington from Houston and back, along with who would travel on the train from Spring, Texas, to College Station.

Something else happened in early September that set a clear, though not unexpected, parameter. Arizona senator John McCain died on August 25 at the age of eighty-one after his long and distinguished career. His congressional funeral held at the National Cathedral was just over three hours long. After that, President Bush 43 reiterated his desire to keep the services being planned for his father in Washington and Houston as close to ninety minutes as possible. That would be a bit more challenging at the National Cathedral, again, because of the many traditional pieces around a state funeral, but we did our best to tailor the worship services with that goal in mind.

This also meant that those giving remarks at both services were now given their charge to prepare their words. In DC, the president chose Jon Meacham; the eighteenth prime minister of Canada, Brian Mulroney; and his longtime friend Wyoming senator Alan Simpson. Traditionally, the sitting president is included among the speakers, but in President Bush 41's case, it seemed far more appropriate and fitting for his son and the forty-third president to round out the laypersons speaking.

In Houston, it would be the president's closest friend, Secretary Baker, and his grandson and son of Governor Jeb and First Lady Columba Bush, George P. Bush.

I was asked to work with the president and his team in suggesting Scripture readings. For the state funeral, I suggested Scriptures that would prompt those in attendance to consider the president's oft-quoted and much-inspired call to be "points of light."

Thus, a passage from Isaiah that begins, "Arise, shine; for your light has come," and a visionary image of life beyond the grave that comes from the book of Revelation and ends with the hope that in God's kingdom, there is no need of "sun or moon to shine … for the glory of God is its light," seemed to fit the bill.[2] For the Gospel lesson, the most fitting choice seemed to be Jesus's reminder from the Sermon on the Mount given to his earliest disciples to be "the light of the world" by letting "your light shine before others."[3]

As I thought about the service in Houston, knowing this was a moment for the president to be honored at "home," I suggested Scriptures that focused on love, for Houston knew well this loving man and loved him in return. A lesson from Lamentations would remind the St. Martin's congregation that "the steadfast love of the LORD never ceases," and Paul's well-known "love chapter" from 1 Corinthians seemed a perfect choice.[4]

Then, keeping in mind that this service would begin to bring the weeklong gatherings and services to a close, I suggested Scriptures that promise beyond these historic moments around the death of the president, there was still the promise of life. So I recommended Psalm 23: "Yea, though I walk through the valley of the shadow of death … thou art with me," and Jesus promises that he is, in fact, "the resurrection and the life."[5] I did wonder if the president or family members were considering any readings outside of the Christian tradition, but these selections were received well and given the stamp of approval, and so I could then, using these, begin to consider my own remarks.

In both places, I was invited as the clergyman to offer the homily. Being, as I was at Barbara's funeral, last up to bat, it was essential that I had access to everyone's remarks before taking the pulpit so as not to repeat or be put in the position of editing as I went.

---

2. The full texts were Isaiah 60:155, 60:18–20, and Revelation 21:1–4, 21:6–7, 21:23–25 (NRSV).

3. Matthew 5:14–16 (NRSV).

4. The full texts were Lamentations 3:22–26, 3:31–33, and 1 Corinthians 12:31b–13:13 (NRSV).

5. The full texts were Psalm 23 (KJV) and John 11:21–27 (NRSV).

I literally took a week off and left Houston to spend a number of hours each day writing and rewriting, cutting and adding. When I finished, I reached out to John Williams, longtime assistant and speechwriter for Secretary Baker, and asked if he would review my remarks for accuracy, clarity, and also length.

He was quick and to the point, editing massive pieces out and offering comments on how to make things clearer or sharper. When he finished, I reached out to Jean, thinking perhaps it was time to pass them on to President Bush 43. I told her John finished editing my remarks and he "lovingly" cut both homilies by 50 percent!

Jean agreed but, before passing them on to 43, emailed me back on September 18, 2018:

> Russ,
>
> Both are of course excellent. You are a great writer...
>
> Please do not kill me but I think the St. Martin's one is still too long. By the time you speak, the family and TV audience will have heard from 6 eulogists, and you already once.
>
> How much more is there to say?
>
> Not a lot.
>
> Yes, we are going to be shorter than McCain...but I think people will still be tired from it all...
>
> So I would do yourself a favor and cut out 5 minutes. It is slightly repetitive in several places. And yes, I'm happy to try to do it for you.
>
> Everyone raved about 43's eulogy at McCain's funeral. It stood out for one huge reason: It was short. People will adore you if you make this one very short, very meaningful, very sweet.
>
> Don't you love John Williams and me?
>
> Jean

Ouch! But it is what I needed to hear! I did not care if people adored me, but I absolutely did not want to drone on, nor make anyone think,

Didn't this guy already speak? When will this be over? So it was back to the chopping block.

Evidently, in the days that followed, 43 asked everyone to submit their remarks for review by his staff—which, honestly, helped everyone. On September 24, Jean wrote to all of us:

So please keep in mind I am just the middle man...

President Bush 43 asked his personal aide to read all the eulogies and look for redundancies.

The good news is—he found very few.

His report is below.

So you can do what you want with this information.

But especially if you come after the other person saying what you wanted to say...well, take note!

A reminder of the order of the speakers:

Washington:

Jon Meacham

Brian Mulroney

Alan Simpson

Russ Levenson

Houston:

James Baker

George P. Bush

Russell Levenson

Let me know if you have any questions.

Jean

Jean was right: there were just a few redundancies—among them, Brian Mulroney, President 43, and I were all making reference to the president's favorite motto, "CAVU," and thus 43 said he would remove his reference and leave it up to the prime minister and me to decide how, or if, we wanted to keep ours. That was about it, so I emailed Jean back: "Very helpful...I'll edit appropriately...Russ+," and she responded, "It doesn't help you come last...Sorry! But it is helpful. I am smiling 43 had his aide do that..."

At the same time that lessons were under consideration and remarks were being written, edited, and rewritten, the music was being selected for both DC (and here, Mike Wagner was tremendously helpful) and Houston. At the National Cathedral, the choir, under the direction of Canon Michael McCarthy, would play the primary role, but there would be additional musical tributes before and during the service by the United States Marine Chamber Orchestra, the Joint Armed Forces Chorus, and the United States Coast Guard Band, and offerings by two very special friends of the Bush family, Christian performer Michael W. Smith and Irish tenor Ronan Tynan.

In Houston, at St. Martin's, it was pretty much up to music director Dr. David Henning, choral director Kevin Riehle, roughly one hundred or so members of the St. Martin's choir, and again, several special friends of the Bush family—country music legends the Oak Ridge Boys and actress and singer Reba McEntire.

Despite this tremendous effort, there was no fly in the ointment— not one. There were literally legions of participants in the design and preplanning for what would happen when the president left this life for the next. But everyone—every single person from top to bottom— wanted to do their best for this president, not because he asked for it or required it, but because they wanted to honor this man and the incredible impact he had made on their lives. They wanted to honor someone who was truly honorable in every way.

The Fearless Journey

Athanasius of Alexandria was one of the ancient church fathers responsible for helping to structure some of the earliest theology of the Christian faith. Christians believed, as they do now, that many, if not all, of the essential truths of the Christian faith were ratified, so to speak, by the promise of life beyond death, realized first in the person of Jesus of Nazareth.

I logged a quote of his some time ago, which bespeaks of what I saw in President Bush when he had returned from Maine to Houston in the fall of 2018:

> For man is by nature afraid of death and of the dissolution of the body; but there is this most startling fact, that he who has put on the faith of the cross despises even what is naturally fearful, and for Christ's sake is not afraid of death.[6]

After Bar's death, there was the promise of Kennebunkport and the revolving door that provided time with friends and family. Mercifully, for a number of reasons, the president did not die in Maine. And, as Jean shared with me, he did want to come back to Houston, but he would be coming to a very quiet house—a home without Bar.

For this reason, and many more, soon after Laura and I returned from overseas, we began to visit 41 regularly—once or twice a week. On our first visit, I could tell his health had declined. He had, almost constantly, it seemed, struggled with bronchial issues—sometimes born of illness, other times exacerbated by allergies—and of course, his lack of mobility impacted not only his respiratory system but also the ongoing day-to-day health everyone needs to maintain a vibrant lifestyle.

The average bear, and certainly this priest, believed the president had every good reason to be frustrated, to be sad, to be depressed—to be afraid. I never once saw any of this in those last months of his life.

Though he talked less and listened more—and when he did talk, it was often whispered or in between coughs—he was far more interested in the lives of his visitors than he was in complaining about his own circumstances.

It was clear he missed Barbara. He would bring that up from time

---

6. Athanasius died in AD 373.

to time. And once again, as we did previously, we discussed death and life after death. Once again, he wanted to know if he would get to see Robin. "Yes," I said, "and you will see Barbara again too." I remember that conversation well, and when I said that about Bar, he smiled and his eyes filled with tears. But they were tears, I think, of joy, of faith, of gratitude, and of want—he wanted to be reunited with Bar and Robin.

But he was going to make the best of whatever days he had left—and he did. The president loved to eat, and he had not given up drinking his favorite adult beverage, Grey Goose. And he did have his new companion, Sully.

The first time I met Sully was on that first visit after we were all back in town together. By now, there were no longer security checks for the Levensons, and after passing beyond the large metal gate, I would go into the house without knocking. Sully would often be the first to greet me. With his thick blond fur, he would saunter up to the door and drop his head for a pat or back scratch. He was a great companion, and there was never any danger of being bitten by Sully!

Then there were "the boys," as Barbara used to call them. While all of the Bush children and grandchildren were attentive to their "Poppy," perhaps none were more so than the president's son Neil and grandson Pierce. Virtually all the other family members lived out of town, and I suspect a day did not go by without 41 getting a call from Doro and at least one, or perhaps all, of the boys.

But Neil lived across the street with his wife, Maria, and Pierce lived nearby as well. I rarely found the president alone on my visits, and often when I came over, I could hear Neil's buoyant voice reading to his father. This did not happen just in those last months, but more and more in the last several years of 41's life. Neil was, and remains, an active businessman, community leader, and also the driving force behind the Points of Light Foundation.

But being present with his dad was a chief priority. Among some of 41's favorite reads were the Candice Millard books. The president much enjoyed history, so Neil would read David McCullough's *1776* and *John*

Adams; Walter Isaacson's *Benjamin Franklin*; and Doris Goodwin's *Team of Rivals*. And it's no surprise to know that the president enjoyed reading Jon Meacham's books, including his book on Thomas Jefferson, *The Art of Power*, and his biography of 41, *Destiny and Power*.

Pierce learned well from his father and often came over to eat with the president or watch television with his "Gampy." And when Doro or Marvin came to town to visit, they would pick up the reading mantle as well. Neil once told me that he believed they read about fifteen books to the president during that last season of his life.

Laura and I were often fortunate to witness the unbridled affection among the family members, but especially between Neil, Pierce, and 41 that fall. I had been asked to come by and bring Communion on the evening of November 6. By then, the president was spending more time in his bedroom and less in the sitting room.

When I arrived and came upstairs, I heard the news on. It did not occur to me until I got there that the midterm election results were being broadcast by the hour. When I came in the room, I found Pierce lying in bed beside the president, the two of them talking about the election. It was a precious memory. Pierce, like Neil, would always hug and kiss his grandfather and never leave without saying, "I love you"— to which the president would almost always reply, "Love you more."

Neil and I grew closer as friends in the last years of Barbara's life and certainly during her decline, death, and the events that followed. Before and after Barbara's death, he often shared Communion and prayer time with us when we visited.

Another constant in the last few years of the president's life, as you have likely discerned by now, was Evan Sisley. While he was daily with the president for years up until the fall of 2018, there was hardly an hour that went by that Evan was not in some way at the president's side. He and his husband, Ian, purposefully rented a townhome within walking distance of the president's home so that should the need arise, which it often did, he could be there in a matter of minutes.

In the months leading up to 41's last days, there was a steady stream of family and friends that visited with the president, perhaps most often, Jim and Susan Baker.

As the frequency of the visits increased so did their intensity. They were not long visits, for the president's energy level was declining, but we always ended our visits with my anointing his head with a cross of oil, sharing Communion, and then holding hands to pray. What I noticed as those weeks went by was that his grip became stronger in prayer, not weaker.

Our last time alone was Thanksgiving weekend. Evan kept a small office with a single bed near the president's bedroom so if he needed to stay overnight, he could. On this visit, I stopped and talked with him some.

He made it clear to me that the president's health was quickly declining. There was no timetable and no clarity about when, exactly, the president would die, but the certainty of its growing nearer by the day was clear.

Then Evan shared yet another "thin place." He said, "He saw Barbara the other night."

"What?" I said, not surprised but wanting to know more.

"He was sitting in his chair and he looked at me and said, 'Isn't she beautiful?' And I said, 'Who, Mr. President?' and he responded, 'Bar— she's sitting right over there . . . She looks so beautiful.'"

I think Evan and I both teared up. We had both seen and experienced that when people are near death, they begin to see, hear, and sometimes even talk with loved ones who have already died. Some physicians and scientists would say this is merely hallucination. That is not what I believe, and it was not what Evan believed. The president was being welcomed to his next life by the woman he so loved.

I came into the master bedroom, and he was in his sitting chair watching television. He smiled and warmly welcomed me. "Let me turn this off," he said, and then, as always, immediately turned the attention away from himself. "What are you going to do for Thanksgiving? Are the kids coming?" and on and on. Selfless to the core.

We shared Communion, and then we did something we had never

before done. I said to the president, "I'd like to go through the service of Compline with you—it's a beautiful service, a great way to end the day—if you would like that."

He raised his eyebrows and smiled. "Sure."

Most historians trace the origins of Compline to the fourth century AD, and over time it became the last of seven worship times held throughout the day in monastic communities. I loved the comfort of the prayers and thought it a good fit for a first Thanksgiving without Barbara. As we began this little personal service, I had no idea it would be his last Thanksgiving, nor did I know it would be the last time we would be together alone.

The liturgy contains Psalm 31, which includes the same words Jesus offered on the cross before his death—"Into your hands I commit my spirit"[7]—as well as these two lovely prayers:

Be present, O merciful God, and protect us through the hours of this night, so that we who are wearied by the changes and chances of this life may rest in your eternal changelessness; through Jesus Christ our Lord. Amen.

Keep watch, dear Lord, with those who work, or watch, or weep this night, and give your angels charge over those who sleep. Tend the sick, Lord Christ; give rest to the weary, bless the dying, soothe the suffering, pity the afflicted, shield the joyous; and all for your love's sake.[8]

And then it closes,

Guide us waking, O Lord, and guard us sleeping; that awake we may watch with Christ, and asleep we may rest in peace.[9]

---

7. Psalm 31:5, cf. Luke 23:46.

8. Book of Common Prayer, 133–34.

9. Book of Common Prayer, 135.

Little did I know how appropriate each of these prayers would be for what would soon begin to unfold. As I finished, he said, "Thank you... That was very nice."

We held hands once more—a firm grip. I stood, kissed him on the cheek. "Have a good Thanksgiving, Mr. President."

"You too," he said.

"I love you," I said.

"Love you more..."

Farewell...

In the days that followed our last get-together, the president's health declined all the more. Neil; Maria; Pierce; Marvin's daughter, Marshall, who also lived in Houston; Jim and Susan Baker; Jean; and, of course, Evan came together in ways so that the president was constantly with someone.

There were some serious discussions about end-of-life care, but like Barbara, the president had made his wishes known.

Publicly, many times, he had said he hoped to live to be one hundred. One goal he had was to see the fruition of years of discussion of a yet-to-be-determined high-speed rail project making travel between Houston and Dallas possible in ninety minutes. The president said he wanted to be on its maiden voyage.

But these, and other things, were not to be.

A week or so before his last day, he and Jim Baker had a wonderful visit that Jim told me about later. They were sharing a drink together and Jim asked 41 if he still wanted to live to be one hundred. The president said, "Yes, I do... but I don't think I am going to make it." His words were, of course, prophetic.

As the last week of November rolled around, the contact with the Bush family and staff became more frequent and more intense. Jean and the president's staff were working at full tilt. There was no start or end to the workday.

I went by the house most days, sometimes twice a day, and Neil,

Pierce, and Evan were virtually omnipresent, as were Susan and Jim Baker. I confess that those days were a bit dreamlike. We were all running on little sleep and pins and needles.

I got to the house on the afternoon of Thursday, November 29. Jim and Susan Baker were there. The president acknowledged our presence with a smile or squeeze of hands, but he was not talking on this day and was really slipping in and out of a deep sleep.

Susan was sitting by the president's bedside, her head bowed, eyes closed, silently praying. Jim went over to sit on a nearby sofa and I joined him. We sat there for a while just talking a bit. And then Jim pointed toward the president and whispered to me, "That man changed my life." He went on to tell a story I had heard him tell before. When his first wife, Mary Stuart, died at the age of thirty-eight on February 18, 1970, Jim was left to raise four children on his own. He often said, privately and publicly, that if ever there was a time he would have become an alcoholic, that would have been it.

But his tennis partner and friend jumped in to be a rock in Jim Baker's life at a time when he needed it. The president asked Jim to manage his Senate campaign in the same year, which helped pull Jim out of the downward spiral anyone would likely face under similar circumstances. That friendship, forged in the fire of a traumatic life event, sealed the two forever.

It was then that Baker got up and walked over to the president's bed and stood near his feet. He patted them and then, slowly, but very deliberately, started to rub and massage the feet of his dear friend for perhaps thirty minutes. Frankly, I was brought to tears. I could palpably feel the pain Jim was feeling, and yet, at the same time, his only desire was to bring comfort to his dear friend.

And it was hard, at that moment, not to think of Jesus washing the feet of his own disciples the night before he went to his own death. He told them, "I have set you an example that you should do as I have done for you."[10] Jim Baker incarnated those words in that half hour.

---

10. John 13:15.

Sometime that afternoon, the president's physicians, Dr. Clint Doerr and Dr. Amy Mynderse, came and we all had a discussion about end-of-life care once more. That decision is often hard for a family to make. As the doctor described the various possibilities available should, say, the president's heart stop, I looked over at Evan, and I could tell that he and I were both thinking the same thing—the president's body was saying it was time to go.

Neil asked me, "Russ, is he ready for heaven?" It was not my place to contribute to the decision, but it was my place to answer that question.

"Neil, without a doubt—he is ready when the time comes."

After some more talk, we surrounded the bed, and I anointed his head with oil, said a brief prayer, and left. Though the president was very weak, death did not seem imminent, so I asked Evan to please stay in touch.

When I got home, I told Laura that I thought that death was close. We shared a glass of wine or two. Laura and I watched something on the television but went to bed early. I could only sense that his death was coming, and I wanted to be as rested as possible.

I woke early and tended to several things before heading over to the house. When I got there, the president was actually awake. I was surprised to learn from Evan that he had eaten breakfast—eggs, yogurt, some juice. He was certainly not the picture of health, but he was also not the picture of death. Was the president rallying? He had several times before, and there was no need to think he was not going to rally now.

Jim Baker had already been by early that morning. It was then that a now rather famous exchange had taken place. When Jim came in the room just after 7:00 a.m., the president opened his eyes wide and said,

"Hey, Bake, where are we going today?" he asked.

"Jefe, we're going to heaven," Jim answered.

"Good, because that's where I want to go," the president said.

The president fell in and out of sleep and became less and less talkative. At one point, Susan Baker placed her hand on the president's head and said, "We love you so much, Jefe."

Forty-One, with humor even then, opened his eyes a bit and said, "You better hurry."

I headed back to the office, as it was clear that every last detail had to be in order. If indeed the president did die, I had to meet with the St. Martin's staff to go over what was to happen in the days to come, and Laura and I had to be prepared to leave Houston for Washington. Evan and Jean promised to keep in touch.

Almost everyone I have ever served prays and hopes for a good "last day," and the president certainly got one. Jean Becker had arranged for Ronan Tynan to be at the house. The world-famous Irish tenor sang "Silent Night." Jim Baker said he could tell the president was actually mouthing the words as Tynan sang. He finished with a Gaelic folk song.

Family members were calling throughout the day. I returned in the late afternoon, and there, once again, were Jim and Susan. If one of the children called in, Jean or Evan would put the call on speakerphone. In a moment like that, I felt the need to leave the room. At some point, 43 called in, and again I left but later learned that is when the president spoke his last words. Forty-Three said, "I love you, Dad." And 41's last words were, "I love you too."

Jean, Evan, Jim McGrath, and I spent a good deal of time in the small office just off the master bedroom. If there was any rally earlier, it was subsiding, but the president did not seem to be in any sort of pain or distress. He was resting comfortably, so I decided to head home.

My phone battery was low, so I plugged it in in another room while Laura and I sat down to try and take our minds off of things by watching a little television. Something prompted me to go check the phone, and when I did, there were three missed calls from Neil and one from Evan.

I immediately called Neil and apologized. Neil said, "We are getting very close," and I told him I would be right over. I called out to Laura in the other room and said, "It's time; I am going to head over."

When I arrived, the house was intensely quiet. The Secret Service agents were clearly upset; they welcomed me with quiet whispers as I walked across the driveway, into the house, and up the stairs.

I think I saw Jean, Jim, and Evan first, and gave them all a big hug. We had all been planning for this for a long time, but we were not ready for, or wanting, the moment to come.

We just sat around the bed quiet for some time. Whispering. Susan Baker never once let go of the president's hand, never once ceased in her prayers, as if to respond to the apostle Paul's injunction to "pray without ceasing."[11]

Neil said, "Perhaps it is time to pray." I looked over at Evan and he nodded. I suggested we all kneel and place our hands on 41. We all knelt—Neil and Maria, Pierce, Jean, Evan, Marshall, Drs. Doerr and Mynderse, Jim McGrath. I was to the president's left, and placed my right hand upon his. Jim Baker was kneeling next to me.

So, there we were, this little band of mourners who so loved and respected this great man, circling around him as the life of our forty-first president began to wane away, and we prayed together.

I anointed the president's head with a cross of oil in the same way he was anointed as a babe at his baptism. We offered the prayers that only months ago we had offered at Barbara's bedside.

As we began the Lord's Prayer, I could feel Jim weeping next to me and wrapped my left arm around him as my right arm stretched across my prayer book so that I could rest my hand on the president.

The prayers are the kind we would all want at the end...

Dear Friends: It was our Lord Jesus himself who said, "Come to me, all you who labor and are burdened, and I will give you rest." Let us pray, then, for our brother George, that he may rest from his labors and enter into the light of God's eternal sabbath rest.

Receive, O Lord, your servant, for he returns to you...

Wash him in the holy font of everlasting life, and clothe him in his heavenly wedding garment...

---

11. 1 Thessalonians 5:17 (NRSV).

May he hear your words of invitation, "Come, you blessed of my Father"...

May he gaze upon you, Lord, face to face, and taste the blessedness of perfect rest...

May angels surround him, and saints welcome him in peace...

Into your hands, O Lord,

We commend our brother George...

Almighty God, our Father in heaven, before whom live all who die in the Lord: Receive our brother George into the courts of your heavenly dwelling place. Let his heart and soul now ring out in joy to you. O Lord, the living God and the God of those who live. This we ask through Christ our Lord. Amen.[12]

After a few more prayers, we just knelt in silence for a good long while, until he took his last breath. It was 10:10 p.m.

We all knelt quietly awhile longer before saying our final good-byes. As it was at the moment of Barbara's death, the intense, unmistakable, and unambiguous presence of God's Spirit was with us in that room.

We slipped out of the president's bedroom, one by one, leaving only family members behind. Jean, Jim, and I stepped into the small office, hugged one another, and then we each went to different areas of the house. Jean had to put into place basically everything. Jim had to contact the press. We had all prepared, but now it was time to put things into motion.

My first call was to Laura, then to my father, as I wanted him to hear it from me before he heard it on the news. Then I called Marty Bastian and Carol Gallion. Everyone I called I asked to please pray—pray that what would unfold in the next week would honor our forty-first president and his faith. Those were my most pressing prayer requests.

---

12. Book of Common Prayer, 465–66.

While it is not always possible, when it is, it is sometimes customary for a priest to wait for the body of a member to be taken away and to see the body safely into the hands of who will prepare it for burial. So I contacted the George Lewis funeral home and told them I would be over shortly and would wait until the president's body was safely in their care.

His remains did not arrive until around midnight, but I waited in the lobby. Since coming to Houston in 2007, I had worked with members of the George Lewis team for an untold number of funerals and perhaps just as many meetings around President Bush's funeral. They were not strangers to me and they knew how important their solemn duty was at this moment.

Bob Boetticher, who had attended virtually every funeral-planning meeting since I first came to Houston in 2007, came out and told me the president's body had arrived and would soon be prepared for burial. I joined Bob and the rest of the small band of preparers. They stood quietly aside as I anointed his head one last time, placed my hand on his forehead, and used the same prayer I had used for Barbara:

Into your hands, O merciful Savior, we commend your servant George. Acknowledge, we humbly beseech you, a sheep of your own fold, a lamb of your own flock, a sinner of your own redeeming. Receive George into the arms of your mercy, into the blessed rest of everlasting peace, and into the glorious company of the saints in light. Amen.

I finished my prayer and stood upright and looked over at the small team ready to do this sacred work. A few of them were in tears.

I leaned over, kissed my friend George's forehead, and said, "Farewell, Mr. President. Farewell."

CHAPTER FIFTEEN

RECEIVED INTO THE ARMS OF MERCY

O death, where is thy sting? O grave, where is thy victory?
1 Corinthians 15:55 (KJV)

And so we ask, as we commend his soul to God, and as he did, "Why him? Why was he spared?"
Jon Meacham, state funeral, National Cathedral

And we're going to miss you . . . a great and noble man, the best father a son or daughter could have.
The Honorable George W. Bush, forty-third president of the United States, state funeral, National Cathedral

Preach Christ at all times.
Levenson, quoting a plaque President Bush gave him, state funeral, National Cathedral

The Beginning of the End

It is difficult to encapsulate everything that occurred beginning in the last hours of November 30 right after the president died, through the six days that followed until his burial on December 6, 2018.

Almost immediately, the nation and world were spellbound with grief. Statements from national leaders across party lines were immediately released, and dozens more from world leaders, virtually all expressing prayers and thoughts of sympathy but also gratitude and praise, not just for all the president did but, perhaps especially, for who the president was.

It is no secret that Barbara's and the president's deaths occurred in a season in our nation's history when civility in the political arena seemed to be tossed to the wind. The president's death seemed to offer a cultural pause button in a nation increasingly exhausted by leadership that was growing comfortable with the verbal assaults of character assassination and juvenile vulgarity under the guise of power and strength.

It was easy to assume a great deal of this was flowing from our forty-fifth president, but he was only part of the equation. The extremes of both the Republican and Democratic parties were doing their fair share to contribute to this poisonous climate, as were the political pundits.

President Bush's death recalled for those old enough to remember that his hope was, in fact, for a kinder and gentler nation and world. So that is what everyone who played any kind of role in the days ahead set out to do—lift up 41's memory, with the hope that it might inspire some, if not all, to recapture his vision.

Back to Washington

With a tremendous measure of gratitude for the plans pulled together by the family, Jean Becker and the president's staff, Mike Wagner and his staff, Dean Randy Hollerith and the staff of the National Cathedral, and the incredible team at St. Martin's, there was very little about which to fret.

The National Cathedral was adept at hosting state funerals and, having only recently hosted Senator McCain's funeral, had somewhat of a practice run, though on a much smaller scale.

The staff of St. Martin's had actually had two practice runs, so to speak. In the latter years of his life, I had developed a deep friendship with Captain Gene Cernan, known to many as "the last man on the moon." We spent a great deal of time together and he became somewhat regular in his attendance at St. Martin's. When mobility became an issue for him, I would visit Gene and his wife, Jan, at his home in Houston for conversation, Communion, and prayer, much like my visits with 41 and Barbara. But sometime before his death, he asked if I would officiate at his funeral. Sadly, it came sooner than I had wished, but I was able to be with him when he died on January 16, 2017, and I officiated and preached at his funeral, which we hosted at St. Martin's on January 24.

There were a number of elected officials, former astronauts, media personalities, and NASA officials who came from all over the US to attend Gene's funeral. It was a moving and appropriate tribute to a man who had done so much for the space program of our nation, but it also gave St. Martin's clergy, staff, and support teams an opportunity to get somewhat of a handle on what it meant to host such a service, including meeting the challenges of parking, security, reserved seating, and the like.

Then, of course, in all honesty, Barbara's funeral gave us a chance for nearly a practice run for the president's service in Houston—with one exception: most of the dignitaries would be at the service in DC, which, frankly, was a relief to those of us back home. St. Martin's would fittingly be the last major gathering before the president's body was to be transported to College Station for burial.

I received calls from friends and family around the country wanting to know how they could support St. Martin's and her rector. My answer was simply "Pray for us." And I felt those prayers the whole way through to the end.

Blessed am I to be married to my best friend. Laura has been with me through life's ups and downs, the moves and transitions, parenting and grandparenting—and the illness and death of beloved friends and family members. But if ever there was a time I needed her constant companionship and presence in my life, it was in those moments and the days ahead.

Not only did Laura love the president deeply, but he loved her. We had not just suffered the death of a church member in President Bush, but someone who had become a friend, a mentor, a prayer partner. We had seen him at his best and, frankly, at his worst—and in either or any condition, all we ever witnessed was decency, kindness, and nobility. Laura and I were virtually inseparable for the week ahead.

The press began again to set up shop in the designated parking lots of St. Martin's. My friend Pastor Ed Young, of Second Baptist down the street from St. Martin's, worked with Mike Wagner, city officials, and the Houston Police Department to put the same parking plan we used for Barbara's funeral in motion.

The schedule we had agreed to some years before would now become the road map for the days ahead, though we did make a few changes.

Initially, the president's body was going to be moved to St. Martin's overnight and then the extended family was to gather in the chapel at St. Martin's for prayer prior to leaving for nearby Ellington Airport. But there were (and are) so many members of the family that adding this to the mix seemed like an unnecessary burden.

So the "departure point" became the Houstonian Hotel, not far from St. Martin's, where virtually all the Bush family members who were not already in or near Washington were gathered. Essentially, President Bush 43 was our host, so once he launched the day's activities, we followed his lead. It was time to get started, so we loaded up buses, SUVs, and cars and made our way to Ellington Airport.

I cannot adequately convey the penetrating intensity that began the moment we stepped off of that bus and inaugurated this historic journey. As a priest and pastor, I have been fortunate to stand, and to pray, in many places that I would consider to be "holy ground." Such was the experience that began with the first official ceremony at 10:30 a.m. on December 3 and continued until the president's burial.

Though there were meals, interviews (more about that later), conversations, tears, laughter, and some rest, all of it seemed to be seasoned with God's abiding presence—in large part, due to the president's desire to fold Christian hymns and music into the many traditional elements of a state funeral.

Several steps along the way, traditions appropriate to protocol were carried out, which included thirteen moments when honors were rendered consisting of four measures of ruffles and flourishes, the playing of "Hail to the Chief," and the simultaneous firing of a twenty-one-gun salute with five-second intervals between rounds. But these were interspersed with renditions of the hymns.

For instance, when the president's remains were received at the east Capitol Rotunda and placed on the same catafalque used in President Lincoln's burial service, the United States Army Band played "Fairest Lord Jesus" and "A Mighty Fortress Is Our God."[1] As the service in the rotunda began, led by the chaplains of the Senate and House of Representatives, wreaths were placed by the Speaker of the House and the majority leader of the Senate while the United States Army Brass Quintet played and the members of the United States Naval Academy Glee Club sang "Eternal Father, Strong to Save."[2]

The next morning, as the president's coffin was departing the Capitol Rotunda for the National Cathedral following the traditional honors of ruffles and flourishes, "Hail to the Chief," and the twenty-one-gun salute, the United States Navy Band played "My Faith Looks Up to Thee" and "Nearer, My God, to Thee."[3]

Keep in mind that up to this point, no official religious service had begun. There is an old saying among believers that "singing is praying twice." The president and those who planned these holy moments

---

1. A catafalque is the base upon which the coffin is placed. Lyrics of "Fairest Lord Jesus" were written by an anonymous German composer, whereas "A Mighty Fortress" was composed by German reformer Martin Luther (d. 1546).

2. Lyrics by William Whiting (d. 1878).

3. "My Faith Looks Up to Thee" was written by Ray Palmer (d. 1887); "Nearer, My God, to Thee" was written by Sarah Fuller Flower Adams (d. 1848).

created a roving chapel from beginning to end, and whether or not they knew it, those present at one, any, or all of these stops along the way were being soaked in prayer, all the way up to the doors of our nation's National Cathedral.

But before all of this, we had to get from Houston to Washington, so after stepping onto Ellington Field, Laura and I, along with members of the Bush staff, stood behind members of the Bush family as the president's coffin was placed into Air Force One, which was designated "Special Air Mission 41" for this solemn occasion.

Then, we were all welcomed aboard. Since this was a first for some of us, including the rector and his wife, the mood lightened some. This would be about a two-and-a-half-hour flight, including lunch and, frankly, about anything else one could want.

Laura and I were seated near a large conference room, along with members of 43's and 41's staff. Evan brought Sully on board, who, for whatever reason, found his way to our feet, where he lay quietly for most of the flight.

To be honest, I think one of the best parts of the experience was there was no "announcement" about seat belts, placing our seats in the upright position, and putting our tray tables away. When it was time to depart, frankly, it was just up and away. The large television screen in the conference room was broadcasting our departure, which happened just after noon. Laura smiled at me and said, "I could get used to this."

"Enjoy it while you can ... I think this is a one-off!" I said.

I think what surprised me the most is that Air Force One looks pretty much like the Air Force One of the movies—same galleys, conference rooms, seating areas—but we were free to roam about, and we did, as did most of those on the aircraft, including President George W. Bush, who came through several times and visited with us for a few moments as we went through the worship bulletins for the services at the National Cathedral and in Houston. He did make a point of saying to all of us gathered that a lot of people, and a lot of press, would want us to compare the current state of politics, and those in leadership, with the days that 41 was at the helm. "That's what they would want, but now is not the time for that. Now is the time to talk about Dad...to lift up my dad." His counsel was simple—now was not the time to curse the darkness—that was all too easy. Now was the time to light a candle.

But I think my favorite moment was when Jim Baker came to talk with us. Of course, we knew him very well by now, but he sat on a small table in front of us and propped his feet up on the armrest between Laura and me. He also wanted to take a look at the bulletins, but as he began to thumb through them, he began to talk about his dear friend— what an incredible man he was, what a great president and leader, a man of character and decency. "And then there is now..." Laura said, going on to share what we all felt—what happened to those days?

We landed at Joint Base Andrews for another ceremony before those present went their separate ways. The president's body was taken to the US Capitol, where it would lie in repose from the evening of December 3 through December 5. The family and the president's staff had tremendous responsibilities and social obligations, but several of us who did not peeled off. It was at this point that Laura and I were given somewhat of a break. We were taken to the Omni Shoreham Hotel, where many of the president's staff members were staying.

I had family nearby in Northern Virginia, so Laura and I had one night to take a deep breath and be with them. Before being picked up for dinner out, Laura and I decided to get a glass of wine. We were sitting in the bar area when my phone rang. It was Evan Sisley.

"Hey, where are you?" he asked.

"We are in the bar. What's up?"

"This is not from me—this is from Forty-Three...He wants to see everyone's remarks again."

"He has seen mine...a few times."

"Yes, he's asked to see everyone's—Mulroney's, Meacham's, Simpson's. He's still really concerned about time—he wants to try and cut them all in half."

Laura was looking at me across the table, probably noticing me turning white at that point.

"Well, Evan, I am working for the family, so I will do whatever they ask of me. I will try and email you a copy before we go out to dinner."

"Okay. I'll let you know if he makes any changes."

I closed up my phone and told Laura what Evan had said. My remarks came to four single-spaced pages in fourteen-point type. "The thing is," I said to Laura, "I have read everyone else's remarks, and I think Meacham's and mine pretty much stick to the guidelines, but Mulroney's and Simpson's are much longer!"

Since I did not have my computer, I had to finagle a copy from my phone. Though not well, I knew the president, and I knew him to be a plainspoken man who appreciated the same from those speaking to him, so I sent it on to Evan, but I added a bit of commentary:

> I will do whatever the President wants, but let me say that I am the only one speaking about the President's faith, and my remarks are only four pages, less than Senator Simpson's and less than Prime Minister Mulroney's. I just want to make sure the President's faith is lifted up, but at the end of the day, I will do what he wants.

I left it at that but fretted a bit trying to figure out how I was going to edit, print, and get a newer version into my brain before the state funeral less than forty-eight hours away.

Aside from that, I really was concerned that we would be, in some way, weakening the Christian message. It really was not about me— I was going to get plenty of airtime. I just wanted to make sure we lifted up 41's faith as much as possible—along with our Christian hope. But I also knew that 43 was, and is, a deeply committed believer, and I felt like my point would sit well with him.

Over those days, the interview requests began coming in again— they would be filtered through Jim McGrath and then members of my staff who were managing my schedule from afar. I did some print interviews—one with my old hometown paper, the *Birmingham News* out of Birmingham, Alabama; our local *Houston Chronicle*; and the *New York Times*. Neil Cavuto, with whom I had interviewed several times now, was one of the first to reach out to me. Before leaving Houston, I did an audio interview with PBS. I also sat down with NBC journalist Kelly O'Donnell, who, by the end of our visit, was in tears thinking about the loss of this great man. Bianna Golodryga, who was still with CBS at the time of the president's funeral, and I sat down for an interview as well. That one felt more familiar since she had interviewed me around the time of Barbara's funeral. And again, Bianna was brought to tears off camera for basically the same reason.

The next day Laura and I had a chance to go up to the National Cathedral. Though the dean (Randy) and I had talked several times on the phone, this was the first time we got to meet face-to-face, and I think he and I both knew how important the day ahead would be for our nation and for our faith.

At the National Cathedral, Jan Naylor Cope and Rose Duncan walked us through the service. There was press everywhere, some of whom did not seem to take notice that we were actually having a rehearsal. I had to smile when the verger, Scott Sanders, lined up those who would be part of the procession into the cathedral's nave (perhaps one of the most important moments in the service). At first, he kindly asked an audio-visual technician who was blocking our path to please move out of the way. When the technician ignored him, he said in a loud, clear voice, "We need you to move, please."

I looked at him and said, "Now I know why you are the verger!"[4]

As all of this was going on, we were heading into the next day and less time before the state funeral. I did not want to pester Evan (or the

4. While not every Episcopal Church has a "verger," many do, and they are often responsible for aspects of orchestrating pieces of worship that involve procession and movement. In medieval times, the verger was charged with dispersing the crowd so as to make way for the clergy! Mercifully, Episcopalians have softened that role!

forty-third president!), but when midday got to afternoon, I finally called Evan.

"Any word on the homily from Forty-Three?"

"Oh, yes…He said leave it alone—it's fine."

I was relieved—no editing for the evening!

Late that afternoon, I was surprised to get a call from Karin, who said the assistant of CNN's Anderson Cooper reached out and wanted to know if I would do an interview that evening during his broadcast.

"Did you check it out with Jim? Is he okay with that?"

"Yes, he's fine. If you want to do it, they will come pick you up, and it will be live this evening."

"Okay, I'm in."

Mr. Cooper was a professed agnostic, so I wondered what his angle might be, but he could not have been nicer. We got there a bit early and had some time to visit.

The program was coming out of a commercial when Laura started to come over to take a photo with the two of us. At which point, the director seemed a bit unnerved as we would soon be on the air, but Cooper pointed at Laura and said, "Come join us—let's get a photo of the three of us." I think the director rolled his eyes, the photo was snapped, and we were given a countdown. "Back in three, two, one…"

Of course, Cooper is a master at his craft, but I was struck by the sincerity and sensitivity of his questions—not just the nature of them, but the tone and the tenor. Like, "If you are comfortable sharing, what was it like at the end?"

Laura and I thanked the crew, and on our way out, we were caught by CNN journalist Jamie Gangel. She greatly admired President Bush, which led to a conversation about him, my role, her faith (Jamie is Jewish), and my Jewish roots (Levenson—of course). Before I knew it, we were all exchanging cell phone numbers, and we have stayed in touch since that day. Another gift from 41.

On the way back to the hotel, my phone rang. I looked down and it was Ron Kaufman, whom I had first met when 41 orchestrated that meeting with Governor Mitt Romney. We had not talked in a long time, but he had just seen my interview with Anderson Cooper and wanted to tell me he thought I handled it well.

But I will never forget how the conversation went from there. Laura and I were driving through downtown Washington, and he wanted to talk about life after death. "What do you think happens when we die?" he asked.

"I believe we live on. I do not know what that life will really look like, but I do believe we will live on. We will know one another. It will be better than this life!"

Ron laughed a bit, but then it got a bit deeper. "I think we are just given life...to live a good life, and then, maybe that is all there is?"

Ron is Jewish, and I tried to remember him regularly on Jewish High Holy Days with a text or phone call. I said, "Ron, Jews believe in an afterlife!"

This conversation continued all the way back to the front door of the Omni, and then Laura went into the lobby, but I sat outside until Ron and I finished up. I am not sure where he landed, but we both spoke our minds and our hearts. And we stayed in touch...and, well, in time, I sent him some things to read! And, well, we would not have had that talk about death, and life after death, if 41 had not brought us together.

Entering the House of Prayer for Everyone

The United States Congress granted a charter to the Protestant Episcopal Cathedral Foundation of the District of Columbia in 1893, which allowed the foundation to establish a cathedral and institutions of higher learning. President Benjamin Harrison signed the charter, which now rests in the National Archives.

While it began as, and remains, an Episcopal church, it has always been seen as the "nation's cathedral" and rightly boasts that it is a "house of prayer for everyone," as millions from virtually every walk of life, race, and religion have sought and found comfort, solace, and inspiration within its magnificent spaces.

While the National Cathedral has hosted some sort of memorial service for every president who has died, it has been host to only a few state funerals—Presidents Dwight D. Eisenhower, Ronald Wilson Reagan, and Gerald R. Ford, and on the morning of December 5, 2018, it would open its doors to its fourth state funeral, for George H. W. Bush.

In 1990, Laura and I were not too many miles away, and I had entered my second year of seminary training. I remember what a lift to the spirits it was to know that the president of the United States was an Episcopalian and that he would be present to celebrate the completion of the National Cathedral with the placement of its capstone on September 29.

The moment was publicized nationally but particularly in Washington, Northern Virginia, and in various Episcopal news outlets.

The speech the president gave was heartfelt. For him, this was not a civic duty; it was a spiritual one, and a listener could tell that by his well-crafted words:

> What an extraordinary moment this is…And so, we have constructed here this symbol of our nation's spiritual life, overlooking the center of our nation's secular life, a symbol which combines the permanence of stone and of God—both of which will outlast men and memories—a symbol that carries with it a constant reminder of our moral obligations. You know, whenever I look up at this hill and see the cathedral keeping watch over us, I feel the challenge is reaffirmed.[5]

My mind floated back to that historic moment several times in the waning years of the president's life and, more poignantly, when I began preparing my homily for his state funeral service.

---

5. The Honorable George H. W. Bush, "Remarks at Washington National Cathedral Dedication Ceremony," September 29, 1990.

For in those remarks, he also prophetically spoke of a moment those of us in Washington in December 2018 were about to share . . .

> I want my grandchildren to come here. I want them to feel reassured that there always will be comfort here in the presence of God, and I want them to delight in the colors and the sounds and the tapestries and mosaics to the fine old hymns. And I want them to know a very special way of understanding this wondrous place—studying the brilliant stained-glass windows. From where we now stand, the rose window high above seems black and formless to some, perhaps; but when we enter and see it backlit by the sun, it dazzles in astonishing splendor and reminds us that without faith we too are but stained-glass windows in the dark.[6]

I would borrow that last sentence in my homily, but the "want" he expressed in that speech was also something that I kept in mind. He did, as did the whole family, want those who would gather for his state funeral to feel reassured of the comfort and presence of God. That pre-eminent goal and desire of the president remained first and foremost in my mind, heart, and soul in the days, hours, and even minutes leading up to the beginning of that service.

There were several things that made that want a reality. Allow me to turn to those before we finish out this chapter.

From Reception to Commendation

By the morning of December 5, thousands had participated in the opportunity to pay their respects in the Capitol Rotunda. Their stories alone spoke volumes. Laura was my rock and was next to me every single step of the way. Not too long before the funeral, someone asked me if I wanted a

---

6. G. H. W. Bush, "Remarks."

list of who was coming—presidents, first ladies, world leaders, and dignitaries. I declined. Honestly, the attendants were not my concern. I kept in mind throughout that the focus would be the worship service in memory of 41, and in honor of the faith that beckoned us to this holy space.

I would later learn that, well, yes, the crowd was auspicious in the world's eyes. Among those from our own United States, in addition to President and Mrs. George Bush (43) and all the children and grandchildren of 41, would be President and Mrs. Barack Obama; President and Mrs. Bill Clinton; President and Mrs. Jimmy Carter; President and Mrs. Donald Trump; and Vice Presidents Dan Quayle, Dick Cheney, Al Gore, and Joseph Biden and their wives. There would, of course, be members of the Senate and Congress and Supreme Court.

And then there were dignitaries from around the globe, many of whom felt a special friendship, if not kinship, with 41: the secretary-general of the United Nations António Guterres; Charles, Prince of Wales; prime minister of the UK John Major and his wife, Norma; president of Poland Andrzej Duda and the former president Lech Walesa, who worked with 41 to help forge democracy in the beleaguered nation after the collapse of the Soviet Union; chancellor of Germany Angela Merkel; king of Jordan Abdullah II and his wife, Queen Rania; prime minister of Japan Yasuo Fukuda; emir of Qatar Hamad bin Khalifa Al Thani; president of Estonia Toomas Hendrik Ilves; and prime minster of Kuwait Nasser Al-Mohammed Al-Sabah.

A total of over thirty-six hundred people attended the funeral service, and by the time it was over, a worldwide audience of over seventeen million people would watch it. But honestly, I did not want to know any of that. All I wanted to know was that the people were praying, not just for me, but for the service—and they were.

The night before the funeral, Laura and I were preparing for the day ahead. Keep in mind that the next day, we would leave the service at the National Cathedral, drive with the motorcade to Air Force One, and fly back to Houston—no dropping back by the hotel to pick up anything, so there was much to be pulled together!

As we were doing so, my cell phone rang, and it was Jon Meacham.

"Father."

"Jon, what's up?"

"How do I get into the cathedral?"

"Well, as you know, that is not my shop ... but I have Randy's number. I can call him. What's up?"

"I'd like to practice in that space before tomorrow."

"Let me check with Randy and I'll get back with you."

I hung up and called the dean, and he was more than willing to make whatever accommodations necessary for Jon—he gave me a few directions and I called Jon back. He thanked me and said he planned on going up to the church, going through his remarks, then smoking a cigar before praying the Evening Office.[7]

"Do you pray the Office daily?"

"If I can ... most days."

I was deeply impressed. Jon had publicly spoken as many times as, if not more than, the father with whom he was speaking. He had certainly done so before just as many distinguished crowds and had done an innumerable number of television interviews and yet he wanted to— *prayerfully*—rehearse before tomorrow and would not let the day end without the poetic, though efficacious, prayers of the Daily Office:

> Lord Jesus, stay with us, for evening is at hand and the day is past; be our companion in the way, kindle our hearts, and awaken hope, that we may know you as you are revealed in Scripture and the breaking of the bread. Grant this for the sake of your love. Amen.[8]

---

7. The Evening Office is the prayers and Scripture readings assigned at day's end in accordance with the Book of Common Prayer. It is practiced by many in and out of the Episcopal Church as a regular spiritual discipline.

8. Book of Common Prayer, 125.

Prior to the beginning of the funeral service, I was blessed to have two memorable moments of prayer. The first occurred on the heels of a well-needed smile.

Evidently, it is customary in such a funeral service for participating clergy to line up and greet the incoming presidents and first ladies. The presiding bishop of the Episcopal Church, Michael Curry, whom I had come to know since his election and to admire as he began living into the ministry required by his new role, was the chief clergyperson among us. He would participate in the service and offer the final blessing. He had visited a bit with Laura and me prior to the service when I was vesting in my robes.

Laura was ushered into her seat, to the left of the great stone lectern, which was left of the great Canterbury Pulpit of the National Cathedral. All participating clergy lined up and greeted the Clintons and Obamas. President Carter and First Lady Rosalynn had already been seated. We were waiting... and, well, waiting some more on our forty-fifth president.

It suddenly occurred to me that I was the only clergyperson in this line who would participate in the full service from beginning to end, accompany (mercifully with Laura) the funeral procession from the National Cathedral to Joint Base Andrews, and have another set of full military honors. As we waited on President Donald and First Lady Melania Trump, I leaned toward the verger, Scott Sanders, and said, "After we greet the president, I am going to have to make a pit stop." The presiding bishop leaned in and said, "Me too!"

We waited a bit more, the Trumps arrived, and we greeted the president and first lady, and then the presiding bishop and I hightailed it to the nearest restroom. We came out and found our place in the procession. There was still some waiting to do, and the presiding bishop came up and tugged my sleeve and said, "Let me pray for you."

"Absolutely."

He made the sign of the cross on my head and then prayed, addressing me as "my brother." He finished with a hearty "Amen" and then said, "Now... go preach the Gospel." I could hardly speak. Not because of who was praying for me but because God had sent what I needed in that moment—prayer. And really, George H. W. Bush made that happen—none of us would have been there were it not for him.

We walked together to the back to line up and wait for the arrival of the president's coffin into the narthex area of the church.[9] The clergy was a mixed bag. I have already shared that I am fairly conservative theologically. Most of the clergy at the National Cathedral are more progressive. The bishop Mariann Budde has certainly been widely recognized as one of the more liberal bishops in the Episcopal Church. We were all hunched together as Mike Wagner was giving us our final instructions. I was listening closely, and when he finished, I turned around and found Bishop Budde standing behind me, her eyes closed, her hands held over my back, praying for me. Whether or not this was the state funeral for a president, or if we were burying someone whom few if any knew—it was a wonderful reminder of how our faith can bring people together under the very large and expansive umbrella of God's love. George H. W. Bush had brought us together that day, but the God of all had as well, and that God was ever present.

We were all ready. By the time the coffin arrived on the steps of the National Cathedral, the great bell of the cathedral had tolled forty-one times. The congregation was seated as the presiding bishop received the body of "our brother George" and prayed that he would be raised to "perfection in the company of the saints."[10] Then Bishop Budde prayed for all who mourn, asking the Lord Jesus to grant them comfort, goodness, and peace.

And the service began, with the music and lessons we so carefully prepared and the tributes given one after another, like stairs lifting one to a climactic moment of celebration.

Jon Meacham asked the question that 41 had so often asked, but then Jon answered it as well, in such a way as to invite the thirty-six hundred gathered in that holy space to consider the ways of God:

---

9. The narthex is the area just outside the primary worship space in an Episcopal church, which is called the nave. In your home, the narthex would be your foyer.

10. Book of Common Prayer, 466.

And so we ask, as we commend his soul to God, and as he did, "Why him? Why was he spared?" The workings of Providence are mysterious, but this much is clear: that George Herbert Walker Bush, who survived that fiery fall into the waters of the Pacific three quarters of a century ago, made our lives and the lives of nations freer, better, warmer, nobler.

...That's why him. That's why he was spared.

The Right Honorable Brian Mulroney, the president's longtime friend and brother, revealed to those gathered that despite many of the scourges that life can throw your way, President Bush had endured them and had come out on the other side not bitter but better:

"Come with me." He led me down the porch at Walker's Point to the side of the house that fronts the ocean and pointed to a small, simple plaque that had been unobtrusively installed just some days earlier. It read C-A-V-U. George said, "Brian, this stands for 'ceiling and visibility unlimited.' When I was a terrified 18- to 19-year-old pilot in the Pacific, those...were the words we hoped to hear before takeoff. It meant perfect flying. And that's the way I feel about our life today, CAVU. Everything is perfect. Bar and I could not have asked for better lives. We are truly happy and truly at peace."

The president's longtime friend and political partner Wyoming senator Alan Simpson tracked the beginning of their relationship to 1962 and then lifted the spirits by speaking effusively of the president's humor, which revealed not his irreverence but his affection for everyone he met:

He never lost his sense of humor. Humor is the universal solvent against the abrasive elements of life...He never hated anyone. He knew what his mother and my mother always knew. Hatred corrodes the container it's carried in.

And then what for many, if not all, was the most moving moment in this service, our forty-third president rose and spoke so potently about the lessons he learned and the life he observed—not so much the president who was his father, but his father who was the president. As he came to a close, his head dropped a bit, his voice cracked, the tears flowed, and the entire cathedral—and I suspect the audience of millions around the world—was speechless:

> And we're going to miss you. Your decency, sincerity, and kind soul will stay with us forever. So through our tears, let us know the blessings of knowing and loving you, a great and noble man, the best father a son or daughter could have. And in our grief, let us smile knowing that Dad is hugging Robin and holding Mom's hand again.

I have seen grief do all kinds of things to people. It can make one irretrievably depressed. It can make another irrevocably angry. It offers a mystifying and endless path of unanswerable questions. And at times, when it is shared openly, honestly, brazenly, it can draw people together.

As the president finished his remarks for his father, the congregation broke out in applause, then cheers, and then they stood together. Our forty-third president had lifted the veil that almost every human being has had to carry, and the heartstrings of God's fragile earth, our island home—for a moment, if only for a moment—sang together.

Republicans, Democrats, independents, conservatives, liberals, moderates, Jews, Muslims, Christians, the weak and strong, the prideful and the humble for one brief, shining moment became as one and sang together. Applause was rendered for the attribute that stands above all others—love.

We had heard of historic significance, of friendship, of honorable character, and of familial love, but we had gathered in God's house, as was the wish of President Bush, and as is the tradition in an Episcopal church, the priest offers any final remarks before the close of the liturgy.

I will share my homily in the appendix, but I will offer one caveat. As you know from reading, most of my remarks were complete months before the president's death, but I kept thinking about a way to convey, as best I could, the presence of Jesus in and around us on the day 41 died.

Many things stood out, but in particular were Jim Baker rubbing the feet of his dear friend and then our long prayers at the end. I would not share that story without Jim's permission, so I emailed him through Susan. (Jim does not "do" email...or texts—he still has a flip phone for goodness' sake!) I asked how he felt about my sharing those last few minutes.

A few hours later, through Susan, Jim would email me back perhaps one of the most touching bits of correspondence I ever received from him:

> Of course you can use whatever you wish in your remarks at either or both of the services...
>
> I can't tell you what a source of comfort and strength you are to me and to Susan, and we love you very much. God bless you, Jim.

A few hours after the email, he called me from the car. I saw it was him and picked up the phone. "Hello, Mr. Secretary, how are you doing?"

"I'm fine. We actually went out to eat for some sushi."

He sounded good and I was glad they were getting out.

"Russ, it's fine with me if you want to talk about that...to use that story if you think it helps..."

"Well, I did not want to do anything without your permission."

"No, I'm fine with it."

We talked a bit more, and wished each other well, knowing we would be spending much more time together in the days ahead.

If you watched the service, you know that when I began speaking of that moment, the news cameras zeroed in on Jim. I had no idea—and I think neither did he—that when I talked about it, it would bring him to tears.

I will tell you, reading now, I have never watched this service or the one at St. Martin's from beginning to end. I have watched that moment, and while my heart sinks every time I see it, I am glad we decided together to use it, because it gave us a chance to talk about what it really means to be a disciple of Jesus—to preach Christ at all times, and if necessary, to use words.

Before the reading of the Gospel lesson from John, the Joint Armed Forces Chorus accompanied by the United States Marine Chamber Orchestra offered a moving rendition of "O God, Our Help in Ages Past," which is based upon the text of Psalm 90:1–5.

As they did, I got up from my seat and knelt behind the Canterbury Pulpit where no one but a few could see me, closed my eyes, and prayed that God would use my words:

> May my look be your look, my touch be your touch, my words be your words. In all that I do, may I decrease that you might increase in and through me. May only your word be spoken, and only your word heard. Help me, Lord Jesus, to honor George and to honor you, through Christ our Lord. Amen.

I made the sign of the cross over my chest and stood. As Dean Hollerith began to read the Gospel lesson, I sought to make eye contact with Laura, who was seated with the staff in the large transept to the left of the pulpit. I needed that connecting point just a moment before I offered my prayer and then my homily.

After it was over, we all had a chance to meditate and pray on all that had been said as Christian singer Michael W. Smith performed one of his own beautifully crafted pieces, "Friends." This was done at the president's request, and I was actually asked months before the service to listen to it and decide if it was appropriate for an Episcopal burial service. It was—and not just for an Episcopal burial service, but perhaps any service offered in the church:

> And friends are friends forever
> If the Lord's the Lord of them
> And a friend will not say never
> 'Cause the welcome will not end...[11]

As the service came to a close, we offered our allegiance to the historic faith by standing and saying the Apostles' Creed, and then we listened to Ronan Tynan fill that holy space with his pealing tenor voice as he sang "The Lord's Prayer."

After a bit more music, we moved into place. Bishop Budde, Randy, and I walked over to the coffin, held our hands above the remains of our friend and president, and commended him for all the world to see: "Into your hands, O merciful Savior, we commend your servant George."[12]

Bishop Curry blessed us, Randy dismissed us, and we left singing William Walsham How's celebratory hymn, "For All the Saints," reminding those gathered, and those watching,

> But lo! There breaks a yet more glorious day;
> The saints triumphant rise in bright array;
> The King of Glory passes on His way.
> Alleluia, alleluia![13]

---

11. "Friends," Michael W. Smith (b. 1957) and Deborah Kay Davis (b. 1958), arr. David Hamilton.

12. Book of Common Prayer, 483.

13. Words by William Walsham How (d. 1897); music: *sine nomine*, Ralph Vaughan Williams (d. 1958).

We departed the National Cathedral not thinking of death but speaking to it, as if we were echoing Paul's words, "O death, where is thy sting? O grave, where is thy victory?"[14] We left thinking not of death but of the victory beyond it, made possible by the gracious hand of our loving God.

And One More Thing before We Leave Washington...

For that all-too-short moment on a brisk December morning, in God's house that stood taller than all the seats of power in our nation's capital, the world came together. The world sang and wept and laughed and prayed and was reminded of the noble qualities of what truly makes a human, or a nation, great. The world witnessed the unmistakable qualities of a godlike life—civility, decency, humility, kindness, and love. And we did so at the invitation, and by the design, of George Herbert Walker Bush, who had now been received into the divine arms of mercy.

---

14. 1 Corinthians 15:55 (KJV).

CHAPTER SIXTEEN

AMEN

The steadfast love of the LORD never ceases, his mercies never come to an end; they are new every morning; great is your faithfulness.
                                        Lamentations 3:22–23 (NRSV)

We rejoice, Mister President, that you are safely tucked in, now and through the ages, with God's loving arms around you.
                    The Honorable James A. Baker III, funeral, St. Martin's Episcopal Church, Houston, Texas

There is but one just use of power, and it is to serve people. Help us to remember it, Lord. Amen.
                    The Honorable George H. W. Bush, the last words, as a prayer, of his inaugural address, January 20, 1989

And Back to Houston . . . Back to Home

When the service at the National Cathedral was over, the family who were coming to Houston, the Bush staff members, members of Mike Wagner's team, and members of the Secret Service began our procession to Joint Base Andrews. Laura and I rode in a heavily armored security vehicle and struck up a good conversation with the detail who were with us. As we began driving through the streets of Washington, they were struck by the number of people who were lined up along the streets—most with hands over hearts, many holding flags or posters, some saluting. It was impressive, but as I shared with these young men, it was nothing like what we would see back home in Texas.

Laura and I both said with certainty that the highways and byways in the president's adopted home state would be filled with untold numbers—a prediction that proved to be truer than we could have expected.

We arrived at the airfield. There was another set of honors, and then members of the United States Air Force Band played the haunting and yet most appropriate song—"Goin' Home," from Antonin Dvorak's ninth symphony. The lyrics that go with the music were written by Dvorak's student William Arms Fisher and were the perfect background in preparation for the flight home:

> Goin' home, goin' home, I'm a goin' home;
> Quiet-like, some still day, I'm jes' goin' home.
> It's not far, jes' close by,
> Through an open door;
> Work all done, care laid by,
> Goin' to fear no more.

There was a measure of relief as the doors were closed. I had been dressed in a black cassock and wanted to pull that off for the trip home. The security agent on board said I was welcome to go down into the hold below where our luggage was and stow it there if I wanted.

Having watched the film *Air Force One*, I was surprised that we were given the freedom to roam about in such a way. "Isn't there an escape pod down there?" I asked. (For the record, I will not tell.)

But Laura joined me, and after a rather long and exhausting two days, we both got a bit tickled as I was fiddling with my bag and we just took off! No announcement, no request to be seated or secure. We were headed home.

The flight back was full of activity. There was still a great deal of work to be done, primarily by Jim McGrath, Jean Becker, and the rest of the president's staff. A good many more family members flew back from DC than had flown up, so Laura and I were seated a bit farther back in the plane but still had the freedom to roam about as we did flying up. Governor Bush made a point to come back and find us and personally thank us.

A little while later, we walked back up to the conference room. We sat and talked with Bush 41's staff, Evan, Jon Meacham, and a few others, and then President Bush 43 came through. Someone—I cannot recall who—was commenting on the beauty and touching nature of the service, and the president asked, "Well...have you ever heard the St. Martin's choir?"

"No," the person said.

"Just wait—you are in for a real treat!"

With some measure of humility, I would have to certainly agree!

As we got closer to Houston, it was clear we were dropping in altitude—quickly—when Mike Wagner let us know we were going to do a flyover above the Bush library in College Station. It was quite a moment as this gigantic office building in the sky descended to about fifteen hundred feet—so close we could see the cheering crowd below—then went back up for the last little bit before touching down on Ellington Field.

In that last thirty minutes or so, Laura and I found a small conference room and sat by ourselves. We were exhausted. Thinking of the very public life and nonstop schedule that a president and his or her team had to keep, I said, "I absolutely do not know how anyone does this."

"Me neither," Laura said. "I am whipped."

"We have only been at this for about a week...Can you imagine living this way?"

"No." Laura smiled. "So don't ever get any ideas about going into politics!"

Mike came and fetched me—there would be another set of honors and I was to walk with the president's coffin from Air Force One to the waiting hearse. About 4:30 p.m., once everyone was in place on the tarmac yet again, we were treated to the beautiful music from the hymn "Abide with Me," played by the 77th Army Band from Fort Sill, Oklahoma. It was Henry Francis Lyte who later added the words to this ancient monastic tune:[1]

> Abide with me, fast falls the eventide;
> The darkness deepens; Lord, with me abide.
> When other helpers fail and comforts flee,
> Help of the helpless, O abide with me.

It is a beautiful hymn that invites God's presence when it is sorely needed...and we would need that presence as the evening and day ahead unfolded.

We made our way to St. Martin's and were once again greeted with musical honors. Members of the United States Air Force Band of the West from Lackland Air Force Base in San Antonio set the tone with Isaac Watts's hymn "O God, Our Help in Ages Past."[2]

The "holy ground" that began this journey was still with us, and the roving chapel designed by the president and his family was an audible and visible reminder that the Judeo-Christian faith of the president was not superfluous to his life but central. That was evident as we now, family and the clergy team, helped bring his remains into his home church for the very last time.

I received his body as we received it in Washington. The family had a brief moment of silence and prayer before we opened the doors of St. Martin's to a visitation wherein the body of the president would lie in repose from 6:00 p.m. until 6:00 a.m. the next morning.

---

1. D. 1847.

2. Watts died in 1748 and is considered one of the greatest hymn writers in the Christian faith, writing some 750 hymns during his lifetime.

As was the case with Barbara's visitation, vestry members, parish leaders, the St. Martin's clergy team, and other staff members took hourly shifts for the twelve hours that followed. People who wished to visit began at Second Baptist, many waiting hours for their opportunity to pay their respects.

By the morning of December 6, over eleven thousand people had come through the doors of St. Martin's. And as with Barbara's visitation only months before, it was the great tapestry of humankind who made this journey—African American, white, Asian, Hispanic, and Native American; Christians, Muslims, Sikhs, Jews, Buddhists, and I suspect some who did not believe at all. In twelve hours, with thousands of visitors, we did not have one incident that was cause for concern. Those coming and going and waiting were respectful from beginning to end. This was the Houston family. This was a Houston moment. It was a beautiful, reverent, and uplifting experience for everyone involved.

The Last Big Good-Bye

The church was closed, and over the next few hours there was yet again one large security sweep of the campus and church. The president's remains were moved off the platform and taken to the back of the church to be prepared for the procession into the nave.

Laura and I arrived very early—hours before the service. As she did for Barbara's funeral, Laura donned black and joined the sisters of St. Martin's altar guild to serve the many duties behind the scenes.

We had the preselected guest artists—the Oak Ridge Boys and Reba McEntire—who would be singing during the service. I think perhaps everyone at that point was looking for a bit of humor. We had "held" the Oaks and Ms. McEntire in a makeshift greenroom. The Reverend Peter Cheney and his wife, Kiki, were back in Houston, where he would assist in the service, and Peter and I were asked to go take a photo with the artists. As we lined up, I learned Reba had performed in Las Vegas the night before and had flown all night to get there. One would never have known it, as she looked fresh as a daisy, and the rest of us—Peter, the Oak Ridge Boys, and me—well, we pretty much looked like old soldiers. So as we lined up, I suggested Reba be in the middle and the rest of us surround her. Before the photographer snapped his photo, I said, "A blossom between the opossums…"

"I've never heard that one before," Reba said, which ushered us all into an appropriately "fitted" smile for the photo.

Keep in mind that most of the national and international dignitaries had paid their respects in Washington. This would be a "homecoming," so most of the guests were Texas friends, associates, government officials, and religious leaders.

A number of athletes who knew and loved the Bushes and were loved by them attended, including Baseball Hall of Famers Tommy Lasorda of the Los Angeles Dodgers, and Astros players Craig Biggio and Jeff Bagwell; NBA player Yao Ming of the Houston Rockets; and professional football player J. J. Watt. Country singers Larry Gatlin and Crystal Gayle were in the congregation, as were the actor Chuck Norris and the actress Teri Hatcher. Unbeknownst to me until later, the actor and former governor of California, Arnold Schwarzenegger, also attended.

On the front row of the church, in front of the pulpit, I noticed our governor, Greg Abbott; our mayor, Sylvester Turner; and next to them, several religious leaders from various denominations. I took a moment to go over and greet them, but particularly, I wanted the religious clerics from a variety of faiths and traditions to know they were welcome to St. Martin's, so I greeted each one by one with a handshake.

A bit later, some of my clergy told me they had met Governor Schwarzenegger, but I had missed him. "Where did he go?" I asked.

"He is sitting on the front row with the clergy."

I peeked back in the church. He was sporting a full beard at the time, and frankly, the Terminator was a lot shorter than I imagined. I went back and told the clergy, "I met him…I just thought he was an orthodox priest!"

Again, thanks to Barbara, the St. Martin's team was ready—and they were outstanding. As Marty Bastian, the vice rector, told me, while I was away in Washington, the prevailing effort of nearly two hundred staff members at St. Martin's was to honor the president, his faith, and our Lord. Everyone had worked so hard, and that was evident from the moment I returned to campus.

All the years of planning and preparation paid off. And honestly, the heaviness of the previous week had been lifted. There were lots of smiles and hugs and laughs as people came into this holy space where the president and Barbara had worshipped for over half a century.

> Lots o' folk gather'd there,
> All the friends I knew,
> All the friends I knew.
> Home, I'm goin' home!

Indeed, he was coming home to his friends. By 10:00 a.m., the family arrived and the service began. President Bush was right—the music *was* glorious. But in many ways, the remarks offered, first by Secretary Baker and then by 41's grandson, George P. Bush, were simply perfect for this "hometown" crowd.

I knew, after what had happened during the service in Washington, that this was not easy for the president's best friend, but it was a noble task and no one was better suited to it.

Jim, like President Bush, has a wonderful sense of humor. The secretary had been on Air Force One on our flight back from DC to Houston. He was doing his best to keep his spirits up. Secretary Baker and the forty-third president were actually in a small conference room near the front of the aircraft as we neared Houston. He evidently slipped his finger against a piece of metal, which made a small cut. He began bleeding and then jokingly made something more of it than necessary—if only to lighten the mood.

Rear Admiral Ronny Jackson, who was physician to both the

forty-fourth and forty-fifth presidents, was on board with us, and Secretary Baker began to yell out to him. "Ronny, I've cut myself on Air Force One! You need to get a Band-Aid for me...I am wounded here!" Then a moment later, he said, "I'm going to sue!" Honestly, it was a moment we all needed. It provided one of the few smiles in those last moments before we returned to Houston.

But when he stepped up to give his remarks before the "Houston family," one could have heard a pin drop. Here was the man who, outside of 41's wife and family, knew President Bush better than anyone and missed him. But the former secretary of state did not shrink back from the spiritual context in which his words would be offered.

> My friends, we're here today in the house of the Lord to say goodbye to a man of great faith and great integrity...
>
> For more than 60 years, George...has been my friend, and he's been my role model.

And then he spoke an irrefutable truth about his good friend:

> ...As history will faithfully record, he became one of our nation's finest presidents, and beyond any doubt, our nation's very best one-term president...

Then Jim spoke of 41's undeniable traits:

> ...They expressed his moral character, and they reflected his decency, his boundless kindness and consideration of others, his determination always to do the right thing, and always to do that to the very best of his ability. They testify to a noble life, well lived.

If you read or heard those words, you know what they aspired to do: honor the president, lift up his example of life, and unapologetically celebrate his faith, which Jim did with crystal clarity in those last words. On behalf of the president's friends sitting in the pews, his friends across America and throughout the world, the former secretary of state's voice began to tremble and his emotion touched us all as he said, "We rejoice, Mr. President, that you are safely tucked in now and through the ages, with God's loving arms around you."

Here, we had no political speech, no effort to sway the listeners' ideology one way or another—just a pure, unfettered celebration of this man and the Christian hope.

It would be easy, as Jean Becker suggested when we were all thinking of how many people would have spoken after these many days, to believe all that needed to be said had been said. But I can tell you from sitting there in that moment that I am not sure anyone wanted this service to end. It was as if we were peering into a kaleidoscope that turn after turn revealed one beautiful image after another. And this was so well crystalized in the remarks of that last layperson to speak, the president's grandson and an elected official in the great state of Texas, George P. Bush.

> Gampy once said: "God is good, but His love has a cost: We must be good to one another." It was his faith and his love for others that drove him, that fulfilled him, and that led him to a calling in public life.

After all of the gatherings, attention, and public and private moments over the last seven days, the message of ninety-four years of life poured out for the sake of others was even more fully solidified in these last few words: "It was his faith and his love for others that drove him."

I knew I was last up to bat, and I did not want those present or those watching to miss the great hope that had already been suggested by the secretary and 41's grandson—our Christian faith. You will find my words in the appendix of this book.

We were, in fact, "home," and the feeling in that holy space was one of home.

The congregation loved hearing the Oaks and Reba. The music was indeed glorious, seen visibly in the forty-third president's response to the St. Martin's choir's rendition of "The Battle Hymn of the Republic." As they sang those wonderful words, "Glory, glory, hallelujah...," George W. Bush could hardly contain himself—smiling, rocking back and forth, singing along with many others in the crowd. In a very atypical response for stoic Episcopalians, the congregants broke out in applause at the conclusion.

The service came to a close, and we again departed this holy place, as we did only seven months ago with Barbara's remains—as the congregation belted out "Onward, Christian Soldiers."

"Nothin' Lost, All's Gain, No More Fret nor Pain...Goin' Home..."

When we, once again, gathered with clergy and immediate family in the narthex, 43 made his way around the space, and as he stepped up to me and thanked me, I held up my watch as I did after Bar's funeral and said, "Under ninety minutes, sir." He smiled and patted me on the back. The press was, as they were before with Bar's service, piled aplenty outside the doors of the church. Remembering our extended departure after Bar's service, I was a bit on pins and needles to make sure we lined up the procession and got out to the motorcade in a timely way.

I am not sure who the fine young marine was who was assigned to come alongside and give me some directions about "waiting until just the right moment," but as he was talking, Evan came up behind me and said, "Forty-Three says it's time to go..."

The marine was still talking when I gently said to him, "The commander in chief just said it's time to go, so we're going to go now..." I think I heard a "But..." as we made our way out the doors, but I was not going to disobey that order!

So, out we went, and once again, from St. Martin's all the way to Spring, Texas, people lined the roads with signs, hats and caps pulled off, hands over hearts or held up in salute. It is no exaggeration to say there were tens of thousands.

As we arrived in Spring, we loaded onto the custom-made Union Pacific 4141. A gentle rain had begun, but the mood aboard was buoyant. The crowd made up of family, very close friends, the Bush staff, and some members of the press settled aboard. While many of us older folk had traveled long distances by train, many of the younger crowd had not, and they were fascinated.

The locomotive had been painted blue and gray to look similar to Air Force One. Once we got a brief orientation, off we went, but we were to pass through five small Texas towns over the next two and a half hours.

No sooner had we pulled out of Spring, Texas, than we were all treated to what could only be described as a living, breathing tribute to 41. Myriads of supporters lined the tracks—thicker through the towns, of course, but there was never an unbroken moment when you could not look out and see dozens upon dozens of God's children offering their own farewell to their Texas brother. As we passed through a rather barren field, there were several cowboys on horseback, hats to the side, hands over hearts. Children waved flags; adults held signs. Still others stood with the aid of walkers or rolled up as close as possible in their wheelchairs. The good people of Texas, and throngs of others who came from states around, seemed incapable of missing this moment.

Those who designed 4141 converted its sixth car from a baggage hauler called Council Bluffs into a car with transparent sides to allow the multitudes of mourners a chance to view the president's flag-draped coffin.

About 3:30 p.m. the train arrived, welcomed by the Singing Cadets of Texas A&M singing "Mansions of the Lord," the lyrics of which were written by film producer Randall Wallace, who was a descendant of well-known Scottish hero William Wallace. It was a battle tune, though it offered a reminder that all soldiers are to be brought to the care of the Lord at the end of their earthly journey.

> To fallen soldiers let us sing
> Where no rockets fly nor bullets wing
> Our broken brothers let us bring
> To the Mansions of the Lord[3]

Indeed, whether those present knew it or not, the roving chapel continued to move on.

Then the last hour began. For days now, everything had been moving toward this moment. Though we had seen it on the day of Barbara's funeral, we were just as struck with awe as we pulled onto the campus and hundreds of members of the Texas A&M University Corps of Cadets lined the motorcade along Barbara Bush Drive as we approached the library complex.

We arrived at the library about 4:15 p.m., and the United States Air Force Band of the West again set the perfect tone by playing John Bacchus Dykes's beautiful tune to accompany Reginald Heber's lyrics, "Holy, Holy, Holy."[4]

If ever there was a time we were standing in the circle of the Holy Trinity, it was now.

"No More Stumbling on the Way, No More Longing for the Day..."

Though this moment was much like the last hour of Barbara's funeral, there was a difference that was hard to describe. Only months before, the president had been there with us as we made that journey from the

---

3. The song was written for the 2002 film *We Were Soldiers* and was also sung at President Reagan's funeral.

4. Written in 1861. Dykes died in 1876.

library to the place of burial. Now, Bar and the president were both gone from our sight, but not gone.

I suspect most of us were thinking the same kinds of things as the motorcade came to a stop on the plaza between the library and school buildings. The president was being welcomed by our Lord, by those he so loved, and by so many others who were part of the strands woven throughout his life, and they were now, by God's grace, reuniting in life in its most abundant and eternal form. Thus, our grief was coupled with a measure of comfort and peace.

As I wrote in that letter to the president some years before, we believers in the Resurrection actually know very little about what that life will be like. But it does not hurt—and it is, in fact, helpful—to capture images from this world to help unveil some of what rests beyond this life.

In that moment, I imagined the president—without the physical barriers that had become so much a part of his daily life—stretching out those long arms and taking hold of his loved ones in those large, beefy, and now restored hands. His voice strong, clear, loud—free from any hindrance caused by physical health, now healed and made whole—whispering, perhaps, "Barbara...Robin...Mother...Dad...Bucky... Pres...Sadie...Millie."

As the coffin was removed from the hearse and placed on the bier, honors were rendered. One memory that has stuck with me was the weather. For most of that last day, it was gloomy, misting rain on and off, and the president's coffin was covered in a large plastic tarp. The metaphor of a world weeping was not too hard to stir up.

Then we were witnesses to a first-time-ever salute. A military flyover is sometimes part of a memorial service for a deceased veteran. But in President Bush's case, the United States Navy flyover on the day of his burial was the largest of its kind in history. A total of twenty-one F/A-18 Hornets and Super Hornets from the Naval Air Station in Oceana, Virginia, flew directly over us. And then, as is the tradition, one of the jets left the formation to signify the death of an aviator—in this case, the forty-first president, whose name was painted on the side of the aircraft, along with "Barbara, First Lady."

As we began these last few steps with our president, Father Peter Cheney, a navy chaplain, and I walked behind an American flag, carried by a soldier, and in front of the president's casket as the United States Air Force Band of the West played the hymns "I Need Thee Every Hour" and "How Firm a Foundation."[5] President Bush 43 and First Lady Laura followed, then the other children and grandchildren. The interment was to be a private gathering, with the only exceptions being Jon Meacham and Jean Becker.

As we arrived at the burial site, the United States Army Chorus began to sing "God of Our Fathers," a fitting hymn to remind us that despite the grief of the moment, there is more for the faithful soldier of God:

Refresh Thy people on their toilsome way,
Lead us from night to never-ending day;
Fill all our lives with love and grace divine,
And glory, laud, and praise be ever Thine[6]

As their voices closed in perfect unison, I offered a prayer to consecrate the grave:

O God, whose blessed Son was laid in a sepulcher in the garden: Bless, we pray, this grave and grant that he whose body is to be buried here may dwell with Christ in paradise,

---

5. "I Need Thee" was written by Annie Sherwood Hawks (d. 1918), but the authorship of "How Firm" remains a mystery, though it was used during the funerals of Presidents Teddy Roosevelt and Woodrow Wilson.

6. Written by Episcopal priest Daniel C. Roberts (d. 1907).

and may come to your heavenly kingdom; through your Son Jesus Christ our Lord. Amen.[7]

And then, commending George H. W. Bush to the eternal care of God and the heavenly companionship of Barbara, all of his loved ones, and all of God's resurrected children, I offered these words:

In the sure and certain hope of the resurrection to eternal life through our Lord Jesus Christ, we commend to Almighty God our brother George.[8]

Peter led us in the Lord's Prayer, adding one of the beautiful prayers from the Episcopal burial liturgy: "O heavenly Father, grant that we, who now serve thee on earth, may at last...be partakers of the inheritance of the saints in light."[9]

I have actually been present at the burial of many veterans over the years and have experienced the pealing tunes of a final graveside twenty-one-gun salute, but none was more moving and powerful than the one that followed Peter's words: "May his soul, and the souls of all the departed, through the mercy of God, rest in peace. Amen."[10]

The wonderful St. Martin's team had produced a graveside bulletin and had wisely and thoughtfully included a lovely photo of the president and Bar seated between their five children on the wall that overlooks the Atlantic at Walker's Point, only steps away from the president's little bronze plaque that reads CAVU. I watched these same five jolt just a bit with each successive round of reports.

I then offered one more prayer before the final blessing for the family.

---

7. Book of Common Prayer, 503.

8. Book of Common Prayer, 501.

9. Book of Common Prayer, 486.

10. Book of Common Prayer, 486.

Afterward, I stepped back next to Peter as nearby we heard three volleys of musketry, followed by a United States Navy Band bugler playing taps.

The United States Army Chorus then blessed us all with a soft, somber, and moving rendition of "Eternal Father, Strong to Save."[11] Also known as "The Navy Hymn," written by the English hymnist William Whiting, it is a plea for God's presence to always watch over his soldiers and God's steadfast promise to hold them for all eternity...

> The soul that on Jesus has leaned for repose,
> I will not, I will not, desert to its foes;
> That soul, though all hell should endeavor to shake,
> I'll never, no never, no never forsake

The American flag that had been draped over the president's coffin since we began the journey a week ago was now folded carefully into a firm triangle and handed to Doro.

> On behalf of the President of the United States and a grateful nation, please accept this flag as a symbol of our appreciation for your loved one's honorable and faithful service.

Peter and I went and stood with Jon and Jean as the family began to hug and hold one another, each passing for a moment to place their hand on 41's coffin.

Peter and I were thanked, and then, as I did before, I waited until everyone had gone and walked back over to the coffin, where I knelt one last time in prayer, in remembrance, and in thanksgiving for this, my president, this member of St. Martin's, this brother in Christ, and my friend. Amen.

---

11. Whiting, d. 1878.

Shadows gone, break o' day,

Real life jes' begun.

There's no break, there's no end,

Jes' a-livin' on;

Wide awake, with a smile

Goin' on and on.

Goin' home, goin' home, I'm jes' goin' home,

Goin' home, goin' home, goin' home.

CHAPTER SEVENTEEN

A FUNERAL SHARED AROUND THE WORLD

The foolish fear death as the greatest of evils, the wise desire it as a rest after labors and the end of ills.

Ambrose of Milan

I have been to a number of State Funerals over the years, and I have never been to one that had a message that was so far reaching . . . It was an Episcopal Service . . . it was about faith and hope . . . but the symbolic importance of washing the feet which goes back to the days of Jesus obviously, I think for a lot of people was the distillation of a message we all need to hear.

Tom Brokaw, NBC journalist, December 5, 2018

Thank you for your inspired messages for President George H. W. Bush. Now many more have heard the Gospel of Jesus Christ.

Karlene Shea, widow of George Beverly Shea,
December 4, 2018

America at Its Best

As occurred after the funeral of Barbara Bush, within hours of President Bush's funeral I began receiving text messages from family and friends and emails from church members and strangers; and then within a week, I began to receive literally hundreds of letters and bits of correspondence.

Each person who wrote spoke of how they were inspired not just by the worship services (though many, if not most, mentioned that) but also by the testimonies about the forty-first president. In addition, one letter after another referenced that in those historic few days the nation and world were reminded of better times, when civility, decency, and unity were the hallmarks of our nation's leadership.

Allow me to share portions of just some of the words I received as the dust settled and the page of history turned. Almost all of these were addressed to me, so I will forgo the salutations. It is the meat of the words that speak.

December 8, 2018

I watched closely...I was moved and uplifted...

The Reverend Penelope
Edison, New Jersey

December 6, 2018

I don't normally reach out or write to people I don't know or politicians as such. However, after watching both ceremonies for 41, they were truly moving...beautiful...

...I turned 18 the year 41 was running for President and have to say I was heavily influenced by friends and did not vote for him ☺. I did however vote for W. and have always been struck by the Bushes' humanness and morality. Although I am not really a person of faith, I can see how it has shaped that family and have great respect for them...

Karen
Boise, Idaho

December 7, 2018

    The service in Washington brought me to tears. It encapsulated a great man...the faces of those who were in attendance gave proof that [the] message of love found its mark...

Jeff

Houston, Texas

December 5, 2018

    Watching the Bush Funeral here in London...a real gem and help in so many ways, for so many reasons...

The Reverend Canon Tim

London, England

January 7, 2019

    ...Having watched both the State funeral in Washington, D.C. and the service at St. Martin's Episcopal Church in Houston of President George H. W. Bush...what moving and dignified services for a great son of America...

Shaun

Port Elizabeth, South Africa

December 10, 2018

    The funeral services for our Dearest late President Bush... magnificent...inspirational time with our needy nation...I am praying that with all the good things said and seen of God's people—that our nation will take notice of the good example and act upon it...

Sister Mary

Charleston, South Carolina

December 10, 2018

    A few years ago when you kindly hosted me as a guest preacher at St. Martin's, we had a nice visit about the experience of officiating at a Presidential funeral. Last Wednesday ... far exceeded any thoughts I may have shared.

What impressed me especially was that your homily, or at least its conclusion, must have been written no more than a few days before it was delivered. What you said went right to the heart. Jim Baker was weeping when you told of his rubbing the feet of his friend, as I admit was I while watching on television.

Your homily was an important gift, not only to the family, but also to our country. Thank you, Russ, for preaching the Gospel so powerfully at a critical time for a nation in need.

Jack Danforth[1]
St. Louis, Missouri

December 15, 2018
... Beautiful!

The Honorable Rick Scott, governor of Florida

December 7, 2018
... Wonderful job of capturing another side of President Bush...

Even Barbara Bush would say it was good and the right length!!

Kay Bailey Hutchinson,
United States ambassador to NATO

---

1. The Honorable Jack Danforth is an Episcopal priest, a former United States senator from Missouri, and a former United States ambassador to the United Nations.

December 31, 2018
Dear Russ...

Thanks for everything you did for both our beloved parents. You were with both of them when it mattered most.

Marvin[2]

Not too long after the president's death, the Miller Center, a presidential think tank at the University of Virginia, produced an outstanding documentary on the accomplishments of President Bush and his team in four short years. *Statecraft: The Bush 41 Team* includes a number of interviews with members of the president's cabinet, along with photos and video recordings capturing his world-changing policies and the fruit they bore for the betterment of the world community. It ends with reflections on his funeral.

In the documentary, the late Colin Powell, the president's chairman of the Joint Chiefs of Staff, was brazenly honest about the grief in the moment:

> For all of us who were part of the team at one point or another, it was a very sad moment, and there were a lot of tears; even us hard-core infantry guys were tearing up because he was such a great guy.

No question the grief was palpable, but I know the president wanted the services to lift the spirits of those watching, and it was heartwarming to hear the president's vice president, the Honorable Dan Quayle, offer his experience:

---

2. From Marvin Bush—one of the most moving letters I received. Knowing this is how the family felt was a gift to me—because it only happened because the president and Bar had been there for us so many times when it mattered most to us.

The funeral was extraordinary...Everyone was there... leaders from around the world...And the spirit of that funeral was just uplifting...no bickering...no partisanship... no cheap shots...all just celebrating the wonderful life of George Herbert Walker Bush.

Former secretary of state Condoleezza Rice, who served as part of the national security team during President Bush's years, suggested that the gathering at the National Cathedral was, in many ways, a distillation of what was truly great about our nation. She took note that German chancellor Angela Merkel was in the congregation:

And I walked up to her and said, "Chancellor, you honor us by being here." She said, "I had to come for my country. Without President Bush, we would never have unified." And I thought it was the ultimate testament to the way he had conducted this. In fact, the Germans flew their flag at half-staff when George H. W. Bush died. And it said to me, this is America at its best.[3]

No one could disagree with any of these three statements—the gathering was sad, but it was inspirational and uplifting. And as Secretary Rice said, it was in many ways a reminder and a revelation about "America at its best."

Indeed, I think it was.

---

3. Lori Shinseki, producer and director, *Statecraft: The Bush 41 Team* (Richmond: Virginia Public Media and the Miller Center, the University of Virginia, 2020).

And the Forty-Third President Took Time to Pen a Handwritten Note

December 7, 2018

Dear Russ,

The services for Dad were great. Your remarks (two in two days) were perfect. The Cathedral Service was nice; the St. Martin's service was emotional and beautiful. Thank you!

You and Laura have been great caretakers to my parents. What a kind gift!

God bless,

George Bush

An Invitation from the Family ... That Was Accepted

The letters I have included here are only a small sampling of those I received. Many asked for copies of the service bulletins or the remarks or homilies offered. Some asked for sources for the music or liturgy (that was an easy request—the Episcopal Book of Common Prayer), and still others just sent a word of thanks. A few, actually, still stay in touch.

I wrote back every single person without exception and tried to respond to every request.

But as I have looked back over all the words shared from places near and far, one letter sticks out for me in particular. It was from a retired United Methodist pastor who lived in Otsego, Michigan, at the time. He wrote,

I am a retired United Methodist pastor in Michigan ... My wife remarked, "The Bush family brought our nation and world to church today!"

The Service of Resurrection lifted our spirits to God, gave God the glory and left us feeling more hopeful for the future

of our nation...especially [the] reference to Christ wash-
ing the disciples' feet as a symbol of service so well demon-
strated in the life of our late President...

Reverend Dan
Otsego, Michigan

It is not an exaggeration to say that hardly a day has gone by since the spring and winter of 2018 when I have not thought of my friends, the forty-first president and his lovely wife, Barbara. And the same is true of their funeral services.

It is good to know all the years of planning and preparation did, in fact, accomplish all that the Bushes had hoped—a moment to come together, to weep, to laugh, to remember, to worship, to recall the vital importance of friends, family, and faith, and to, when all was said and done, experience the presence of God. Indeed, is that not what is supposed to happen in gathered houses of worship?

CHAPTER EIGHTEEN

THE HOLE FOR YOU AND ME TO FILL

I appeal to you therefore, brothers and sisters, by the mercies of God, to present your bodies as a living sacrifice.

Romans 12:1 (NRSV)

You cannot be president of the United States if you don't have faith.

President George H. W. Bush

Love to you . . .

Barbara Bush

"Some have said this is an end of an era," Bush's pastor, the Reverend Dr. Russell Jones Levenson, Jr. *said during his eulogy in Washington. "But it doesn't have to be. Perhaps this is an invitation to fill the void that has been left behind." We can only hope. Because this moment is haunted by a curious and sobering duality. Some people mourn for George H.W. Bush, yes. But some of us mourn for America, too.*

Leonard Pitts, columnist, The Miami Herald, *December 8, 2021*

So...Why?

In that decade-plus of service and friendship with George H. W. and Barbara Bush, I often found myself asking, *What am I doing here?*

What on earth was I doing reading the sports section of the paper with the forty-first president, his cabinet member Brent Scowcroft, and a Chinese official on a breezy morning at Walker's Point in Kennebunkport, Maine? What on earth was I doing at a country club with my wife, having drinks with the president and first lady and the 103rd archbishop of Canterbury and his wife as they waxed on about a past G7 summit celebration at Buckingham Palace? Why was I there on a grandstand at the invitation of the president to pray at the tenth-anniversary celebration of his presidential library? Why had he invited me to his office, along with my young son, to meet with potential presidential candidate Governor Mitt Romney? Why did Laura and I get to sit with the president and Jim and Susan Baker during a crucial moment in American/Jewish/Palestinian relations and take in their reflections on all they accomplished in that arena in four short years? And why...why was I with both Bar and the president when they took their last breaths on this earth?

Because...

Because a witness has a responsibility to do two things. The first is to observe; and the second is, when given the opportunity, to convey those observations in such a way that it clearly reveals the truth.

I was not invited into many of these moments because of who I was or because of any qualifications I brought to the table or contribution of insight or wisdom I could impart. I know now, looking back, that by the grace of God and the compelling way in which circumstances can place anyone at a specific place and time for a reason, that the reason for all of this was to allow me to serve as a witness—a witness to observe, and a witness to tell that from the first moment of our relationship to the last moments of the same, and everything in between—a witness to *dignity*.

The three great Abrahamic faiths—Judaism, Christianity, and Islam—believe that all dignity is derived from God, because God created humans in his image.[1] In other words, dignity is a "godlike" quality.

I invited someone whose counsel I take seriously to read an early draft of parts of this book, and he said to me, "You make them out to be almost perfect...but of course, they were not." I cannot argue with my honest critic's assessment, of course. Forty-One and Barbara were not perfect—they, like all of us, had their moments. But honestly, when it comes to authentic lives of dignity, they were about as close as any two people I have ever known in my sixty-plus years of life.

Here you have in your hands the story of these two incredible people who were reared in the Christian faith. And while there were certainly moments that would challenge their faith—even test it—they never abandoned it.

When the youngest navy pilot in history was shot down by enemy fire over the Pacific Ocean, his question was not "Why me?" but "Why did God spare me?" When World War II ended, the young navy airman and his new bride delayed their celebration until they could find a vacant church to go in and offer their prayers of gratitude.

When Robin was diagnosed with and fighting leukemia, the future president never doubted God's existence and prayed daily for the healing of his daughter. And for Barbara, brushing her dear Robin's hair when she died was one of the most intense encounters she ever had with God. They agonized over the death of their daughter, but unlike many who travel that path of woe, they continued to hold fast to God and to one another.

The Bushes would rely on regular prayer as a source for guidance and strength. Such prayer became a lifeline that would prepare 41 and sustain him as he entered the Oval Office with an honest assessment of his need: "You cannot be president of the United States if you don't have faith." It was that same lifeline to which he turned after a bruising

---

1. Genesis 1:26ff.

defeat that returned him to Houston. "The way I got through that time," he said, was by drawing on the strength of family, friends, and his faith.

For the president and Bar, church was not only a holy place but a central place. "Worship is central to our life" is something that he and Barbara would not only say but prove with their regular attendance at churches around the globe when they traveled. Or in Washington during their years of service there. Or in Maine where they vacationed, or in Houston—the place they called home. I have often told new and longtime members of St. Martin's who wrestled with coming to church on a weekly basis that, in the years I served as their rector, unless the Bushes were ill or traveling, they were in church at St. Martin's, so I would ask those listening, why not follow their lead?

In their later years, they did not let mobility or pride get in the way of going to church. The president went from standing upright on the way to his favorite pew to using a cane, then a walker, then a wheelchair. Barbara, as she was able, was always at his side, and in her last years, when her back often gave her trouble, she would take one of the prayer books in the pew back and place it somewhere between L1 and L5 on her lower spine to give her the strength and support she needed to make it through the entire worship service. And if there was a special event, speaker, or concert, there they were—present before, during, and after, always making a point to greet new faces and spend time with church family members.

In my business, we clergy types talk about the "three Ts" of personal sacrifice: time, talent, and treasure. The apostle Paul counseled the earliest Christians to be "living sacrifices," pouring out their lives in such a way as to bless others.[2] And he would write to the members of the church in Ephesus, "For we are God's handiwork, created in Christ Jesus to do good works, which God prepared in advance for us to do."[3]

---

2. Romans 12:1.

3. Ephesians 2:10.

This kind of understanding of the Christian faith was a driving force in virtually every policy decision the president made. His question was not whether it was the "politically astute" thing to do or the "popular" thing to do or the "most personally advantageous" thing to do, but whether it was the right thing to do.

When he led a coalition of nearly thirty nations into war, he turned not only to strategy but to theology, seeking counsel from clergy and the ancient historical framework for "just war" devised by the church father Augustine of Hippo. Prior to almost every major decision he had to make as president, he would gather his staff—anyone who would join him—for prayers in the White House, or in nearby St. John's in Lafayette Square.

In 1990, when President Bush made the decision to break the "no new taxes" promise he made at the 1988 GOP convention, many in his inner circle said it would be the kiss of death. Years later, he would say in public and in private, "It was the right thing to do then, and I still believe it was the right thing to do."

The president was driven not by power but by principle, not by self-serving ideology but by sacrifice and service to others. Indeed, he fully lived his life's motto: "There can be no definition of a successful life that does not include service to others."

Barbara did not follow his lead—she was in lockstep with him. Her causes in every arena were to benefit and bless the lives of others. When the nation was cowering in fear over the spread of the AIDS virus, Barbara took sufferers in her arms. She never doubted the power of literacy. Laura and I often heard her say in public and private, "If you help a person to read, then their opportunities in life will be endless." And that belief was the driving force behind a foundation that has made literacy a reality for untold millions of people around the world.

She opened her home and her arms to people of every color, language, and faith tradition. She was a hostess extraordinaire to kings and queens, prime ministers and presidents, and to neighbors and craftsmen, lobstermen and clergy.

She spent endless hours with her Saintly Stitchers, crafting kneelers for the church she so loved and supported. And she lovingly pushed her rector and priest each year to increase giving from the church to outreach agencies that served the hungry, poor, homeless, and needy of the greater Houston community. In the eleven years that we knew each other, St. Martin's supported various outreach and mission initiatives to the tune of almost $30 million, with an annual commitment of roughly 25 percent of its overall budget to be given beyond the doors of the parish.

Yes, they gave of their time and their talent. They also gave of their treasure—sacrificially and generously—yearly to support the ministries of the churches that had supported them, and they stood behind and supported every capital campaign and building project in the history of their homes of worship.

And as they grew older, their desire to pray only grew. Their literal and spiritual hunger to receive that eternal meal that Jesus bid to "do in remembrance" of him became for them, as Jesus promised, the bread of life.[4]

The ancient church father John Chrysostom, whose figure is etched into the great pulpit of St. Martin's and whose preaching and teaching ability afforded him the nickname of "the golden tongue," once wrote, "Faithfulness in little things is a big thing."[5]

In the commitment to owning and living their faith, the president and Barbara were, within the best of human limits, faithful in virtually all things.

How?

I think a fair question at this point might be "How?" How did 41 and Bar get the power to so faithfully live the Christian life into which they were born up until the day they left this world for the next?

I used to kid with the president and Bar that I thought they had secret twins (or triplets) hidden away somewhere in their house. Laura

---

4. Luke 22:19 and John 6:51.

5. D. AD 407.

and I just simply could not take in all they were able to accomplish and at the same time still remain so attentive, caring, and, frankly, loving toward others.

Let us face it—we all have those times when we run out of juice and reach the edge of our physical limits, and when that happens, we can be frustrated and snippy with those around us.

I think I have already mentioned this, and it is something that everyone who was closest to the president and Barbara would say, especially their aides Jean Becker and Evan Sisley, not to mention the revolving door of friends and family: one would never see them out of sorts in a way that would be played out negatively on others.

They could be out of sorts, mind you, but they turned that inward and not outward.

I was with them at their best times and at their worst times. I confess to you that I was with them in times of great weakness, pain, and discomfort—and they managed, remarkably, perhaps almost miraculously, to hold up without giving way.

"How?" is the question I asked. I honestly believe that the answer is found in two places of Holy Scripture.

The first is Paul's letter to the churches in a region known as Galatia. The Apostle Paul, writing to a variety of Christian communities in what is now Turkey, would describe what he called "life in the Spirit."

The fruit of the Spirit is love, joy, peace, forbearance, kindness, goodness, faithfulness, gentleness and self-control. Against such things there is no law...Since we live by the Spirit, let us keep in step with the Spirit.[6]

The president and Barbara were followers of Christ and in doing so were filled with the Spirit of God. The "fruit" of that Spirit, Paul

---

6. Galatians 5:22–23, 5:25.

teaches Jesus's disciples, is, frankly, godly living exemplified in the kind character traits he lists for us here.

So the pervasive expression of their innate goodness was a gift of burying themselves, if you will, within that goodness—through their faith, their prayers, their worship, and the core belief that it behooves those created in the image of God to do one's best, by the grace of God, to live in what the church's theologians call the *imago dei*. Literally translated—"*image of God.*"

I think if 41 or Bar were sitting beside me at this moment as I type these words, I would likely get a tap on the shoulder with a whisper: *Russ, what on earth are you suggesting? We were, with God's help, just doing our best to be Christians.* And I might say, *By George, you've got it!*

One who embraces the *imago dei* within them—whether they make a conscious decision to do that or not—is actualizing the special qualities of human nature that allow God to then be manifest in humans.

The second place within Holy Scripture that explains "how" 41 and Bar lived out their faith is actually sprinkled throughout the entire Bible.

Going back to the Hebrew Scriptures, we find the foundational teaching that faithful Jews call the Shema, a noun used to proclaim the basic teaching of all Jewish belief:

> Hear, O Israel: The LORD our God, the LORD is one. Love the LORD your God with all your heart and with all your soul and with all your strength.[7]

That love, much like Paul's description of the life in the Spirit, would cause a natural response that poured beyond the individual, for faithful Hebrews were also commanded, "Love your neighbor as yourself."[8]

This ethical imperative, of course, became the very basis for all of the teachings of Jesus, who, when asked by a lawyer what the greatest of all

---

7. Deuteronomy 6:4–5.

8. Leviticus 19:18.

laws was, answered simply by pointing back to the Shema and Levitical teaching.

> "The most important one," answered Jesus, "is this: 'Hear, O Israel: The Lord our God, the Lord is one. Love the Lord your God with all your heart and with all your soul and with all your mind and with all your strength.' The second is this: 'Love your neighbor as yourself.' There is no commandment greater than these."[9]

I like the way the Christian author Frederick Buechner explains this. He writes,

> When Jesus said to love your neighbor, a lawyer who was present asked him to clarify what he meant by *neighbor*. He wanted a legal definition he could refer to in case the question of loving one ever happened to come up. He presumably wanted something on the order of: "A neighbor (hereinafter referred to as the party of the first part) is to be construed as meaning a person of Jewish descent whose legal residence is within a radius of no more than three...miles from one's own legal residence unless there is another person of Jewish descent (hereinafter to be referred to as the party of the second part) living closer to the party of the first part than one is oneself, in which case the party of the second part is to be construed as neighbor to the party of the first part and one is oneself relieved of all responsibility...whatsoever."

"Instead," Buechner writes, "Jesus told the story of the Good Samaritan (Luke 10:25–37), the point of which seems to be that your neighbor

---

9. Mark 12:28–34; Matthew 22:34–40.

is to be construed as meaning anybody who needs you." He adds, "The lawyer's response is left unrecorded."[10]

From my observation, our forty-first president and Barbara did all they could to help anyone who needed them, because they were loving people.

They loved their children and grandchildren—and anyone whom they brought along. As divorces began appearing within the family tree, as they do, and new family members became part of the scene, the president and Bar would do their best to include them. Bar often joked, "You know, like *Modern Family.*"

But the Christian ethos is crystal clear…Christians are known, as the old hymn goes, "by their love."[11]

I often use the word *generous* whenever I speak about the way that the president and Barbara would love on others—because there seemed to be no circle too large for them to draw in order to take others into the love they knew and the love they wanted to share. They had friends from every walk of life and every nation, language, race, gender, sexual orientation, and political persuasion.

In the reams of emails, notes, and letters Laura and I received from the president and Bar over the years, they often ended with "Our love to you" or "Love you." Every time they ended a phone call with a dear friend or family member, or if they were bidding farewell to the same after a visit, their words were "Love you." And of course, Laura and I grew to love the president's favorite comeback to an expression of love: "Love you more." And you know, I believe he did.

They did not see it as their job to decide where to draw the line, so they embodied American poet Edwin Markham's pithy, ethical bit of verse:

---

10. Frederick Buechner, *Wishful Thinking* (San Francisco: Harper, 1973), 65–66.

11. "They'll Know We Are Christians" was written by the late Roman Catholic priest Peter Raymond Scholtes (d. 2009).

He drew a circle that shut me out—
Heretic, rebel, a thing to flout.
But Love and I had the wit to win:
We drew a circle that took him in!

While all things churchy, I think, are fairly important to the Christian way—for instance, the way we worship, our adherence to and study of Holy Scripture, our practice of spiritual disciplines, and so on—in the end, without love, as Paul wrote in his great "love chapter" often read at weddings, everything else is meaningless.[12]

Jesus's closing salvo of ethical and moral doctrinal teaching to his disciples was crystal clear: "By this everyone will know that you are my disciples, if you love one another."[13]

And this imperative is sifted throughout the entire New Testament, perhaps especially in the Epistles of John, who compelled his readers to embody love, "Dear children, let us not love with words or speech but with actions and in truth."[14]

This is the central thesis of this book you now hold in your hands: I give witness to dignity, the dignity of George H. W. and Barbara Bush, from the beginning of life to its natural end.

Barbara's last word? "Home"—the eternal reward for a child created in God's image who lived life to its fullest and loved everyone God sent her way.

The president's last words? "I love you too." Because he did. What better way to slip out of this room we call planet earth and take that next step into the place we call the kingdom of God?

To have lived faithfully through and through and to have loved fully to the end—this is dignity.

---

12. 1 Corinthians 13:1–13.

13. John 13:35.

14. 1 John 3:18.

The Hole for You and Me to Fill

Toward the end of my homily from the pulpit in Washington DC, I referenced that many people in the public arena between the day of 41's death and burial began to say, "This is an end of an era." Instead, I suggested that era does not have to end and that perhaps the president's death is actually an invitation to fill the hole his death had left behind.

That was a late addition to the homily after I had heard one too many times on news outlets that the past is the past—that the good old days of dignified leadership are gone.

There is no question, I think, that politics has always had the propensity to be nasty business. We have, it seems, grown accustomed to histrionic speeches that bear more of a resemblance to a grade school debate than an intellectual exercise of revealing qualities of leadership and statesmanship. And we religious folk—folk like me—have gotten all too comfortable with candidates and elected leaders who live lives and speak in ways that in no way resemble essential Judeo-Christian principles. And that is to our peril.

It is not just a peril to our great nation—though I think that is true—but a peril to faith. For me, of course, that would mean the Christian faith. But anytime a person of faith embraces, ignores, or in any way endorses brutality, obscenity, and vulgarity as acceptable practices in the public square of politics, it weakens our witness to the world.

There are increasing numbers of studies that reveal the droves of people who are abandoning organized religion or spirituality altogether. The reasons given for this exodus vary, but one major reason considered is the apparent inability of adherents to faiths that have been on planet earth almost since the dawn of civilization to uphold the most basic tenet of those faiths—to love one another.

We are now in a season when in our world and culture—and yes, in the arenas of politics and the church—we hunger for those days that do seem altogether elusive. We are nostalgic for a better day, but as I suggested at the beginning, that nostalgia is not just a reflection on "the good old days," but a desire to see them return.

I would ask you, as you consider the current state of our nation's health, are we in the athletic arena of health and vitality or the ICU ward headed toward hospice?

And an important question for people of faith to ask is this: Are we complicit in the decline of a culture, in the decay of a nation's health, when we abandon our central tenets of beliefs, ethics, and morals by being caught up in the elusive web of the culture of personality, a corrupt ideology, or a self-serving movement that only furthers division and distrust between God's children?

I think the answer to all of those questions, to anyone who is intellectually and spiritually honest, is obvious.

Is there hope to turn things around? Yes, of course—there is always hope. As Martin Luther King Jr. often preached, "We must accept finite disappointment, but never lose infinite hope."

But we must do more than hope. And what you hold in your hands provides a road map.

The qualities of character, decency, and integrity are not unattainable, nor should they be abandoned.

Take this volume to heart. Consider as you read, as you reflect, and as you—as perhaps we all do—seek to deal with that ache about the way things are and that desire to turn the tide, that we can not just long for better days, but see them return.

George H. W. and Barbara Bush did that, and in doing so, they changed our nation, changed our world—changed all of our lives—for the better.

They were living points of light. They showed us what it meant to serve and to love. They remind us now of what it means to live with dignity.

By God's grace, may we find our way there again...and again...and again.

CHAPTER NINETEEN

AND THEY LIVE...

In him was life, and the life was the light of all people.

John 1:4 (NRSV)

Jesus said... "I am the resurrection and the life. The one who believes in me will live, even though they die."

John 11:25

Heaven must be in thee before thou canst be in heaven.

George Swinnock[1]

In that sweet by and by, we shall meet on that beautiful shore.

Ira David Sankey[2]

I would like to end on a happy note. More than happy: a hopeful note—a promise, if you will.

So before you close this book and put it away, let me ask you to consider this question: Where are George H. W. and Barbara Bush? Did

---

1. D. 1673.

2. D. 1908.

they leave us and go to heaven? Are they really together? Are they safely "tucked in" the loving arms of God, as Jim Baker proclaimed? Will we see them again?

Recall the things said in those remarks by those closest to the president and Bar in those memorial services. Were the historian, the governor, the prime minister, the senator, the president, the grandson, and the friends just saying things we all wanted to hear? Or were they speaking a deep truth?

The answer to that question, according to the faith that sustained the president and Bar, is a firm, unequivocal, unshakable yes...they were speaking truth.

A few weeks after the president's death, as the proverbial dust began to settle, Jean Becker called me and asked if I could come by the office. "I have something I want to give you," she said.

I made my way over to 10000 Memorial Drive, wondering how many more times, if any, I would return to this place that I had visited so often in those last eleven years. When I arrived, Jean welcomed me and walked me back into her office.

My heart was heavy for this, my friend. I had lost friends in the president and Barbara as well, a brother and sister in Christ, but nothing like the loss Jean—who literally had spent nearly three decades in service to these incredible people—was feeling.

"I have something I want to give you," she said again, but this time to my face. She reached over and handed me the Book of Common Prayer. "This was theirs."

On the front were their names: BARBARA AND GEORGE.

"Jean, I don't think I should have this...maybe the library, or one of the kids?"

"They would want you to have this."

I was overwhelmed. We talked. I think we probably cried. We hugged and said good-bye.

And so my hope and prayer is that this book has made some difference in your life. I hope and pray—and I do mean that—that it inspires you to be, well, more like Barbara and George. Two of the finest people who walked planet earth.

But let me go back a few paragraphs to that thing I called an "unshakable yes."

In Barbara and George's Book of Common Prayer, there is a section called "An Outline of Faith," or what we members of the Episcopal Church call "The Catechism."

In its closing pages, there are three questions that speak to this matter of the "unshakable yes."

Q. What do we mean by the resurrection of the body?

A. We mean that God will raise us from death in the fullness of our being, that we may live with Christ in the communion of the saints.

Q. What do we mean by everlasting life?

A. By everlasting life, we mean a new existence, in which we fully are united with all the people of God, in the joy of fully knowing and loving God and each other.

Q. What, then, is our assurance as Christians?

A. Our assurance as Christians is that nothing, not even death, shall separate us from the love of God which is in Christ Jesus our Lord. Amen.[3]

Can we believe this? Or is this just something in a red book with BARBARA AND GEORGE stamped on the cover?

You will recall the discussion I had with the president about life after death—we had that discussion more than once. I also shared with him a reflection I wrote some years ago and that I send to friends and to every member of St. Martin's who experiences the death of a loved one. It is not as weighty as, let us say, a papal encyclical. But the truth of the matter

---

3. Book of Common Prayer, 862.

is there is a lot of mystery about "what kind of life" rests beyond the grave. But for Christians, there is no mystery that life does, in fact, exist.

My saying that this is what Christians believe is not my way of saying that what everyone else believes about life after death is wrong. That is not my business—that belongs to the One for whom I work. So, with that caveat, this is what I shared with President Bush, and I hope and do pray that it is of help and perhaps reassuring to you.

What Christians Believe about Life after Death

All of us have questions about life after death. While Christians do believe in the promises of our Lord that his followers will indeed experience life after death, some may still be asking, "What *kind of life* is there after death?"

To begin answering that question, I have to utter four very honest words: I do not know. The apostle Paul shared a word about his own ignorance on this question when he wrote to the church in Corinth, "Now we see only a reflection as in a mirror; then we shall see face to face. Now I know in part; then I shall know fully, even as I am fully known" (1 Corinthians 13:12).

I believe we see glimpses behind death's door throughout Holy Scripture. Consider the scene from the Transfiguration, in which Jesus is "visited" by what appears to be Moses and Elijah (Matthew 17:1–13 and Mark 9:2–13). In this visitation, the figures are recognized and even speak with Jesus.

When Jesus rises from the grave, he appears to Mary Magdalene, who first recognizes Jesus's voice and then his face (John 20:11ff.).

Jesus also appears to the disciples and even invites the doubting Thomas to touch him (John 20:24ff.). Later, Jesus visits with them, eats with them, and I can only imagine that he also laughed with them! (See John 21:25.) We are told in Luke's sequel, Acts, that the resurrected Jesus walked the earth for about forty days, continuing his work of sharing the good news of the kingdom (read all of Acts!).

But then again, remember—this risen body was not a medically resuscitated one. It did not come to life as a result of an injection of adrenaline and a jolt of electricity from a defibrillator. It was the power of God that did this. The resurrected body that contained Jesus on earth had been transformed in a way that expressed that very power. We still do not see that type of resurrection in our day-to-day lives—so the question remains: What kind of life is there after death?

I think that these appearances tell us just a few clear things:

First, that we will remain who we are: God created us as unique beings, and we will but only die once (see Hebrews 9:27). Thus, for Christians at least, we do not believe in reincarnation. Each person is uniquely created, and uniquely loved—as they are in their creation. They do not have to be refashioned over and over again until they become something else; what they are as they are, is the object of God's love. Thus, again, for Christians, we believe we will move from this life to the next and continue in God's kingdom.

Second, we do not become angels either. Angels are heavenly beings created by God to assist him in his work. Humans, we are told, are greater than angels; and by the way, we are also told that sometimes we entertain them without knowing it! (Read Psalm 8:5 and Hebrews 2:7 and 13:2.)

Third, there is still much mystery about what lies after death! But the certainty to which Christians cling is the certainty that, for those who trust in the lordship of Jesus Christ and surrender to his grace and mercy, death is merely a moment that opens the door to eternal life.

This I *do* know—it is ultimately a matter of trust. We find that hard these days because we so often want to know the whys and hows about everything. Modern humans sometimes have trouble with unanswered questions and unsolved mysteries. Parker Palmer, in his book *Let Your Life Speak*, notes this cultural trend, writing, "Our culture wants to turn mysteries into puzzles to be explained or problems to be solved because maintaining the illusion that we can 'straighten things out' makes us feel powerful. Yet mysteries never yield to solutions or fixes—and when we pretend that they do, life becomes not only more banal, but also more hopeless."[4]

My mentor, the Reverend Dr. John Claypool, used to say to me all the time, "When my life is over, if there is anything else, it's up to God." That is a powerful statement not only of fact but of faith.

If someone were to have told me in the comfort of my mother's womb that I should jump from my luxury hotel with twenty-four-hour room service into a bed-and-breakfast where I would begin with a slap on the bum, a limited menu, and a life that included eating, breathing, and communicating in another way I could not at that point understand, I would have said, "No way! I am fine just where I am!"

Now that I am here, I would never choose to go back to the womb. And Christianity tells us that there is indeed something even greater waiting past the door of death. I wish I had more evidence of what it really is like, but my guess is that when I get there, I will never want to come back here.

Perhaps a story that the late, great chaplain of the United States Senate, Peter Marshall, used to tell of a woman in his church will offer an image worth clinging to as we ponder our own deaths.

It seems a mother in a church where he was serving had a young son who had succumbed to the ravages of leukemia, and as his body weakened, their greatest joy was to spend afternoons with her reading stories to him—particularly those of Camelot and the Knights of the Round Table.

As she read about one particular battle scene, her son looked at her with a childlike innocence and said, "Mom, what is it like to die?" She knew that he was not asking about the story—he was asking about himself. He was asking the same question many of us innocently ask.

Marshall said that the woman was so overcome with emotion that she paused, closed the book, and looked at her beloved son. She told him she would be back in a minute and excused herself. She went out

---

4. Parker Palmer, *Let Your Life Speak* (Hoboken, New Jersey: Jossey-Bass, 1999), 60.

into the kitchen, knelt on the floor, and literally prayed—asking God to give her an answer to her son's almost unanswerable question. She opened her eyes and lifted her head, and as she did, her eyes lit upon a photo of her older son tacked on the refrigerator—and she was given her answer.

She went back, sat next to her son, and said, "You just asked me what it is like to die. Well, son, I have not died, so I do not know. But I have to believe it is something like this.

"Do you remember back when you were healthier that you could run and play in the afternoons? Some of those days you would come in and plop down on the sofa; you were often so tired that you would fall asleep in front of the television. Some nights, I just did not have the heart to wake you and so I would ask your older brother to pick you up and take you to your room.

"The next morning, you would wake, not in your old clothes, but in your clean pajamas and in your own bed. You did not know how you got there; but all that happened is you went to sleep in this room of your father's house, and you woke in another. That is what I believe it is like for the children of God," his mother said.

So in the end, if there is anything more after death—and I believe that there is—it is up to God. And knowing God as I do, I believe that it will be better than we could ever ask or imagine. Indeed, "whoever believes in him may have eternal life" (John 3:15 NRSV).

This is one of the many reasons we call our faith "the good news"—for it is good news indeed that what Jesus offers his followers is the promise that at death, life is changed, not ended. And that beyond death's door, we will be welcomed by his words, "Come, you who are blessed by my Father; take your inheritance, the kingdom prepared for you since the creation of the world" (Matthew 25:34). That is good news indeed!

I invite you to consider these words. Those who stood at the lecterns of our National Cathedral and in the pulpit of St. Martin's—they all attested to these deep truths.

And these deep truths are what the president and Barbara believed. And because of God's love, and because of their faith in that love ...

George H. W. Bush and Barbara Pierce Bush ...

live happily ...

ever after ...

Homily for Barbara Pierce Bush

April 21, 2018
St. Martin's Episcopal Church
The Reverend Dr. Russell J. Levenson Jr.

G anny's Garden," given by friends and loved ones of Barbara Pierce Bush, is a lovely spot to rest and reflect near downtown Kennebunkport. There you'll find, on a sculpted bench, a wide-brim sun hat—the kind Barbara wore in her garden—and an open copy, facedown, of her favorite book, Jane Austen's *Pride and Prejudice.*

Though I am taking the quote slightly out of context, because the one who spoke it was pretentiously touting her love of reading, nonetheless, Jane Austen used one of her characters in that book to utter a wonderful truth: "I declare...there is no enjoyment like reading! How much sooner one tires of anything than of a book!" There was nothing pretentious about Barbara Bush; she loved reading, and literacy—for all—was, as you know, Barbara Bush's great passion.

Every great book has a good beginning—but also a wonderful end. And so, the life story of Barbara Bush is best described as the consummate "good read."

We gather today in this holy space that has been the worshipping community of President George H. W. Bush and First Lady Barbara Bush for more than fifty years. It is a humbling privilege to speak as her pastor, priest, friend, and confidant—but what an interesting thing to be a confidant to a woman who has no secrets. What you saw was what you got—what was in here [pointing to head] often came out here [pointing to mouth].

The author of our lesson in Proverbs muses on the gifts of a loving wife and mother—a godly woman—all of which Barbara had. She believed in, and practiced, the principles of honesty, tolerance, decency, courage, strength—and humility. She lived according to the mantra of the Bush family for many years—"Don't get caught up in the big 'me.'"

One day we were walking together on the beach in Kennebunkport. Barbara was washing off her own shoes and a fella came up to her and said, "Hey, you look a lot like Barbara Bush." Without missing a beat, Barbara just said, "Yes, I hear that a lot."

She was a friend to people of every political persuasion, race, religion. Her generosity of spirit did not draw *lines that kept others out*; hers was a life of *circles that sought to bring others in*. Here in Houston, we saw her at major galas, behind home plate at the Astros games, praying here in the pews, catching up with a neighbor while pushing her own buggy through Walgreens.

Oh, her humor—a hundred stories we could tell. One day after sharing prayers and Communion with the president and Bar, my wife leaned over to kiss the president on the cheek, at which point Bibi, one of her beloved dogs, nipped her on the calf. Apologies came; but the next morning, on our doorstep was a beautiful orchid with a handwritten note: *Dear Laura, I am so sorry about the bite, you just looked good enough to eat.*

Oh my word, we could all talk endlessly, could we not, about how great this woman is? But then we are reminded in the lesson from Ecclesiastes that there comes a time for everything—*even the end of a great story.*

The least of Barbara's virtues was patience. If you were sharing a meal, or waiting on her favorite drink (a manhattan, for the record), and things were slowing up, she would ask "Why the holdup?" Barbara liked to see things move along—and I think that is why we are here today. I think Barbara was becoming impatient; she was tired of waiting on that next chapter...So, well, she welcomed it on April 17th—but perhaps this will help those of us she left behind.

Jesus was her pathway to God. She honored and believed that others *found God in their own way.* But for her, being a Christian mattered. We were talking one day when she looked me in the eye and said, "I am a Christian. I do believe. I want to be confirmed." She asked if she had to take a class. I said to her, "Take one? Bar, you could teach one!"

So, in May of 2015, she and some family gathered in our chapel as she confirmed her faith in Christ: not something she wore on her shoulder—just something very personal, but very real.

She confirmed simply what we believe in the lesson from 2 Corinthians—that we live not by what we see, but by faith and those things we don't see. So, as Paul wrote, even on days like today, we do not lose heart. Yes, Barbara's health declined, but as we just heard, "Though our outer nature is wasting away, our inner nature is being renewed every day...for what is mortal," Paul writes, by the grace and mercy of God, is "swallowed up by life."

We find Barbara's Jesus in the Gospel lesson—a Jesus who says, "All that come to me will be welcomed." Her Jesus offers the hope that life here, when it comes to its natural close, is changed, not ended.

Some good books have no true ending; some offer an epilogue, a hint to imagine what rests beyond the closing chapter...

Can we imagine this day? A reunion with her parents. With your parents, sir. And with your dear Robin. My guess is she has already hunted down Jane Austen and has said, "Well, how did things turn out with Mr. Darcy and Elizabeth Bennet?" Or, knowing Barbara as we all do, she may be telling Jane how things "should" have turned out!

In the meantime, until each of our times come, she would want us to carry on...to live as she lived—fully, deeply. To laugh—and laugh often. To love all that God sends our way. And to serve one another, the common good, and especially the purposes of God.

So leave here today, not to grieve, but to rejoice. And as we do, we will sing—by Barbara's choice—"Joyful, joyful, we adore thee..."

Barbara would want us to celebrate her great next chapter. She has been raised to new life, for in this story, you never turn the page and see the two words "the end."

Barbara Bush's story has just begun again—and the best is yet to come!

Amen.

Homily for the Honorable George Herbert Walker Bush

State Funeral
December 5, 2018
Washington National Cathedral
Washington DC
The Reverend Dr. Russell Jones Levenson Jr.

It is an honor and privilege to follow the wonderful speakers today, particularly someone for whom I have so much respect—our forty-third president. Mr. President, I will share with you that your father always seemed to enjoy our visits. He was never much in a hurry. He was very generous and always thanked me for our time together. Your mother, on the other hand...well, sometimes she would say, "Good sermon...too long!" Sir, you are a lot like your mother!

So, ladies and gentlemen, children of God, when death comes, as it does to us all, life is changed, not ended—and the way we live our lives, the decisions we make, the service we render *matter*. They matter to our fellow humans, to this world God has given to us, and they matter to God.

Few people have understood this as well or lived their lives as accordingly as *President George Herbert Walker Bush*. Hear what I said—*lived it*, not earned it, or strived to achieve it. It was as natural to him as breathing is to each of us. President Bush was a good man; he was a godly man...full of grace, love, and a quality absolutely necessary to enter the kingdom of God—humility, grounded in a desire to serve his God and all God sent his way.

How do I know this? Because for nearly a dozen years, my wife, Laura, and our children have laughed with him, fished with him. The president just mentioned how much his father enjoyed going full throttle on *Fidelity.* We have had that pleasure with the forty-first president. One time, we were out, with the Secret Service following close behind. We saw them reaching into their coats for what I thought might have been some form of protection—it was only then we realized they were crossing themselves!

We have been blessed to share meals, tears, moments of silence, and prayers in times of great strength and in times of great weakness.

Never, *not once,* did I witness anything but care and concern for those around him. The job of a pastor, a priest, an imam, a rabbi, when dealing with someone he or she is called to serve, is to call on that person to look to God, to do the right thing, to serve others and to love. And President Bush made my job so easy.

Our lesson from the Hebrew Scriptures reminds us that God is light—and the president reflected that light his whole life through. He once said, "I am a man who sees life in terms of missions defined and missions completed." We recall with delight when he reminded America and her citizens of his mission and ours—to be "points of light" with but one aim: to leave our world better than we found it.

I have a political cartoon of 41 with caricatured big ears and glasses. He's at his desk, looking at his watch, and saying to himself, "Communism is dead, the wall is down, apartheid is falling, Mandela is free, the Sandinistas are ousted, Germany is reuniting, the Cold War is over, I've returned my calls, and heck, it's not even lunchtime."

We sometimes forget all President Bush did for us, in large part because he preferred to shine not upon himself, but to shine attention on others.

Several years ago, President Bush gave me this plaque, and on the back is a note: *Russ, A good friend gave this to me some years ago. It may be of help to you in some way.* It reads—simply—PREACH CHRIST AT ALL TIMES...IF NECESSARY, USE WORDS. It remains on my desk as a reminder that faith means more than words. Jesus Christ, for George Bush, was at the heart of his faith—but his was a deep faith, a generous faith, a simple faith, in the best sense of the word. He knew and lived Jesus's two greatest commandments—to love God and love your neighbor.

The president loved and served not just some, but all God sent his way. He lived his own adage—"Tolerance is a virtue, not a vice." He respected and befriended Christians of every denomination as well as Jews, Muslims, Buddhists, and Sikhs. His comrades were from every nation and race. Yes, he was a Republican, but for him, political parties were but a line in the sand to brush away in the times of the greater good of working toward his goal for all of us to be a "kinder and gentler nation."

The Gospel reminds us that Jesus told his followers to be the light of the world so that the world could turn their hearts toward God and others—"Let your light shine before others so that they may see your good works and give glory to your Father in heaven." And so was President Bush. His life was defined by his faith and service that are worthy of all of those made in God's image.

In September of 1990, President Bush spoke to those gathered outside these doors for the dedication of this great cathedral. He pointed inside to that beautiful rose window and said, "From where we now stand, the rose window high above seems black and formless to some, perhaps; but when we enter and see it backlit by the sun, it dazzles in astonishing splendor and reminds us that without faith we too are but stained-glass windows in the dark."

The president understood that even the darkest of nights can be transformed if handed over to the redemptive power of the Almighty. No one on that first Good Friday expected Easter Sunday—but it came. It came because the Light that brought creation into being also brought life from the grave—we call that resurrection.

Only days ago, I was humbled, along with the loving members of the president's family, his wonderful medical aides, Evan and Josh—and Sully! Who I think may have gotten more press in the last few days than our forty-first president! Also present was someone that the president liked to call his "little brother": James Baker and his wife, Susan. There had been wonderful and kind words and hugs and kisses through the day. Toward the end, Secretary Baker pointed at the president and whispered, "You know, that man changed my life."

I have been at the deathbed of many people over the years, but what followed is something I will never forget. A bit later, Secretary Baker was at the foot of the president's bed, and toward the end, Jim Baker rubbed and stroked the president's feet for perhaps half an hour. The president smiled at this comfort of his dear friend. *Here I witnessed a world leader who was serving a servant who had been our world's leader.*

And what came to mind was Jesus. On that last night before his own crucifixion, having said everything there was to say, he wrapped a towel around his waist *and without words, he washed his disciples' feet.* As Jesus finished, he said, "I have set an example for you…do as I have done… serve one another…by this the world will know you are my disciples— if you love one another."

At the end, we all knelt, we all placed our hands on the president, we said our prayers together. *And then we were silent as this man who had changed all of our lives, who had changed our nation…who had changed our world, left this life for the next.*

For a moment, *but a moment only,* that dear point of light we know as George Herbert Walker Bush dimmed, but now it shines, brighter than it ever before has.

And now, this godly man, this servant, this child of God is in the loving arms of his Barbara and Robin and the welcoming arms of our Lord, who embraced him with his divine love.

Some have said in the last few days, "This is an end of an era." But it does not have to be. Perhaps it is an invitation to fill the hole that has been left behind.

You know, the president so loved our great country. He loved his church—the Episcopal Church. He loved you—his friends—and he loved every single member of his family. But he was so ready to go to heaven...and heaven was so ready to receive him. Because he lived those great two commandments. If you want to honor this man—if you call yourself a daughter or son of God—then love one another; serve and love one another. There is no greater mission than these.

My hunch is heaven, as perfect as it must be, just got a bit kinder and gentler, *leaving behind a hole for you and me to fill.* How? *Preach Christ at all times; if necessary, use words.*

So, Mr. President—mission complete. Well done, good and faithful servant...Welcome to your eternal home...where the ceiling and visibility are unlimited and where life goes on...forever.

Amen.

Homily for the Honorable
George Herbert Walker Bush

Final Homily
December 6, 2018
St. Martin's Episcopal Church
Houston, Texas
The Reverend Dr. Russell Jones Levenson Jr.

A few days before Barbara Bush's death, I was called to the Bushes' home, where the president asked me to pray with Barbara. When I knocked on her door, she said, "Hello, Russ...I'm not checking out yet!" We talked for a bit, I anointed her head with oil, and then prayed for her. As I left, she called me back into the room.

"Bar, are you okay?" I asked.

She said, "Yes...just tell him I adore him."

Today we are gathered to celebrate *the life of a man we all adored.*

At the beginning of a journey that began June 12, 1924, George Herbert Walker Bush was born into the cradle of a loving family that held fast to the values of friendship, family, and faith; of integrity, honesty, and loyalty; and of character, courage, and service.

Now at the end of the journey, that cradle that sustained him throughout his ninety-four years of life has released him into the loving arms of his heavenly Father. The end depends on the beginning—and this is a good ending—because from the very beginning George Bush was committed to a life not for himself, but for others.

And so we gather today charged with three tasks: saying good-bye, giving our thanks, and lifting our lives to hope.

Bidding farewell is the hardest of those three tasks because we must acknowledge that the world isn't the same without this great man. The tectonic plates of our lives have shifted. In today's world, we sometimes recoil from complex emotions instead of shedding tears of grief that honor our loved ones. George Bush was never afraid to shed tears. And so today, I bid you to follow his lead.

We also gather to give thanks for the actions of a remarkable public servant who improved the lives of so many around the world, across the nation, and in our great state of Texas and our beloved city of Houston.

Each of us gathered here today join untold millions around the globe to mourn the death of one of history's greatest leaders. But we have lost more than a leader. He, like his wife of over seventy years, Barbara, had that unique ability to make you feel like he was your best friend, and you were his—and he pulled it off with charm, humility, and humor with few, if any, rivals. So however you do it—whether through quiet meditation, tearful remembrance, or jubilant story—give thanks that his life brushed up against yours.

Good-bye...and thank you. But there is one more thing we come to do—we also come to raise our lives to hope. *What do I mean by that?* President Bush was a man of faith—a faith that sustained him in this life and that has brought him new life.

The president and Barbara Bush were devoted and active members of St. Martin's for over fifty years. In a talk the president gave here in 1982, he spoke of his love for St. Martin's, his memories of teaching Sunday school, serving coffee...and just worshipping here: "I remember sitting in the back and how my pew wiggled and shook as our four boys and sometimes Doro got the giggles," he said.

Then, he added, "I don't want to hold it over the rest of you, but how many of you can say of the Christmas pageant, 'My grandson was a shepherd in 1980 and his sister an angel. Both in the same year!'" At which point, Barbara spoke up and said, "Did it ever occur to you they both made it because you had just been elected vice president a month before?"

But there was a deeper purpose in his faith. In an open letter to clergy across the United States just days before his inauguration, then president-elect Bush wrote, "Worship is basic to my own life. Our family has endeavored to uphold our faith by participation in the life of our Church."

In an address two years into his presidency, he recalled President Lincoln's response at the height of the Civil War when asked if he thought the Lord was on Lincoln's side. Lincoln responded, "My concern is not whether God is on our side, but whether we are on God's side." Make no mistake about it—George Bush was on God's side. It is why together we carefully chose the lessons for this service—lessons that bespeak of the love of God, the comfort of God, and the hope of life eternal given to us through his Son, Jesus Christ.

Martin of Tours is the patron saint of this parish and best known for tearing his cloak in two to cover a barely dressed beggar. He did so impulsively, instinctively knowing that it was the right thing to do. Only later was it revealed to him in a dream that his selfless act had clothed Christ himself. Those of us fortunate to worship with George and Barbara Bush witnessed a similar selflessness. As we worshipped together, they never made a show of arriving, worshipping, or leaving.

They had a "favorite spot," but if they arrived and someone had beaten them to it, they never created a fuss.

In fact, on particularly crowded days, they often relinquished their seats to a mother overloaded with children or a son coming with his elderly parents.

One particularly cold day, as the president came in the back, he was met by an usher who did not have an overcoat. "Aren't you cold?" the president asked the young man.

"I'm fine," the usher started to say. But before he could finish his sentence, the president whipped off his own coat and placed it around the gent's shoulders. He then walked into worship with a smile and without another word.

George Bush loved our Lord and knew our Lord loved him, and it was THAT connection that birthed in the forty-first president a desire to serve.

A few years back, the president and I discussed his deteriorating health. At the time, he did not know how that struggle would end. He put a question to me about as simply as anyone could. "What do you think heaven is like?" he asked. It was a confident statement, one that bespoke of a resolute faith.

He didn't want to know *if* there was a heaven, or whether he would be there *when* the end came. Instead, he wanted to know *what* it was like. He was ready for heaven...and heaven was ready for him. My guess is, on November 30th, when the president arrived in heaven, Barbara was standing there with her hands on her hips, saying, "What took you so long?" But then, a big old Texas-sized hug from his wife and daughter with the words, "We adore you."

His very first act after being sworn into office as the forty-first president was to lead our nation in prayer.

And, as the end depends on the beginning, and as we say our good-byes, allow me to invite you to pray in honor, thanksgiving, and celebration of this man we know, love—this man we adore. May his prayer be ours:

Heavenly Father, we bow our heads and thank You for Your love. Accept our thanks for the peace that yields this day and the shared faith that makes its continuance likely. Make us strong to do Your work, willing to heed and hear Your will, and write on our hearts these words: "Use power to help people." For we are given power not to advance our own purposes, nor to make a great show in the world, nor a name. There is but one just use of power, and it is to serve people. Help us to remember it, Lord. Amen.

Acknowledgments

No author pulls together a project like this on his or her own, so here is my chance to offer a few important thank-yous. Let me begin by thanking Governor Jeb Bush for his thoughtful foreword and the other children of 41 and Bar—President George W. Bush, Neil, Marvin, and Doro Koch—and lifelong friends to the president and Barbara, Jim and Susan Baker, all of whom kindly gave their permission, and read the book as well, before its first printing.

I deeply appreciate the support of those who have offered endorsements, which you can find on the first few pages of this book. A word of thanks to Jean Becker, Evan Sisley, Sam Waterston, and Karl Rove, who reviewed and helped me lock down some important details.

Thank you to my friend Jim McGrath, who was so helpful in connecting me to Paul Morse and Eric Draper, who in addition to Evan Sisley, provided photographs to include in this book.

Thanks to those in my immediate office—Lesley Hough, Carol Gallion, Brittney Jacobson, and Allie Hippard, as well as St. Martin's communications director, Sue Davis—all of whom played a role in organizing details and pieces of the project. Thanks also to the fine people of St. Martin's Episcopal Church who support me in another venue of ministry, writing as I have for you.

A word of thanks to my two previous publishers, Fisher Humphreys with Insight Press and Nancy Bryan with Church Publishing, who helped launch me into authorship many years ago. And to my friends Ian Markham and Barney Hawkins, who urged me to "tell this story."

Thanks also to David Moberg and Steve Green, who kindly connected me with the most wonderful literary agent a writer could want—Tom Dean with A Drop of Ink, who in turn made possible the connection with Alex Pappas of Hachette / Center Street, who was the consummate cheerleader, counselor, and gentle editor extraordinaire.

I would be remiss not to thank Hachette / Center Street's team of marketers, Abigail Skinner, Rudy Kish, and Katie Robison, as well as the final copyediting team under the leadership of Anjuli Johnson, for making it possible to share what I hope has been a wonderful story with you, my reader.

Of course, thanks to my wife, Laura, who for a season became the "author widow" of our home while I spent more time with the keyboard than with her—but now, we will be making up for lost time.

And of course, finally and most importantly, my thanks to our wonderful God, from whom flow the blessings of friendship, memory, life, and love—all of which I hope you have found well told in the pages you hold in your hands.

Index

Note: George H. W. Bush and his presidential son, George W., may be referred as Bush 41 and Bush 43, respectively. First lady Barbara Bush is referred to as "Bar." Page numbers preceded by "P–" indicate photo insert pages.